AIRCOOLED VW
ENGINE INTERCHANGE MANUAL

**To Joe, Gene and Dean – the
founding fathers of the industry**

AIRCOOLED VW
ENGINE INTERCHANGE MANUAL

KEITH SEUME

BAY
VIEW
BOOKS
FROM
MBI Publishing Company

This edition first published in 1996 by MBI Publishing Company,
729 Prospect Avenue, PO Box 1, Osceola, WI 54020-0001 USA

© Bay View Books Limited, 1996

MBI Publishing Company books are also available at discounts in bulk quantity
for industrial or sales-promotional use. For details write to Special Sales Manager
at Motorbooks International Wholesalers & Distributors, 729 Prospect Avenue,
PO Box 1, Osceola, WI 54020-0001 USA.

Library of Congress Cataloging-in-Publication Data Available

ISBN 0-7603-0314-2
Printed in China

CONTENTS

1. **INTRODUCTION**   7
When in doubt, ask...

2. **CRANKSHAFTS**   11
Getting to the heart of the matter

3. **CON-RODS**   24
From stone stock to trick titanium

4. **CYLINDER HEADS**   35
Breathing life into the VW engine

4. **CAMSHAFTS & VALVETRAIN**   53
Camshafts, lifters, pushrods, rocker arms, springs and retainers

6. **CRANKCASES**   72
From 1131cc to 3 liters and beyond

7. **CYLINDERS & PISTONS**   85
Cylinders, pistons, piston rings, wrist-pins and wrist-pin retainers

8. **CARBURETORS & FUEL SYSTEMS**   93
Bigger is not always better - but it can be

9. **EXHAUST SYSTEMS**   112
One of the most effective ways to make horsepower

10. **IGNITION SYSTEMS**   118
Putting the spark back in your Volkswagen

11. **LUBRICATION AND COOLING**   126
It takes more than air to cool a Volkswagen engine

12. **ADDRESS FILE**   143
Principal product manufacturers and suppliers

The author wishes to thank the following for their help with supplying information and photographs for use in this book:

The late Gene Berg; Dee and Gary Berg (Gene Berg Enterprises); Don Pauter (Pauter Machine); Dave and Judy Kawell (Kawell Racing Engines); Greg Brinton (Rimco); Jeff Denham (Jeff's Speed & Fab); Bill Taylor (Dee Engineering); Tom Lieb and Don Ishimaru (Scat Enterprises); Bill Steiner (Auto-Craft Machine); Jack Sacchette (JayCee Enterprises); Dean Lowry (Deano Dyno-Soars); Steve and Laurie Dunlap (Web-Cam); Luke Theochari (Terry's Beetle Services); Dean Kirsten (Hot VWs Magazine - Wright Publishing); VolksWorld Magazine; Dave Fetherston; Rob Loaring (ICE Racing Engines); Don Larby (Phegre Engineering) and all the others who have helped along the way.

Also thanks to Charles Herridge of Bay View Books for his patience while I pushed deadlines to the limit (and beyond) and to Gwynn for her suggestions and support.

INTRODUCTION

When in doubt, ask...

It is hard to believe that a car as modest as the Volkswagen has become the focal point of a whole industry dedicated to producing high-performance engine components. When first conceived back in the 1930s, as the brainchild of Ferdinand Porsche and Adolf Hitler, the Beetle was intended to be nothing more than inexpensive transport for the population of a new Germany.

In the pre-war period, there was little demand for a mass-produced performance car, for it was only the wealthy who could afford to treat an automobile as a plaything. For everyone else, a car was a luxury - most still made their way to work on a bicycle, motorcycle, or by public transport. However, once the Second World War had reached its conclusion, Ferdinand Porsche's thoughts began to turn to producing a small, affordable sports car which would bridge a gap until better, more affluent, times came once more. The result was a series of VW-derived sports cars which grew into the legendary 356 model and, as soon as it was practical to do so, Porsche turned his back on the Volkswagen engine and began to develop a new design of motor which shared progressively fewer components with its VW forebears.

However, the increased price of these new models was more than many people could yet afford in those still austere times

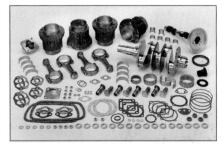

Counterweighted long-stroke crankshaft, modified stock con-rods, large-bore cylinders and pistons and a performance camshaft – but where do you start? Choosing the right parts for your Volkswagen can be a nightmare if you don't plan your project carefully before you start spending your money.

and a number of companies in both Europe and America began to take a fresh look at the Volkswagen to see how the engine could be improved to give better performance at a reasonable cost. Among the first was Oettinger Kraftfahrttechnische Spezialanstalt - better known throughout the world by its acronym, Okrasa - in Germany. Okrasa conversions became available in the early 1950s and consisted of high-quality cylinder heads, with improved inlet and exhaust ports and larger valves, long-stroke crankshafts, dual carburetors and many other optional items such as oil coolers and high-lift camshafts. Soon to follow was Wolfgang Denzel's similar conversion with its aluminum con-rods, special cylinder heads and a long-stroke crank.

Between them, these two companies proved that, despite its humble origins, the Volkswagen engine had plenty of potential to become a performance engine of some note. In the USA, a far-sighted Volkswagen dealer by the name of

There's more to a Volkswagen engine than you might think – and this collection of parts doesn't include the cooling, carburetor, exhaust or ignition systems.

Joe Vittone, who ran a company called Economotors in Riverside, California, took note of what Okrasa and Denzel were up to and began to import their conversion kits. He also developed a unique tool to allow Volkswagen cylinder heads to be fitted with new valve guides, so founding a company which would have a far-reaching effect on the future of the VW: European Motor Products Inc (EMPI).

Over the years that followed, Vittone developed a wide range of performance products for the Volkswagen, ranging from superb replacement cylinders and pistons to camshafts, carburetor kits and exhaust systems. Others would soon follow suit: Scat Enterprises, Deano Dyno-Soars, Gene Berg Enterprises, FAT Performance - all grew up in the wake of EMPI and helped to create a legend where the Volkswagen ruled the drag strips of California for more than a decade.

Today, the Volkswagen industry is at an all-time high as regards the quantity and quality of products on offer. Where once it was difficult to buy off the shelf anything more than one or two aftermarket camshafts for the Volkswagen, today there are over 200 different grinds available to the would-be engine builder! Everything about the industry is bigger and better (although nostalgia may suggest otherwise), for it is now possible for virtually anybody to build a modified VW engine using readily available components which would have been the envy of drag race heroes of days gone by. Once it was only necessary (or indeed possible) to build a race engine with 180bhp to break class records in National Hot Rod Association competition, whereas today there are many street-legal VWs with engines which boast this and more. Nowadays, to make the grade in top-line drag race competition, normally-aspirated engines must develop in the region of 300bhp, while turbocharged motors can be expected to produce 400, 500 or even 600bhp in their quest for glory.

As time has passed, so the performance industry has grown, and better quality components are being developed all the time. Where once there was no alternative but to use a modified VW crankcase, today there are several aftermarket cases available which allow the engine capacity to be increased to over 3 liters - a far cry from the original 1131cc of old. A wide range of aftermarket cylinder heads is also available, some based loosely on the VW factory

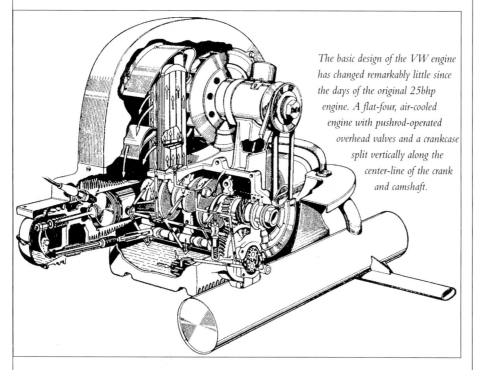

The basic design of the VW engine has changed remarkably little since the days of the original 25bhp engine. A flat-four, air-cooled engine with pushrod-operated overhead valves and a crankcase split vertically along the center-line of the crank and camshaft.

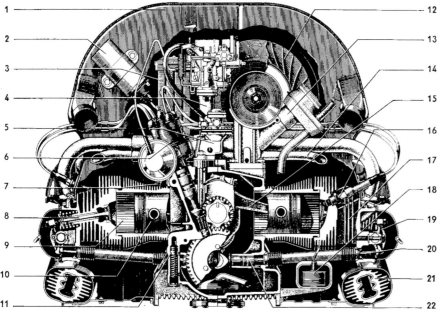

Cross-section of a VW 1500 engine:

1. Fan-housing
2. Coil
3. Oil cooler
4. Inlet manifold
5. Fuel pump
6. Distributor
7. Oil pressure switch
8. Valve
9. Cylinder
10. Piston
11. Oil pressure relief valve
12. Fan
13. Oil filler
14. Pre-heat pipe
15. Con-rod
16. Spark plug
17. Cylinder head
18. Thermostat
19. Rocker arm
20. Pushrod
21. Heat exchanger
22. Lifter

All-out race engine from Pauter Machine is based on the company's Super Pro aftermarket crankcase and heads. Turbocharged, injected and running on alcohol, this amazing engine is used in a sand dragster.

design, others, like those of Scat Enterprises and Pauter Machine, bearing little resemblance to the original castings. Indeed, such has been the development of so many new components that it is now possible to assemble a 'Volkswagen' race engine which uses not one single part produced at the Wolfsburg factory!

For the serious and experienced Volkswagen engine builder, all this is, of course, great news and he - or she - can rest safe in the knowledge that, as every year passes, even more aftermarket parts will be designed, developed and marketed for the aircooled flat-four. These will further help the quest for even greater

performance levels than anyone could ever have imagined. But where does this leave the less experienced enthusiast - the person who maintains his own car, would love to build a hot street VW and maybe even go drag racing at the weekend? How can he be expected to know what parts are best suited to his needs (and, more importantly, his wallet)? With such a

To give an idea of how far the Volkswagen performance industry has progressed, it is now possible to buy every single component for the VW engine from an aftermarket manufacturer: crank, rods, crankcase, cam, heads, induction system – everything!

bewildering array of components on display in the pages of specialist VW magazines, or on the shelf at the local VW store, how is anyone to know which parts work best, which to avoid and which offer the best return for your investment?

Hopefully, this book will go some way towards guiding you through this jungle, offering advice on which components to select, for everything from a reliable, mildly-modified engine for a daily-driver up to a full-blown, out-and-out race engine for a drag car. Much of the advice and comment which is offered is based on personal experience, gained over more than twenty years of 'messing with VWs', while still more is based on the word of the acknowledged gurus of the performance industry, including Dave Kawell, Tom Lieb, Don Pauter and of course, the late, great Gene Berg, among

Built a high-performance engine for your street car? Good, now invest in some instrumentation. Aside from the tachometer, you should consider gauges to monitor oil temperature and pressure and cylinder head temperature. A set of VDO gauges like this is cheap insurance compared to the cost of rebuilding a damaged engine.

many, many others.

If there is one piece of advice that can be wisely given, and even more wisely accepted, it is this: if in doubt, ask. Dave Kawell, of Kawell Racing Engines in Tennessee, once told the author that 'there is no such thing as a dumb question, only dumb people who don't ask questions'. Nobody can be expected to know everything and it is a foolish person indeed who pretends otherwise. For every problem there are frequently several solutions, and when the problem is how to get reliable horsepower from your VW engine, you will be given many different answers, often conflicting ones. All too often people will try to sell you parts you don't need, or suggest ideas which do not - or even cannot - work. If you have any doubt, ask them that not-so-dumb question. If they know the answer, all well and good. If they don't, pass on by for, along with the dumb people who don't ask questions, there are the dumb people who pretend they know all the answers but frequently cannot give them when challenged.

Nothing is more frustrating than owning a hot VW which has all the right components on board, yet runs worse than a stocker. On the other hand, there is nothing more satisfying than the experience of streaking away from the stop-light, or startline, with the opposition trailing in your wake. Believe me when I say that nothing hurts them more than to be beaten by a Volkswagen. Read the book, ask those questions and enjoy that experience.

Keith Seume
Crondall
England

Scat Enterprises' VW race engine is an impressive sight, with its split-port cylinder heads and 48IDA Weber carburetors. However, if you don't have this kind of budget, there are literally hundreds of components on the market which could be right for you.

CRANKSHAFTS

Getting to the heart of the matter

Stock Crankshafts

It is often said that the crankshaft is the heart of any engine, and it's true, for everything, almost literally, revolves around the crankshaft. However, not all crankshafts are the same: a weak crank can destroy an engine, a high-quality one can act as the foundation on which to build a high-horsepower motor. But, before we take a look at the many aftermarket alternatives, let's examine what the factory has had to offer over the years.

The first crankshafts used in the prototype engines in the 1930s were crude castings, which unfortunately broke on a regular basis while the vehicles were on test. A change in the manufacturing process, to drop forging, saw a massive improvement in reliability and set the scene for the next 50 years. From the very beginning, all Volkswagen crankshafts have run in four main bearings, unlike cranks in many other engines which have relied on two, three or five main bearings. The rear main bearing (number 1) is a one-piece flanged bearing located in the crankcase by means of a small dowel pin which, in conjunction with a thrust face on the flywheel and three shims, is designed to take up the end-float on the crank. The center-main (number 2) bearing is a split design, each half also being located by a dowel pin.

Number 3 bearing is situated between the camshaft drive (timing) gear and the web of number 2 rod journal, while number 4 bearing is to be found at the nose of the crank, between the pulley and the distributor drive gear. Both these bearings are of one-piece design and prevented from rotating in the crankcase by a single dowel pin.

Stock Volkswagen crankshaft is a high-quality forging which has proved itself to be extremely dependable. This is a late 'F'-type forging with cross-drilled oilways. Note the four-dowel flywheel fitting.

The crankshaft used in the 25 and 30bhp engines carries the part number 111 105 101 and has a stroke of 64mm. Numbers 1, 2 and 3 main bearing journals are 50mm in diameter, with number 4 being 40mm. Each rod journal is also 50mm in diameter. In August 1960 (the 34bhp unit, starting with engine number 5 000 001) the crankshaft was changed to part number 113 105 101A and the journal diameters grew to 55mm for numbers 1 to 3 bearings, and 42mm for number 4.

While all of these factory crankshafts were high-quality forgings, they lacked the ability to withstand high engine rpm for reasons which will be discussed later in this chapter. The design of the oil-ways within the cranks also precluded their use in high-performance applications, as there is an insufficient supply of lubricant to all bearings at high engine rpm. By high, we mean in excess of 5,000rpm.

When the first 1500cc engines appeared in the Type 2 range, in January 1963, the crankshaft was increased in stroke by 5mm to 69mm and came with the part number 311 105 101B. As can be seen from the '311' prefix, this crank was originally designed for the new Type 3 range which had been introduced in 1962. There were other changes made to the VW forgings: in 1966, both 64mm and 69mm crankshafts were modified to accept a new design of flywheel, which spigotted onto the end of the crank and featured an O-ring to help prevent loss of oil past the dowel pins (older cranks used a thin steel gasket). This necessitated the machining of a 10.8mm-deep relief on the end of the cranks (part number 113 105 101E and 311 105 101E) to accommodate the new flywheel, earlier cranks having a relief of just 7.1mm. For this reason, it is not possible to fit a later flywheel onto an early-style crankshaft. However, it is worth noting that an earlier flywheel can be used on a later crankshaft should the need arise.

Later, towards the end of 1967, this crank was redesigned with further improved oil-ways ('cross-drilled') and given the part number 311 105 101F. This 'F' crank is the finest factory crank available and was used in all air-cooled VWs other than the 1200cc Type 1 and the Type 4/2A models from this date. Featuring extra oil-ways drilled through the forging, the 'F' crank overcame any problems from which earlier crankshafts had suffered in terms of an inadequate supply of oil to both rod and main bearing journals.

Flywheels

The design of the flywheel itself has been changed over the years. To begin with, all flywheels were machined to accept a 180mm-diameter clutch assembly and came with 109 teeth on the starter motor ring gear. The flywheel of the early 25 and 30bhp (US 36hp) engines carried the part number 111 105 271, while the 34bhp engine came with flywheel part number 113 105 271B. In 1962, a 200mm clutch was developed for the Type 2 range, as the 180mm assembly was proving unable to cope with the greater weight of these vehicles, necessitating the use of a new flywheel (part number 211 105 271, later superseded by 211 105 271C). However, the 180mm clutch/flywheel would continue to be used in all 1200cc and future 1300cc applications, with part number 113 105 271C. In August 1966, a new 200mm flywheel was introduced on both Type 2s and Type 3s (part number 311 105 271), which had 130 teeth on the ring gear, in deference to the introduction of the 12 volt electrical system across the majority of the VW range.

Increased horsepower leads to the VW engine shedding its flywheel when driven hard. Drilling the crank and flywheel for eight dowels helps solve the problem. One dowel is always offset to ensure flywheel is refitted the same way every time.

In all cases, the flywheel is located on the crankshaft using four 8mm dowel pins and held in place with a large 36mm-head gland nut which must be tightened to 30kgm (217lbft). This system works fine in most instances, but is inadequate for high-performance applications where it is possible for the dowel pins to shear, causing the flywheel to come loose on the crank. To combat this, the crankshaft and flywheel need to be drilled for an extra set of dowel pins (available in either 8mm or 11/32in diameter). This can be accomplished using a drill jig, available from many of the VW aftermarket suppliers, and the work carried out by any competent machine shop. The advantage of adding the extra dowels is obvious: the load on the four factory dowels is considerably reduced and the flywheel has a far better chance of staying in place. Note that one of the extra dowels is almost always drilled in an offset position. This is so that the flywheel can only be fitted one way onto the crank, thus ensuring that the engine remains in

Stock VW flywheel can be lightened by removing material from around the edge as shown. Flywheel on right has been blanchard ground to ensure perfect finish for clutch to bite more efficiently. Note O-rings used on all cranks from 1966 on.

The stock flywheel gland nut is not strong enough to withstand increased tightening torque. A chrome-moly nut will do the job nicely. Longer dowels help keep the flywheel in place while ground washer adds extra support.

When straight 8-dowelling is not sufficient, having the crank and flywheel assembly wedgemated is the answer. End of crank is ground to a taper, with the inside of the flywheel welded and ground to match. This is the perfect solution for those on a budget.

designed to be used without a washer. Whether these or the chrome-moly type are used, the tightening torque can be increased to as much as 350-400lbft, thereby ensuring the flywheel won't part company with the crank in most instances.

In cases where even this level of security is not enough - for example, in drag race applications where a high-rpm launch can result in the flywheel being torn off the crank, despite the presence of extra dowel pins and a heavy-duty gland nut - there are two options available: wedgemating or the use of a flanged crankshaft. The former was introduced by Porsche back in the 1950s, as a way to prevent the flywheel working loose during the constant cycle of increasing and decreasing engine rpm that comes about as a result of the on and off use of the throttle during a road race or rally.

Wedgemating is the procedure whereby the inside of the flywheel (on the side facing the crankshaft) is welded and machined with a taper. A similar taper is machined on to the end of the crank so that, when the two are mated together, an extremely tight fit results. Indeed, once a such a crank and flywheel assembly has been mated, removal of the flywheel becomes something of a chore for the home mechanic, necessitating the use of an air-driven 'chatter gun' to help break the flywheel loose. Alternatively, it is possible to press the flywheel off the crank but doing so can risk damage to the taper surfaces or even distort the flywheel, so this procedure is not recommended unless there is no alternative.

Volkswagen engineers acknowledged the merits of the bolt-on flywheel when they designed the Type 4 range. Instead of relying on the four small dowel pins and a single large gland nut, the Type 4 used five small bolts to secure the flywheel onto the crank. However, this is not the ideal solution to the problem of a poorly supported flywheel, as the load needs to be spread out over a larger area. Scat Enterprises came up with a solution when it introduced the Volkstroker II Pro-Drag crankshaft, which features a larger flange with no less than six 7/16x20 grade 8 bolts and six dowel pins holding the flywheel in place. This is commonly

balance when the flywheel is refitted. This offset pattern is commonly referred to as the SPG pattern, after the German company who first introduced it.

To get the most from this arrangement, the stock gland nut and washer should be exchanged for a heavy-duty, chrome-moly type which is available from just about every VW performance specialist. This design of gland nut usually comes with a large diameter ground washer, which offers greater protection by covering the entire head of the dowel pins. The stock washer only partially covers the dowel pins and, therefore, does not offer adequate support. Some companies sell forged gland nuts with a larger diameter head - 1⅞ in - which are

For all-out competition use, the only answer is to use a flanged crankshaft which has a bolt-on flywheel. This is a Scat Pro-Drag forged crank which features six bolts and six dowel pins to keep things together.

The major drawback of the flanged crank is that it requires a special split two-piece rear main bearing which is not as readily available as the stock item. The flywheel oil seal is also unique to the flanged crank assembly.

known as a 'flanged crank'. This cured the loose flywheel blues at a stroke but does, however, require the use of a special split two-piece number 1 main bearing and a special flywheel oil seal. For drag racing, especially, this is a small price to pay for the security offered by the flanged design.

Welded counterweight crankshafts

Although the stock VW crankshaft is a high-quality forging, the problems begin when we make greater demands on our engines. The stock crankshaft - and here we are talking about the late 'F' forging - is perfectly adequate for use in a mild engine that rarely sees action over 5,500rpm. Above that, the lack of counterweighting results in the crank flexing and, especially where earlier

model cranks are used, actually failing altogether at high engine speeds. This was a particular problem with the old 30bhp (US 36hp) motors, where broken cranks were a common ailment when the engines were subjected to excessive rpm. Anyone who has heard a VW engine running with a broken crank (yes, they do still run!) will never forget the sound...

An inexpensive cure for this potential ailment is the use of welded-on counterweights, which can be attached to the stock factory crankshaft. Counterweighting is necessary to offset the loads on the crank as it rotates - the rod journals are, of course, offset from the centerline of the crankshaft and therefore result in constantly changing loads being applied, not only to the crank, but also to the crankcase and bearings. At high engine rpm these loads can be sufficient to destroy a crankcase in very little time unless steps are taken to even out the stresses.

Several companies have offered crankshafts with welded-on counterweights, based on the factory forgings, notably Rimco, Scat and Gene Berg Enterprises. Rimco starts with a sound stock crank and welds on a set of counterweights to the crank webs. These rough weights are then turned down in a lathe before the crank is then finish-machined and balanced. Most, if not all, welded counterweighted crankshafts are reground to an undersize bearing diameter, usually 0.25mm (0.010in), on both main and rod journals. This is not only to take into account the fact that almost all such cranks are based on sound used components, but also to ensure the crank is straight, and the bearing surfaces undamaged, following the welding process. These welded 69mm counterweighted crankshafts offer great value for money for the engine builder wishing to stay on a more modest budget. Almost certainly, the most popular conversion carried out on the air-cooled VW engine is to retain the stock crankshaft and increase its capacity to either 1776cc, with the use of 90.5mm cylinders, or 1835cc, by using 92mm cylinders. The maximum size it is currently possible to build a VW engine, while retaining the stock stroke, is

Rimco of Santa Ana, California, starts with a stock F-type VW crank and welds on counterweights as shown.

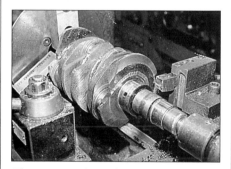

These counterweights are then narrowed on a lathe to reduce weight and provide clearance inside the crankcase.

Material that has to be removed to achieve perfect balance is taken off manually using a belt-sander.

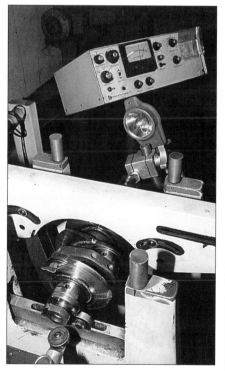

The finished crank is placed in a balancing machine to check on balance. Strobe light shows up areas to remove metal.

This is a finished Rimco 69mm welded counterweighted crankshaft – note that it has been drilled for eight dowel pins.

1915cc, achieved with the use of 94mm cylinders. Beyond this, it is necessary to use a long stroke (or 'stroker') crankshaft to increase the capacity.

Stroker cranks are available in a variety of designs, varying in cost from what can only described as 'reasonable' to 'expensive'! The first stroker crankshafts were, in fact, regular VW cranks that had been offset ground - ie, the rod journals were remachined to a smaller diameter (usually Porsche 50mm) and slightly off-

Stock cranks can be welded and offset-ground to achieve a longer than stock stroke. This is a 74mm crankshaft based on a late F-type forging. Such cranks are excellent for hot street use – if you can find a good quality one like this Berg part.

center from the original. This resulted in a stroke of as much as 74mm being achieved. A better solution was to weld the rod bearing surfaces and again offset-grind the crank to result in a longer stroke. This process allowed cranks with a stroke of up to 84mm to be 'created' from a factory forging, although there are many who feel that 78mm is the practical maximum when Volkswagen bearing journal dimensions are retained. However, by opting for the smaller 53mm Porsche, 2in Chevrolet or even the 46mm VW Rabbit (European Golf) journal size, the strength of the crankshaft need not be unduly compromised for anything other than all-out race applications.

The amount of work necessary to convert a stock crank into an 8-dowelled (or wedgemated), welded, counterweighted stroker is enormous and such cranks really do represent exceptional value for money. However, among the companies that have offered

such cranks in the past, Pauter Machine now no longer advertises the product due to the labour-intensive production process. Gene Berg Enterprises does not list any such crank, stating the same reason, and it is more than a possibility that other companies will also feel the same way in the future.

Aftermarket crankshafts

While welded factory cranks are perfectly adequate for many installations (the author used a Pauter Machine welded 78mm crank in a 400bhp turbocharged drag race engine for four seasons without failure), the best way to increase the stroke of an engine is to use a good-quality aftermarket crankshaft. The first to appear on the scene, back in the 1950s, was the superb, high-quality forged stroker crank

Gene Berg Enterprises no longer manufactures a welded, counterweighted crankshaft as it does not feel the amount of work necessary to produce a high-quality part is not cost-effective in the long run.

manufactured by Okrasa in Germany for the 30bhp (US 36hp) engine. Used in conjunction with the stock 77mm cylinders and pistons, the Okrasa 69mm crank resulted in a capacity of 1285cc (as opposed to the original 1192cc). A 67mm crank was available from Denzel, this being used in conjunction with larger 78mm cylinders and pistons to give 1281cc. Later, in the USA, EMPI began to market the Okrasa conversions and soon after added its own 69.5mm stroker crank for the Volkswagen engine.

Today, there are several companies offering stroker cranks which are not based on a factory forging. The least expensive of these are the cast crankshafts. As the name suggests, these are not forgings but are actually cast by pouring metal into a mould to create a blank from which the finished crankshaft is machined. The manufacturing process is fast and relatively inexpensive but does not result in a crank that is as strong as a forging. However, for some low-rpm applications this need not be a problem and many such crankshafts have been sold throughout the world. Indeed, CB Performance claims in its catalog that its cast crank is the world's most popular counterweighted VW crankshaft, with over 30,000 sold.

For applications where greater strength is required, such as high-horsepower street engines and all-out competition motors, there is no alternative but to use an aftermarket forged crankshaft. These are offered by all the major suppliers and can, in most cases, be considered a worthwhile alternative to either welded or cast stroker cranks. Note we say 'in most cases'. It has to be said that, over the years, there have been some poor quality crankshafts which the suppliers have claimed to be forgings but have proved to be otherwise. Today, to find such a crank on sale new is an unlikely situation but be wary of cheap used cranks which may be on offer at swapmeets.

Forged crankshafts are manufactured from a billet created by pressing the material into the approximate shape of the crank, from which the finished item is machined to size. The major benefit of forging over casting is the more uniform

strength of the finished product, with the grain flow of the material (yes, forged metal does have a grain, just like wood) evenly following the contours of the crank.

CB Performance lists a range of forged crankshafts alongside its cast and welded counterweighted cranks, the latter being available in strokes up 86mm with VW, Porsche or Rabbit rod journals. The forged cranks are manufactured with 78mm, 82mm and 84mm strokes. All cranks are available with 46mm Rabbit rod journals while the 78mm crank is also available with 55mm VW journals. The 82mm crank can be ordered with either VW or Porsche rod journals while the 84mm stroker is available with the Porsche journal. All CB Performance stroker cranks are drilled for 8 dowels in the offset SPG pattern.

Gene Berg Enterprises prides itself in manufacturing forged crankshafts using the original Volkswagen tooling, modified

to suit the new application, and is justly proud of the forging process which results in a crank of exceptionally high quality. By forging a blank (ie, a raw, unmachined crank) that is close to the finished size and shape, it is possible to control the grain flow so that it very closely follows the shape of the journals and counterweights without creating any weak points when the final machining is carried out.

The process of manufacturing a quality forged crankshaft is long and therefore costly. However, the greater expense is more than compensated for by the gains in strength and ultimate reliability. With race engines turning at up to 9,500rpm - or more - it doesn't pay to cut corners. Gene Berg Enterprises' cranks are manufactured from the same material as that used by Porsche in its 911, and the forging, heat-treating and X-ray inspection are carried out by the same Swedish company which supplies VW, Porsche and BMW. They are available in

Forged cranks begin life as a crudely-formed blank such as this from Gene Berg Enterprises. Already it is possible to identify the basic shape of the crankshaft.

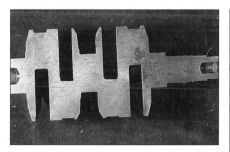

This classic Berg photograph shows one of the GBE forgings cut lengthways to demonstrate the grain pattern which is present in all forged crankshafts. GBE always prides itself on the evenness of the grain structure of its cranks.

Each rough forging is machined on a lathe with the main bearings being the first to take shape. This establishes an accurate center line around which all other machining operations are based.

anything from 78mm up to 94mm (88mm and above are to special order only).

The rod journals are machined to either VW, Porsche or Capri diameters while the number 2 main bearing is always machined to the larger Type 4 (60mm) diameter. The latter feature is designed to give the crankshaft much needed extra strength about the center main bearing and thereby help to reduce flex at high rpm. This requires the use of a special bearing shell (a BMW part) which has the Type 4 inner and stock Type 1 external diameters. Berg does not recommend line-boring the crankcase to accept a stock Type 4 center main bearing, although other engine builders will often choose to go this route so as to make use of the thicker Type 4 bearing shells. Either way, these Type 4 center mains will require a small notch to be cut into each crankcase half to accept the tangs on the bearings which are necessary to prevent the bearing shells from turning in the case.

The main bearing journals are machined with a groove leading forwards from the oilways (in terms of crank rotation) so as to scoop oil into the cross-drillings and force it towards the rod bearings. This characteristic, which Berg refers to as hydro-dynamic oiling, helps to increase the pressure at the rod journal, especially at high rpm. Note that there is no groove leading away from behind the oil-ways, nor a groove all the way round the crank journals, either of which would reduce the amount of oil picked up as the crank rotates.

Once each oil gallery has been drilled in the crankshaft, the closed end is tapped to accept a threaded plug. These plugs may be removed at a later date to facilitate cleaning the oil-ways, a job which should be carried out each time the engine is rebuilt.

After machining, the cranks are stress-relieved prior to drilling the oil-ways, rough ground to 0.015in oversize, stress-relieved a second time and then ground to finished size. Berg machines all the main bearing journals in one fixture, a procedure which is demanding on equipment (it requires the use of four separate dial gauges to check the sizing)

Bugpack wedgemated crankshaft from Dee Engineering is an excellent choice for all-out street and drag race use. Bugpack cranks have an excellent reputation for offering high quality at an affordable price.

A good quality crankshaft is the heart of a high-performance engine. Always buy the best you can afford – you will not regret it.

but ensures total accuracy. Once ground to size, the crank is finally Nitrided - a surface-hardening treatment which ensures long journal life - and then shot-peened to relieve any stress points, micro-polished on the journals and, finally, dynamically balanced. As you can see, the production of a quality crankshaft is no five minute job! All Berg crankshafts come drilled for 8 dowels and can also be

supplied wedgemated to a matching flywheel.

Bugpack (Dee Engineering) markets a range of quality forged stroker crankshafts for use in the Type 1 engine. These are available with a 78mm stroke, with VW journals, or in 82mm, 84mm, 86mm and 90mm, all with Porsche rod journals. The 86mm-90mm cranks are machined to accept the larger Type 4

Photo shows a Scat Pro-Drag billet crank taking shape on Scat Enterprises' computer-controlled CNC equipment. This tooling can cope with virtually any specification of crankshaft a customer might need.

center main bearing. The Bugpack cranks are manufactured from E4340 chrome-moly and come with Nitrided bearing surfaces for long bearing life. They are also Magnafluxed and balanced prior to sale and are drilled for 8 dowels in the popular SPG pattern. All Bugpack forged crankshafts are available wedgemated to a matching flywheel.

Scat Enterprises manufactures a superb line of crankshafts which are available in any stroke from 59mm up to 94mm. Top of the line is the Volkstroker II Pro-Drag billet crankshaft, which is machined from 4340 chrome-moly billet and features a flange to mount the flywheel. As discussed earlier, this system requires the use of a special split number 1 bearing (and minor machine work on the crankcase to accept the new 4in diameter seal), but these disadvantages are far outweighed by the positive method of retaining the flywheel: six bolts and six dowel pins mean that the crank won't part company with the flywheel under (virtually) any circumstances.

Scat crankshafts are manufactured using CNC computerised equipment supported by a CAD (Computer Aided Design) system to ensure total dimensional accuracy at all times. The equipment is truly versatile and can handle the manufacture of any crankshaft up to 60in (1520mm) long and with a stroke of up to 8in (203mm)! It goes without saying that a Volkswagen crankshaft of any description presents few problems for this equipment.

A unique feature of the Pro-Drag crank from Scat is the drilled rod journals, which feature a hole bored longitudinally through the journal and adjoining webs. The thinking behind this is to reduce the overall weight of the crankshaft and thus keep the revolving mass to a minimum. This results in an engine which feels more responsive and is less likely to suffer from case pounding at high engine rpm. This feature is only available on crankshafts of 76mm and above, as below this stroke the holes would interfere with the main bearing journals and weaken the crank. Knife-edged counterweights help to keep the weight down and are also designed to

Scat Enterprises' Pro-Drag crankshafts are drilled through the rod bearing journals in an effort to save weight. Many of the top drag racers in the Pro-Stock and Pro-Turbo classes use these cranks.

slice through the oil in the engine with less drag.

To complement this crankshaft, Scat can supply a 4340 chrome-moly billet flywheel which weighs 12lb and comes ready machined to mate with the flange on the crankshaft. Available with either 6v or 12v starter ring gear, these flywheels can also be supplied to accept the J&G floater clutch assembly for drag racing.

Scat Volkstroker II Pro-Comp crankshaft receives the final touches to number 3 main bearing. Liquid is used to prevent tooling from gauling or overheating the surface of the material.

Scat also offers a range of 8-dowelled crankshafts, with or without the lightening holes bored through the journals. Called the Volkstroker II Pro-Comp, this is a less costly alternative to the Pro-Drag for those who don't need the security of a flanged crankshaft. Manufactured to the same high standard, these cranks are machined from a 4340 chrome-moly multi-die forging. Each crankshaft is Magnafluxed (X-ray crack tested), dynamically balanced and micro-polished before being Nitrided for greater strength and reduced journal wear. All Pro-Drag and Pro-Comp cranks are available with a choice of either Type 1 or Type 4 main bearing journals. Finally, Scat's Pro-Street crank is similar to the Pro-comp but is not available with lightening holes and does not come with the Nitride surface-hardening treatment. Intended as a high-quality part for use in vehicles which won't see all-out race action, this is a fine choice for someone wishing to build a high-performance engine for the street.

Pauter Machine produced a range of billet crankshafts for a number of years and then, due to rising material and manufacturing costs, were forced to withdraw them from the market. However, such is the demand in recent times for high-quality, long-stroke crankshafts for competition use that Pauter Machine decided to retool for production and can now offer its Super Pro 4340 chrome-moly billet crankshafts once again. Machined from a solid billet of steel on state-of-the-art CNC equipment, the Super Pro cranks are designed for everything from high-horsepower street use to all-out competition, such as drag racing or sand dragging. Pauter's cranks are produced with a flange to accept the specially-made flywheel, although this flange is larger in diameter than the similar Scat set-up:

Scat Enterprises' Volkstroker crankshaft shown all finished and ready to go. Note the keyways machined into end of crank to accept Woodruff keys for camshaft and distributor drive gears and crank pulley.

Pauter machine of Chula Vista, California, manufactures a range of superb crankshafts machined from a solid billet of 4340 chrome-moly steel. Flange is a slightly different size to that used by Scat: 3.750in diameter as opposed to 2.562in.

3.750in in diameter as opposed to 2.562in. The flywheel produced by Pauter is machined from chrome-moly and can be ordered to accept single- or two-disc stock-style clutches, a J&G floater or a Tilton multi-disc arrangement.

Pauter Machine offers its Super Pro crank in any stroke the customer requires and can also machine the rod journals to stock VW, Chevy or Porsche dimensions. In addition, the main bearing journals can be finished to VW Type 1, Type 4 or the mighty Ford 351 V8 size, the latter being *de rigeur* for Pauter's billet Big Block crankcase.

Choosing a crankshaft

Today, the VW enthusiast has what is probably the finest ever selection of crankshafts on offer to him, with everything from counterweighted stock forgings right up to Pauter Machine, Berg and Scat's bullet-proof stroker cranks in anything up to 94mm stroke and with a variety of bearing journals. There is even a full-circle-counterweighted crank on offer from Weber Cam for those who feel this is the best solution to engine imbalance at high rpm. However, none of this helps the engine builder to decide what is the best crank for him in terms of stroke and rod journal - two of the most

important factors in choosing a crankshaft. Let's take a look at stroke first.

A stock late-model VW engine displaces 1584cc and this is achieved by use of a crankshaft with a stroke of 69mm and a set of cylinders and pistons with a bore of 85.5mm. Now, to increase the size of this engine to, say, 1900cc or thereabouts, we have three options: increase the bore, increase the stroke or increase both. Each has its own merits. An increase in bore to 94mm would result in a capacity of 1915cc, while an increase in stroke to 84mm would create a 1929cc

Pauter makes a matching flywheel, also machined from 4340 chrome-moly. This is available to accept either a stock type clutch, a J&G 'floater' or a Tilton multi-disc clutch.

engine. The former would certainly result in more horsepower, notably higher up the rpm range, and be a reasonably inexpensive engine to build, but would require machining the crankcase and heads for larger cylinders. The 84mm stroke option would result in an engine with tremendous torque but would be comparatively expensive to build, necessitating long-stroke crankshaft, almost certainly longer conrods, either spacers under the cylinders or 'stroker' pistons, possibly longer pushrods, clearanced crankcase, etc, etc.

The third alternative would be to build a combination of the above with a milder 74mm stroker crankshaft and 90.5mm cylinders and pistons. This would result in a displacement of 1904cc but would require the purchase of both a long-stroke crank and larger cylinders. There would be little need for internal clearancing of the crankcase for the longer stroke although the case and heads would need to be machined for the larger cylinders. However, the stock-length conrods would be satisfactory and the engine would produce both more torque and more horsepower than a stocker.

As you can see, there are a number of considerations to bear in mind when choosing what engine combination to go for and, as the crankshaft is the single most expensive component of your engine, it pays to think carefully before making your decision. However, in most instances, there is no difference in cost between a 78mm and an 84mm crank, although longer stroke cranks than this frequently carry a higher price tag, depending on manufacturer. Where increased costs do arise is when longer rods are needed (usually where strokes above 78mm are involved) or where special stroker pistons are deemed necessary (generally with strokes of 84mm and above). Bearing that in mind, probably the best all round combination for regular fast street use is an engine based around a 78mm crank as it does not necessarily require other exotic (read: expensive) components or excessive crankcase clearancing.

If there is one golden rule about stroker cranks, it is this: the longer the stroke, the greater the torque but also, the greater the hassle factor. Clearancing the crankcase, more exotic parts - all add up to extra cost, and this is compounded by any increase in stroke over and above 78mm. However, for serious performance use, and by this we don't only mean all-out race applications, there is no substitute for a longer stroke crank used in conjunction with larger cylinders and pistons. Anyone who has driven a street car with an 84mm x 90.5mm engine cannot fail to have been impressed with the staggering increase in torque compared to a stocker.

For all practical reasons, an 84mm crank should be considered the largest stroker to use in a stock VW crankcase - above that figure there is so much clearancing required to allow the crank to turn that you are into the realms of considering the use of an aftermarket case designed to accept such cranks. However, it is not unknown for an 88mm or even a mighty 92mm crank to have been squeezed inside a highly-modified Type 1 crankcase, but long-term reliability is brought into question here.

Where aftermarket crankcases are concerned, the sky is not quite the limit, but it's pretty close. The biggest stumbling block with the factory case is the proximity of the camshaft to the conrods at the bottom of the crank's throw. Notching the cam for clearance provides a partial solution, but not when a long stroke crank is used in conjunction with certain conrods. The answer here is to use an aftermarket case with a dropped camshaft bore, which moves the cam away from the crank centerline for more clearance. At the top of the crank's throw, most aftermarket cases allow for extra clearance by providing either a higher roof to the case or by incorporating 'blisters' above each rod which can be seen on the outside of the casting.

As far as rod journal size is concerned, the stock VW 55mm is fine for all strokes up to 78mm, which will make use of VW-type rods. Above this stroke, it is normally recommended to change to the smaller 53mm Porsche rod journal to allow a more compact rod to be used, be it a Porsche 912 or an aftermarket type. This results in the reduced need for excessive clearancing

Nostalgia! While it may be fun to tell your friends that you have an SPG roller-bearing crankshaft, it won't be such fun to tell them your engine is destroyed because you have twisted the crank. Stick with more modern designs and you won't go wrong.

inside the case. The added advantage with using a Porsche-style rod over a VW is that the bearing journal is narrower and therefore the crank is stronger across the webs. The VW rod is 0.895in wide at the journal as opposed to the Porsche's 0.790in. Anything that can be done to improve the strength of a long stroke crank is important as it leads to less flex at higher rpm and therefore a reduction in damage to the crankcase.

Finally, before we leave crankshaft choice, how about the old SPG roller-bearing cranks? Manufactured in Germany during the 1960s and early 1970s, the SPG was a full-circle crank with roller-bearings on each rod. As a consequence, the rods were not removable from the crank which, itself, had to be pressed together in sections. This was a great idea used by Porsche

with its Hirth roller cranks, but sadly not one which proved to be particularly long-lived in high-performance VW applications. The SPG cranks were popular to begin with among the drag racers of the time but they soon discovered, to their cost, that the cranks twisted as the clutch was released on the startline. Pinning each section together helped matters but, by the time people discovered that fix, better and more conventional cranks were appearing on the market, thanks to people like Scat and Gene Berg. Our advice: if you find a good used SPG crankshaft, pass it by or do what a friend of ours did - make a table lamp out of it.

It is recommended that you always use high-quality bearings such as those made by original equipment suppliers KS or Glyco. These feature steel-backed

CRANKSHAFT BEARINGS

Type	Main Bearings	Rod Bearings
Volkswagen (early)	50mm	50mm
Volkswagen 1500/1600	55mm	55mm
Porsche	55mm	53mm
Chevrolet 327/400	-	50.8mm (2.0in)
Chevrolet Capri	-	54mm (2.125in)

The factory grinds all crankshafts with a radius to the edge of each bearing to add strength. Check that your choice of aftermarket crank is machined the same way. This is a Bugpack forged stroker crank.

center-main shells and guarantee long bearing life. Avoid using 'no-name' brands bought on price alone.

Crank Regrinding

It is generally accepted that crankshafts can and do require regrinding on occasion, either following a lot of use or as a result of damage to the journals through oil starvation or component failure. This process reduces the diameter of the journals by a small amount - just sufficient to remove the damage to the crankshaft surface. In extreme instances, this may mean that a crank needs to be re-Nitrided to restore the original surface hardening. Note that each bearing journal has a radius machined on each side adjacent to the crank web. It is imperative that any reground crank is remachined

It is essential that you use a good quality bearing in a high-performance engine. Stay away from 'no-name' brands and stick with well-established makes such as KS or Glyco.

with this radius to ensure there is no loss of strength.

New bearings are available in various under- and oversizes according to whether the crankshaft has been reground or the crankcase line-bored. In general, most bearings can be supplied 0.25mm, 0.50mm and 0.75mm undersized on the crank with up to 1.0mm oversize in the case. However, we feel that for high-performance applications it is preferable not to use a case that has had to be line-bored more than 0.50mm. Note that Gene Berg Enterprises does not recommend using a line-bored case under any circumstances.

End-Float

The end-float on a Volkswagen crankshaft is set by inserting shims between the flywheel and the thrust face of the number 1 main bearing. To set the end-float with the engine disassembled, fit the flywheel onto the crankshaft with the bearing in place and measure, using feeler gauges, the gap between the flywheel and the bearing. By fitting shims of the correct thickness, the desired end-float

can be achieved. Shims are available in six thicknesses: 0.24mm; 0.30mm; 0.32mm; 0.34mm; 0.36mm and 0.39mm. Note that only three shims are to be used at any time.

The factory end-float setting is from 0.065mm (0.0028in) to 0.125mm (0.0047in), with the wear limit being 0.15mm (0.006in), but it is recommended that race engines use a larger setting - as much as 0.25mm (0.010in). The thinking behind this is that, as a hot race engine cools down, the crankshaft tends to remain hot and can cause the rear main bearing to expand and partially seize if insufficient clearance is left between it and the flywheel.

To set the end float with the engine assembled, it is necessary to follow much the same procedure except, instead of using feeler gauges to measure the gap, a dial-gauge is used, mounted on the crankcase via a bracket so as to allow a reading to be taken from the face of the flywheel. Push the flywheel all the way in towards the crankcase and note the reading on the dial-gauge. Next, pull the flywheel as far out from the case as it will come and note the second reading. By deducting the second reading from the first, the end float can be calculated. Once again, three shims of a suitable total thickness can now be fitted behind the flywheel.

Where wedgemated crankshafts are concerned, fitting and removal of the flywheel is not an easy task. To facilitate setting the end-float, manufacturers of wedgemated cranks will always tell you the correct total thickness of shims required to achieve a given end-float.

As far as flanged crankshafts are concerned, it is not possible to fit shims to the end of the crank, so the end float is determined by the thickness of the thrust face on the number 1 bearing. The correct bearing will be supplied by the crankshaft manufacturer.

RECOMMENDATIONS

Street	Stock 69mm F-type crank; welded counterweighted up to 78mm; 8-dowelled
Hot Street	Welded counterweighted up to 78mm; forged up to 86mm; 8-dowelled; wedgemated
Competition	Forged or billet; flanged or 8-dowelled and wedgemated

CON-RODS

From stone stock to trick titanium

The connecting rods - con-rods for short - are, without doubt some of the most important ingredients in the make up of a powerful, yet reliable, engine. However, they are also somewhat taken for granted and few people, other than the serious race engine builder, fully appreciate just what an effect a change of rod can have on an engine's characteristics. By change of rod, we are not only talking in terms of make or material, but also length, for this dimension can, and does, have a dramatic effect on the way in which an engine produces horsepower and torque.

Stock con-rods

Before we get too deeply involved with the subject of rod lengths and ratios, we'll take a look at what the factory has had to offer over the years. The first rods used in the original 25bhp engine were forged

When installing a stock rod in your engine, always make sure this small casting mark is facing upwards. This mark ensures rod is fitted to crank the right way round to take into account rod offset.

Early Volkswagen rod on left was used in 25bhp and 30bhp (US 36hp) engines. Fine for the use for which it was intended, but little else! Later VW '311' rod on right is a far better design and can be used in mild performance engines without any real problem.

(cast rods were tried in some prototype engines but, fortunately for us, proved to be unreliable. We say 'fortunately' because otherwise we might have been stuck with an inherently weak rod for the rest of time!) and came with the part number 111 105 401. They had an I-beam cross-section. These rods continued to be used in the 30bhp (US 36hp) engine up until its replacement by the 34bhp (US 40hp) engine in August 1960 (from engine number 5 000 001). The new 34bhp rod carried the part number 113 105 401. The 25/30bhp rod had a length, measured from the center of the small end

to the center of the rod (or 'big end') bearing, of just 5.086in (129.25mm), compared to the 34bhp rod's 5.120in (130mm). The rod journal diameter increased from the 50mm of the original engine to 55mm at the same time.

In 1962, with the introduction of the Type 3 range, the factory produced a new con-rod with the part number 311 105 401. This was superseded almost immediately by others with the part number suffixes 'A', 'B' or 'C'. The '311' rods were longer and stronger than the earlier rods and came with a small-end diameter of 22mm compared with the previous 20mm. The rod journal diameter remained the same at 55mm but the length was increased to 5.394 in (137mm). This brought about an increase in weight, too, from the '113' rod's 507gms to 617gms for the '311'.

Note that all con-rods you are likely to come across with the 113 and 311 part numbers will have a small casting mark on one side of the beam - only the earliest 113 rods did not. These rods must always be assembled on the crankshaft with the casting mark facing upwards. This is because they have been designed with an offset small end, to center the rod in the piston. Failure to take note of this will result in excessive side-loadings being placed on the piston and increased wear.

The stock VW 311B rods (the most widely used) are more than adequate for the task for which they were designed. After all, the Volkswagen engine was conceived as a low-revving unit which placed little stress on its internal components. It is only when the engine builder starts to increase his demands on the engine that the VW rod begins to show its deficiencies. The weakest part of the Volkswagen rod is the bolt but, to appreciate why, we must take a look at what happens to the rod while the engine is running.

On the induction stroke, there is little or no strain on the rod, for the crankshaft is physically pulling the rod and piston down the cylinder, sucking the air/fuel mixture through the inlet port, past the valve. At the bottom of the induction stroke, the crankshaft begins to push the rod and piston back up the cylinder to compress the mixture in the combustion chamber. This is where the rod first starts to do any real work. At or about top dead center (TDC), the mixture is compressed to the maximum and combustion takes place. Suddenly, there is considerable force applied as the piston is pushed down the cylinder. However, this force is trying to compress the rod and, unless there really is a major problem with the choice of material, there should be no real cause for concern at this point. Rods rarely bend unless they are either subjected to extreme forces due to detonation, or excessive use of nitrous oxide, for instance, or when something breaks in the valve train, allowing the valve to drop and attempt to stop the piston dead in its tracks.

Failure is most likely to occur when the rod and piston assembly swings from travelling up the cylinder to travelling back down again at TDC. Here, the rod and piston are being moved at a quite unbelievable speed upwards and are then suddenly yanked back in the opposite direction. Just think of the forces coming into play: at just 5,000rpm, the rod and piston travel down the cylinder, back up, back down and then back up again, over

Rimco uses this set of scales to measure the weight, end for end, of each of their modified Super Rods. Correct balance is essential for a smooth, long-lasting engine. Rods are sold in matched sets of four.

83 times a second! Spin the engine to 8,500rpm and that rises to 141 per second. At the TDC point on each engine revolution, the momentum of the piston applies tremendous stresses on the rod, trying to stretch it. These stresses act on the weakest part of the assembly, which is usually the rod bolt. This situation is worst at TDC on the exhaust stroke, as there is no air/fuel mixture to compress and act as a cushion when the piston rises up the cylinder.

As far as a stock engine, limited by design to something in the region of a 5,000rpm maximum, is concerned, the rod bolts are just fine. Rarely will a bolt fail in regular use unless it has been incorrectly torqued. However, start to place greater demands - especially higher rpm limits - on the stock rod and problems will begin. In the early days of Volkswagen tuning, efforts were made to strengthen the rod by boxing the I-beam section, either by welding pieces of steel plate across the beam or simply by filling it with weld. This helped but did not really address what was the most common source of rod failure on early race engines: bolt failure. It took some time before people realized that the answer lay in replacing the stock bolt with something a little stronger.

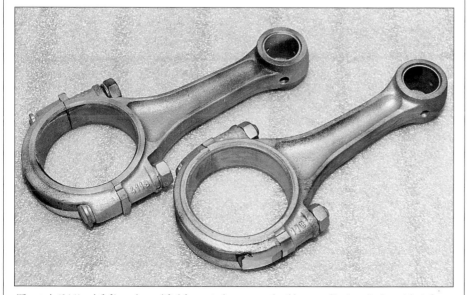

The stock '311' rod (left) can be modified for use in hot street and mild race applications. Rod on right is from Rimco and has been shot-peened to relieve stress, clearanced for use with a stroker crank and then balanced.

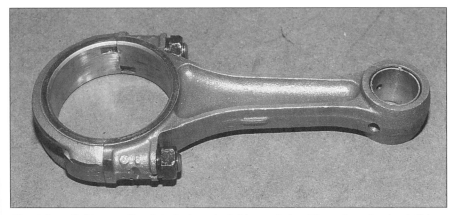

Rimco's Super Rod is an excellent choice for the engine builder on a budget. These rods cost less than half the price of a full aftermarket type yet are capable of use in race engines that frequently see in excess of 7,000rpm.

This fixture holds rod securely while belt sander removes just enough material to allow use with stroker crank without compromising rod strength.

Rimco of Santa Ana, California, along with a number of other companies, has brought the stock rod to as close to perfection as can be achieved by fitting high-strength ³/8in SPS bolts to the 311B rods, together with shot-peening and clearancing them for use with a stroker crankshaft. Such rods are good for up to 7,500rpm (and will frequently withstand more) and are an excellent choice for the engine builder on a budget, as their cost is remarkably low considering the benefits of their use.

This modified stock rod has two major drawbacks as far as the builder of high-performance engines is concerned: the inability to withstand extremely high rpm for prolonged periods and its length. A number of years ago, it was unusual to subject VW engines to exceptionally high rpm. Most were built to operate at up to 7,500 or maybe 8,000rpm. Today it is not uncommon for race engines to be

subjected to as much as 10,000rpm although, it has to be said, opinions are divided as to whether this is the ideal way to extract the most horsepower from a VW motor. Certainly 8,500-9,000rpm is commonplace and there is no way on

Gene Berg Enterprises also offers modified stock '311' rods under its GB191 part number (or GB191S when supplied shot-peaned. GBE does not remove quite as much material from side of rod as others.

earth that a Volkswagen rod, modified or otherwise, is suited to this task. Even with stronger bolts and shot-peening to relieve any stress points, the factory forging cannot be expected to survive under such conditions. The most likely point of failure would be the big-end cap itself, although it is not unknown for the small-end to become elongated and ultimately fail.

In an effort to improve the situation, early engine tuners looked for suitable alternatives to the stock rod. In the days of the 30bhp engine, one of the first to address the problem was the Austrian company, Denzel. Wolfgang Denzel's engine conversion kits were works of art and included, along with special cylinder heads and a long-stroke crankshaft, a set of aluminum con-rods which were both lighter and stronger than the original components.

Porsche rods

The next significant change in thought came when Porsche released the 356C model, powered by what was in many ways the ultimate development of the VW engine. Throughout the 1950s, Porsche had gradually developed its flat-four engine from the basic 1131cc VW unit, which powered the first cars, to a comparatively sophisticated 1600cc motor which shared few components with the contemporary VW powerplant. One of the finest features of the Porsche engine was the conrod, a lightweight, compact design with bolts which were integral with the big-end cap. This allowed the engine builder to assemble a long-stroke engine that required less clearancing inside the crankcase than one which used the more bulky stock rods. This rod was used in the 356C and SC as well as the later 912 model, and comes with a part number R616 103 10101. Earlier Porsche rods, with the part number beginning R502, should not be used as they are not strong enough for our purposes. At 5.352in (136mm) in length, the Porsche 912 rods were slightly shorter than the VW '311' part but, at 540gms, were some 77gms lighter. The rod bearing diameter was smaller than that of the VW, being just 53mm. This allowed machinists to offset-grind the stock VW crankshaft to

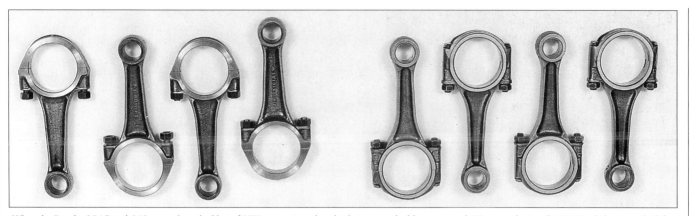

When the Porsche 356C and 912 came along, builders of VW race engines thought their prayers had been answered. However, the Porsche '616' rod shown on the left didn't prove as strong as hoped. Many suffered rod bolt failure. However, design of rod bearing cap allowed use of stroker crank with minimum of clearancing.

the smaller Porsche rod-journal dimension, gaining a small increase in stroke without having to clearance the crankcase excessively, when the 912 rods were used.

Engine builders loved their high-quality forging, the light weight and the need for less crankcase clearancing, but the Porsche design still did not solve the problem of high-rpm failure. As time was to prove, they earned themselves a reputation for breaking at the base of the bolt where it joins the big-end cap, especially as many of the rods used by drag racers in the 1960s were not new and had already been subjected to many miles of road or race use in the original Porsche engine. However, as long as the rpm is kept to a safe level – 7,000rpm is generally reckoned to be a satisfactory limit – the Porsche 912 con-rod can see long life.

The problem today is that Porsche 912 rods are very hard to come by and are also very expensive. Now that early Porsches are themselves sought after (remember, in the mid-1960s, it was possible to buy used Porsches, and especially their engines, very inexpensively), getting hold of a good set of 912 or 356C/SC rods is increasingly difficult. It has to be said, however, that nowadays there really is little point in choosing to use these con-rods, as there are more suitable alternatives readily available at a more attractive price. Note that you should beware of Brazilian replicas, which look exactly like the genuine Porsche article but are not forged from the same chrome-moly material and are, therefore, not as strong.

Rod ratio
Aside from the matter of strength and consequent rpm limits, the main drawback for the competition engine

When you hear your engine detonating, it may not only be the pistons which suffer! Gary Berg had this '616' Porsche rod split along the beam as a result of detonation.

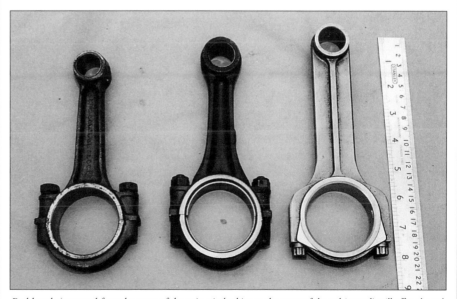

Rod length (measured from the center of the wrist-pin bushing to the center of the rod journal) will affect the rod ratio – that's the ratio of rod length to crankshaft stroke. On the right is a 6.500in billet chrome-moly piece from Pauter Machine while on left is a short 5.086in early VW rod.

builder is the short overall length of the 912 rod. This brings to light the subject of rod ratio. This is the ratio of the length of the connecting rod to the stroke of the crankshaft. For example, a stock VW 1600 engine, with its 137mm long rod and 69mm stroke crankshaft, will have a rod ratio of 137:69 = 1.98. In very general terms, the shorter the rod and hence the lower the rod ratio, the more torque the engine will produce at lower rpm. The longer the rod for a given stroke, the higher the rod ratio and the more the power band will be moved up the rpm range.

With a short rod and lower rod ratio, the piston speed for a given rpm becomes much higher as the piston/rod assembly travels down the cylinder. On the inlet stroke, this makes for better cylinder filling - assuming an efficient inlet port design - and hence greater torque as more air/fuel is made available for the engine to burn at low rpm. An increase in rod length results in slower piston speeds for a given rpm, which means less efficient cylinder filling until higher rpm levels are reached. Only then can greater cylinder filling be achieved.

Obviously there are disadvantages to both options. Short rods result in greater side-loads on the cylinder walls, and hence an increase in both frictional losses and cylinder/piston ring wear. Long rods are easier on the cylinders and rings but reduce the engine's efficiency at low rpm. Engines with long rods and stroker crankshafts are also physically much wider than short rod/short stroke motors and can be a problem to fit into a stock-bodied sedan: with any stroker crankshaft, at TDC the piston crown will end up much further from the centerline of the engine. If a long rod is used, the crown will be moved out even further at TDC. This means that either spacers will have to be placed under the cylinders, or longer cylinder barrels used, in conjunction with short-compression-height pistons in order to keep the pistons within the cylinder bore at the top of each stroke. This automatically requires the use of not only longer cylinder head studs, but also longer push-rods and a wider exhaust system to reach across from one side of the engine to the other. If the engine is to be used in a street-legal vehicle with, a full cooling system, then the sheetmetal of the cylinder head shrouding will have to be extended, too. Note: contrary to popular myth, fitting a longer rod to your engine will not change its cubic capacity! For some reason, that is one old wives' tale which refuses to go away.

Many performance engine builders believe the rod ratio should lie somewhere between 1.65 - 1.70, feeling that this is a good compromise between the ability to achieve a good spread of power across the rev range and yet keep cylinder and piston wear within acceptable limits. However, for a race motor, where longevity and/or a broad spread of power are not prime considerations, there is no reason why the rod ratio could not be well above 2.0 or well under 1.6. There will always be those who don't wish to go with the flow and prefer to experiment with radical departures from the norm. However, unless you have access to a dynamometer and a large pile of parts, it is perhaps best to follow the accepted path.

Chevrolet, Rabbit and aftermarket rods

So far, we have looked in detail only at VW and Porsche rods, but there are many other options available to the engine builder, some exotic, others not so. Of the latter, a popular choice has been the Chevrolet 327 con-rod. The potential of this rod first came to light when people began to look around for a longer rod to go with their stroker crankshafts, but one which wouldn't cost a fortune to buy. As the domestic performance industry in the USA is dominated by Chevrolet products, the prices of most components are well below those of the equivalent VW parts. Indeed, it is somewhat ironic that it is possible to buy a set of eight aftermarket con-rods for a Chevrolet V8 engine for the same price as a set of four for a VW!

The Chevrolet rod measures 5.700inches (144.78mm) center-to-center and weighs a reasonable 585gms. The rod journal diameter is 2in (50.8mm) making it possible to offset grind a stock VW crank if necessary. The Chevy rods are good quality forgings which are readily available, but do require some clearancing of the big-end cap for use in the VW engine case, while the small-end needs to be replaced with a 22mm bushing to accept the VW-pattern wrist (or 'gudgeon') pin. The top of the rod, at the small end, also needs to be machined to provide adequate clearance between the rod and the piston crown to allow the rod to swing back and forth at TDC and BDC (bottom dead center).

In addition to the 327 Chevy rod, Pauter Machine and others offer a modified 400 Chevy component. This is a shorter, 5.55in (140.97mm), rod which

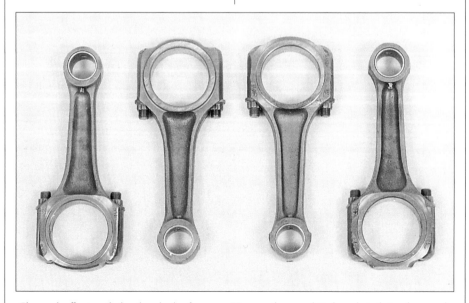

Chevy rods offer strength, length and value for money. However, they are relatively crude in design, heavy and may require some extra clearancing when use with a longer stroke crank. Chevy 327 rod is 5.700in long.

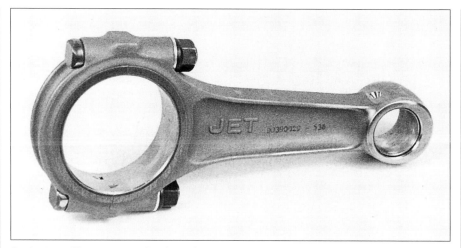

Jet titanium rod has never met with widespread acceptance due to high cost. Titanium is extremely expensive, but very light and strong. Rod is similar in design to original VW-style forging.

can be machined to accept either a stock VW (55mm) or Porsche (53mm) rod bearing and is an acceptable alternative to a modified VW '311' rod where costs have to be kept within reasonable limits. Also available is the Chevy Capri rod with a 2.125in (54mm) journal which, like the Chevy 400, measures 5.55in center-to-center. However, it is worth noting that they are still appreciably more expensive than the modified VW rod.

Chevrolet rods are not the only non-air-cooled VW alternatives, for it is possible to purchase from a number of sources, notably CB Performance, a so-called 'bolt-in stroker kit' which consists of a reground and stroked VW crankshaft

with a set of modified rods from a VW Rabbit (the US version of the European Golf water-cooled VW). These feature a 46mm rod bearing and have their big-end cap bolts reversed to allow more clearance within the crankcase. They are relatively inexpensive and have the advantage of allowing a crankshaft of up to 82mm stroke to be installed in a Type 1 crankcase with only very minor machining - indeed, a 78mm crank requires no crankcase clearancing at all. However, there are some engine builders who believe that the small diameter of the rod journal leads to an inherently weak crankshaft, rendering the conversion unsuited to serious high-performance

applications. There is certainly little doubt, however, that the rods themselves are more than strong enough for the task in hand.

When rods longer, stronger or lighter than Chevrolet's 327 parts are required, for example in high-rpm, all-out race motors, there is only one option: the aftermarket con-rod. The Volkswagen engine builder has several to choose from, ranging from the tried and tested forged rods to the more exotic billet aluminum items. It is also possible to buy a set of titanium rods for the VW - made by Jet, these ultra-light rods have not proved to be popular simply because their initial cost is so high compared with other proven designs.

Without doubt, the most widely-known aftermarket rod is that manufactured by Carrillo. First made available for all popular V8 engines, the Carrillo is a very robust forged H-section rod, made from E4340 chrome-moly, that is available in virtually any combination of length and journal to suit all possible applications. The most popular sizes remain the stock VW (5.394in long with 55mm journal) and 5.5in, 5.6in and 5.7in lengths with, in most cases, the Porsche 53mm rod journal. Each have alignment bushes in the big-end cap to ensure perfect alignment of the bearings every time the rods are reassembled.

Although Carrillos are frequently in

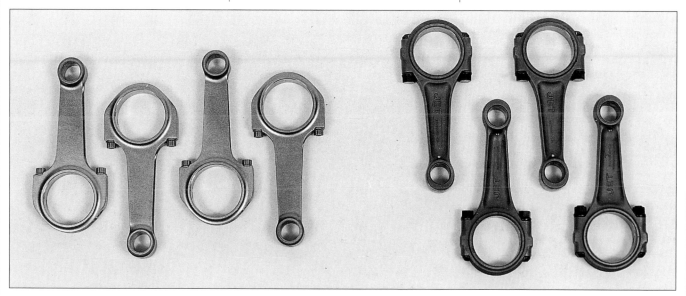

Carrillo rods on the left have almost become the industry standard – basically, you cannot go far wrong with a set of these in your engine. However, often poor availability and a relatively high price tag will make alternatives seem equally as attractive. Rods on right are exotic Jet titanium.

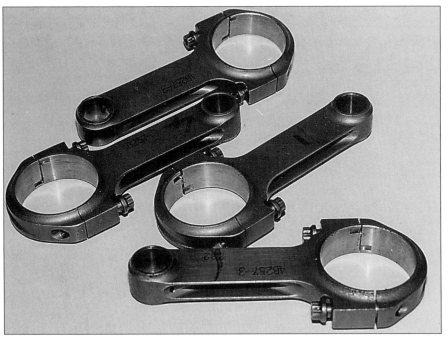

Bugpack's Race Rods from Dee Engineering look very similar to the Carrillo. They, too, are manufactured from 4340 chrome-moly and are available in a wide variety of lengths and rod journals.

short supply, they are generally regarded as some of the finest rods on the market - their SPS bolts are extremely strong and failures are uncommon, unless the bolts have been over-tightened. For this reason, Carrillo recommends that you test-tighten a rod bolt before general engine assembly and measure the bolt stretch. To do this, you need to use a micrometer to measure the overall length of a new bolt and then assemble the rod and gradually tighten the bolts with an accurate torque wrench. Start by torquing the bolts to 35ftlb and then measure the length of the bolt again. Increase the torque wrench setting by no more than 5ftlb increments and measure the bolt length each time. You will note that the bolt will begin to stretch - when the bolt has increased in length by 0.006in, stop and note the torque setting of the wrench. This, then, is the torque figure which should be applied to all bolts. On a set used by the author for

Scat Enterprises' own chrome-moly rod - the Superlite Pro-Moly - has a very different appearance to other makes. Like others, it is also manufactured from 4340 chrome-moly but has a thicker section beam.

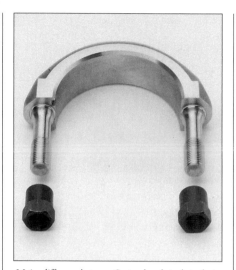

Major difference between Scat rod and rivals is that the rod bolts are an integral part of the rod bearing cap, just like the old Porsche design. This makes for a compact rod which reduces the need for extra clearancing in some applications.

bearing caps, similar to the original Porsche 912 rod. The Scat Superlite rod is available in four different lengths: the popular stock VW 311 and Porsche 912 as well as 5.5in and 5.7in. The Porsche 5.354in, 5.5in and 5.7in rods are supplied with either the 55mm VW, 53mm Porsche or 2in Chevrolet rod journal, while the VW 5.394in version comes only with the stock VW journal. The Scat rods are equipped with 3/8in E8740 chrome-moly nuts, which must be lubricated with a light machine oil and torqued to no more than 36ftlb. Replacement rod nuts are available.

In addition to forged con-rods, it is

Pauter Machine's billet chrome-moly rod differs from others like the Carrillo or Scat in that it is a cruciform design with a beam which is slimmer and features strengthening ribs along each side.

several seasons, while drag racing, the torque figure worked out at 53ftlb, but it may vary from wrench to wrench.

Whenever you assemble Carrillo rods, it is vital that you lightly oil the bolts so that the thread does not stick and result in a false torque reading. Do not use any super-slippery moly-type lubricants - a light machine oil is all that is necessary.

A rod that is very similar to the Carrillo is the Race Rod manufactured by Dee Engineering under the Bugpack name. Virtually identical in appearance to the Carrillo, the Bugpack rod is available in three different lengths: 5.352in (equivalent to the 136mm Porsche) with a VW journal, and 5.5in and 5.6in with Porsche 53mm journals. They are also are forged from E4340 chrome-moly but rely on Bugpack's own 220,000psi fasteners. Also, like the Carrillo, the Bugpack rods come with alignment bushes in the big-end cap. Again, as with the Carrillos, it is necessary to carry out a pre-assembly check on the rod bolts. In the case of the Bugpack Race Rods, a bolt stretch of 0.006in equates to a torque setting of approximately 32ftlb.

Scat Enterprises offers several versions of its Superlite 'Pro-Moly' con-rods, which are also manufactured from E4340 chrome-moly. These rods differ from the Carrillo and Bugpack design, however, in that the rod bolts are integral with the

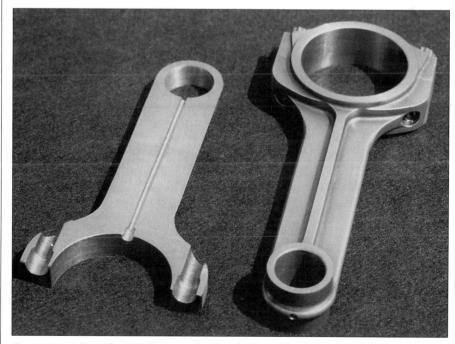

For certain specialist applications where wrist-pin oiling may be a problem, Pauter can manufacture a version of its billet rod with an oilway drilled up through the beam.

also possible to buy billet components. These are, as the name implies, machined from a solid billet of metal which ensures a high degree of accuracy in dimensions and weight. Pauter Machine offers a choice of two styles, one machined from E4340 chrome-moly, the other from a combination of aluminum and chrome-moly. The all-chrome-moly rod features a unique cruciform beam section (referred to by Pauter as a 'slipper configuration'), which is designed to 'redirect critical stress loads to optimum absorption areas', to quote the specification details. By machining from a steel forging, it is possible to produce a rod with a more complex design that adds strength where it is needed most critically and reduces weight without loss of rigidity. The result is a compact con-rod which, although

Unique among all aftermarket products is the AA/Billet from Pauter Machine. This rod features a main beam machined from 7075-T6 aluminum with a rod bearing cap made from 4340 chrome-moly.

Pauter Machine uses CNC-controlled equipment to make its rods four at a time. Machining is carried out to exacting standards.

Here a batch of freshly-finished Pauter Machine billet rods awaits assembly with the SPS or ARP high-tensile bolts which are favored by most rod manufacturers.

more expensive than some forged rods, is far stronger without any weight penalty. The rods come equipped with either SPS or ARP high-tensile bolts. The Pauter E4340 billet rods are available in all the most popular combinations of length and journal diameter, but can also be supplied to order in virtually any configuration to suit the engine builder's individual needs.

Perhaps one of the most exciting rods to have come on the market is Pauter's combination AA/Billet rod. This features a big-end cap machined from E4340 chrome-moly but a beam machined from 7075-T6 aluminum. The result is a substantial-looking rod that combines the light weight of a traditional machined aluminum component with the strength of a chrome-moly rod in the vital big-end area. The advantage of using aluminum for the major part of the rod is that there is a substantial reduction in weight over an equivalent billet steel rod. There is a school of thought which feels that aluminum rods have the ability to absorb some of the shock loads which otherwise punish rod bearings, something which is worth noting when building high-horsepower turbocharged or nitrous-injected engines.

Aluminum rods are, however, considerably more bulky than other types and can present problems when trying to use them with long-stroke crankshafts in a Type 1 crankcase. Pauter's use of a chrome-moly big-end cap, however, does considerably reduce the amount of clearancing that would otherwise be necessary with an all-aluminum design,

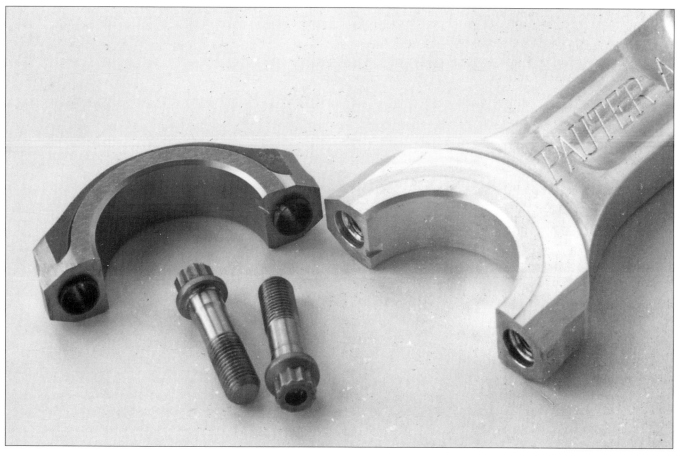

The thinking behind Pauter's unusual rod design is that an all-aluminum rod would be too bulky to fit inside a VW crankcase. By using a chrome-moly rod bearing cap, the rod can be kept slim where it is most needed.

Pauter aluminum rods are manufactured from blanks on this fixture. Note the initial crude billet is designed in such a way that it is possible to make rods of various lengths from the same blank.

but it is still usually necessary to remove more material from under the cylinders, the roof of the case and from around the lifter bores in order to accommodate these rods. Crankshafts of over 78mm throw may require clearancing of the camshaft also, an operation that needs to be carried out with care as it is possible to weaken the camshaft by removing too much material.

The Pauter AA/Billet rods are available with a choice of four different journals: 2in (Chevrolet); 55mm (VW); 50mm (VW Type 4); and 46mm (VW Rabbit). All popular lengths are usually available from stock, with custom orders requiring six to nine weeks notice. In terms of cost, these combination aluminum/steel rods are less expensive than the all-chrome-moly parts from Pauter, but slightly more than some other suppliers' forged components. Whatever the cost, there is no denying that these rods are the most impressive in terms of appearance!

With so many high-quality rods to choose from on the market today, including the Rimco Super Rod (bottom), Carrillo (center) and Pauter (top), there is bound to be something to suit your application.

ROD RATIOS FOR DIFFERENT ROD LENGTH AND CRANKSHAFT STROKES

	912	311	5.5in	5.55in	5.6in	5.7in
Stroke	Porsche	VW	(139.7mm)	Chevy	(142mm)	Chevy
69mm	1.97	1.98	2.02	2.04	2.05	2.08
74mm	1.83	1.85	1.88	1.90	1.92	1.95
78mm	1.74	1.78	1.79	1.80	1.82	1.85
82mm	1.65	1.67	1.70	1.72	1.73	1.76
84mm	1.61	1.63	1.66	1.67	1.69	1.72
86mm	1.58	1.59	1.62	1.63	1.65	1.68
88mm	1.54	1.55	1.58	1.60	1.61	1.64

RECOMMENDATIONS

Mild Street	VW 311; Porsche 912; modified VW311 Super Rod★
Hot Street	Porsche 912; modified VW311 Super Rod★; Bugpack Race Rod; Carrillo; Pauter chrome-moly; CB Race Rods; modified Chevy 327/400/Capri
Competition	Modified VW311 Super Rod★; Bugpack Race Rod; Carrillo; Pauter chrome-moly; Pauter AA/Billet; Scat Pro-Moly; Jet Titanium

★ VW 311 rods which have been shot-peened, clearanced, balanced and fitted with heavy-duty SPS-type bolts, such as Rimco or Berg. Although suitable for some competition applications, they are not intended for all-out race use, such as high-rpm, high-compression or turbo installations.

Side clearance between con-rods and crankshaft

All bearings rely on a regular throughflow of oil to provide adequate lubrication. If oil is prevented from passing across the bearing surface and escaping freely, the bearing will soon break down that oil and overheat. The greater the side clearance on a rod, the better chance the oil has to escape - in theory. In practice, however, too great a side clearance will cause other wear problems, as the rod will be able to move excessively back and forth across the crankshaft journal. While stock engines can cope with a side clearance of as little as 0.004in, a high performance engine requires something in the region of 0.010in to 0.014in to allow the oil to escape at high rpm.

Side clearance is measured by assembling each rod onto the crankshaft and placing a feeler gauge between the thrust face on the big-end cap and the web of the crank. If the clearance is too tight, it will be necessary to have the thrust face of the rod carefully surface ground until the required clearance is achieved. Be sure to remove material evenly from each side of the rod.

It should be noted that different types of rod have different widths: stock VW and Chevy rods are 22.7mm (0.895in) wide while Porsche 912 rods are 20mm (0.790in) wide. When a crankshaft is ground to suit specific bearing journal diameters and rods, this will need to be taken into account.

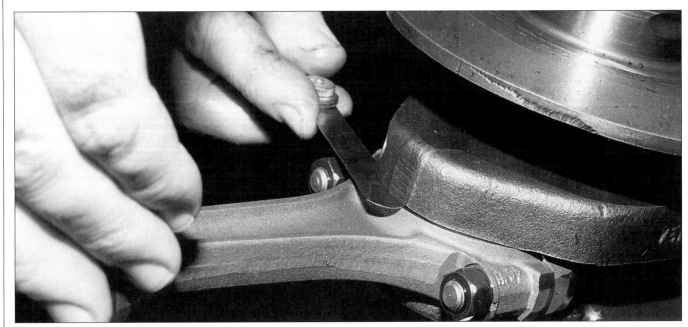

It is vital to check side-clearance on con-rods – use a feeler gauge between rod and crankshaft to check that there is at least 0.010in, or preferably more, to allow oil to flow freely through the bearings.

CYLINDER HEADS

Breathing life into the VW engine

The stock Volkswagen cylinder head is a complex aluminum alloy casting which, although undoubtedly well-engineered and produced, is a major obstacle to ultimate VW performance.

The problem is that the heads were designed to restrict the airflow and thereby act as a rev limiter to ensure a long engine life. The basic design of the cylinder head has changed little since the introduction of the first 25bhp production engines over 50 years ago. Sure, there have been many changes made to the castings to take into account the increases in engine capacity over the years, but the basic layout remained the same until the introduction of an all-new design in 1967.

The first heads featured a single siamesed inlet port which served two cylinders - each cylinder, however, had its own exhaust port. The valves - two inlet and two exhaust per head - run in silicone bronze guides which are an interference fit in the aluminum casting. Initially, these guides were considered to be irremovable so, once they were worn, Volkswagen insisted that brand new heads were installed. However, in the mid-1950s, Joe Vittone of the Economotors VW dealership in Riverside, California, manufactured a tool which allowed new guides to be fitted and thereby saved literally thousands of otherwise perfectly good heads from being scrapped.

The heads are of a wedge design, with parallel valves set at an angle to the head of the piston. Steel-alloy valve seats are shrunk into the head castings and may be replaced by machining out the old seats and driving in new. It is thus a relatively straightforward operation to replace the stock-sized valves with

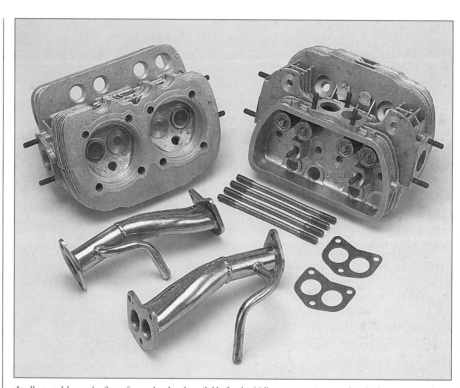

It all started here: the first aftermarket head available for the Volkswagen engine was this dual-port casting from Okrasa in Germany. High in quality and high in price, it was also very efficient. Today, Okrasa conversions are much sought after.

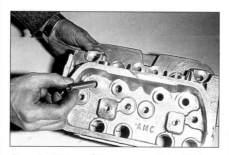

It was Joe Vittone of Economotors at Riverside in California who first discovered that it was possible to replace the valve guides in Volkswagen cylinder heads, thereby saving literally thousands of heads from the scrap heap. From this little acorn, the massive EMPI empire grew…

oversize ones for better flow. The most restrictive aspect of the stock head is the exhaust port, which turns sharply through 90° under the valve seat. The aim of this was to produce a port as short as possible to prevent excessive heat transfer to the rest of the cylinder head. To further aid heat dissipation - a major consideration on any air-cooled engine - the cylinder heads feature extensive finning and also a passageway between the inlet and exhaust ports to allow for the through-flow of cooling air.

The rocker (valve gear) assemblies are supported on pedestals which are an

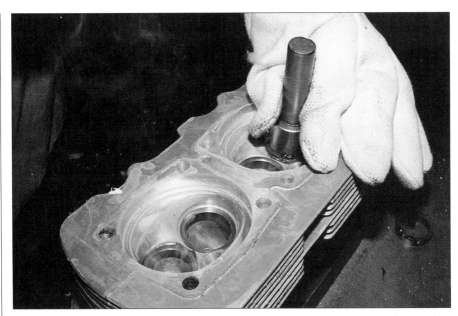

The stock VW head is more than adequate for many high performance applications, up to and including mild turbo installations. Valve sizes can be increased by inserting oversized valve seats, as shown here at Rimco.

integral part of the head casting. Early heads featured semi-circular recesses in each pedestal into which the rocker shafts sat, these being retained by a matching cap, held in place by studs passing through the rocker shafts themselves. Later heads were designed for use with valve gear which had its own mounting blocks. Oil is supplied to the valve gear by hollow pushrods and is allowed to drain back to the sump via pushrod tubes located under each cylinder.

The valves themselves are relatively small so as to limit airflow. They feature single round-wire valve springs which are located by a boss into which the valve guide is fitted. The end of each valve has three machined grooves into which fit a pair of tapered split valve collets and these, in turn, locate the valve spring retainers.

Aside from the small inlet and exhaust ports and valves, the biggest drawback with the stock VW cylinder head from a performance stand-point is the inclination of the valves and the sharp turns in both inlet and exhaust ports. The stock valve inclination is 9.5° to the center line of the cylinder and does not allow for adequate unshrouding of the valve as it opens. Other manufacturers have overcome this problem by adopting a hemispherical head design where the valves are at anything up to 45° to the center line. However, because of the

compact design of the Volkswagen engine, such a layout is not possible.

Incidentally, when Porsche produced engines for its 356 models, the first of which were based on early Volkswagen engines, they improved the design by setting the valves at a much greater angle to the cylinders, operated by long rocker arms which were angled across the rocker shaft. These heads were a logical development of the basic VW design but may not, unfortunately, be used on a Volkswagen engine.

The single biggest improvement was made when the VW factory introduced the so-called dual-port heads, which featured separate inlet ports for each cylinder. First seen on the Type 3 range in 1967, the dual-ports were a major breakthrough as far as VW performance was concerned and literally, almost overnight, changed the VW performance industry. Prior to their introduction, Volkswagen tuners had been forced to rely on costly aftermarket dual-port heads, first produced by Okrasa or Denzel in the 1950s. While the heads produced by both of these companies were of exceptional quality, they were expensive and hard to obtain. In the USA, the Okrasa heads were marketed by EMPI but the Denzel heads, with their Porsche 356-like rectangular exhaust ports, remained hard to come by. These heads represented the first steps taken to produce an aftermarket head which overcame the short-comings of the stock factory casting.

The first heads offered on a production Volkswagen engine came with the part number 101 315C, soon to be superseded by part number 111 101 351 (note the reversal of the last two digits). This was the head used on the 25bhp engine until its demise at the end of 1953. The replacement 30bhp (USA 36hp) engine came with heads marked 111 101 351A and featured 30mm inlet and 28mm exhaust valves. None of these heads really lend themselves to high-performance applications, even on a hot-rod vintage Bug, as they simply cannot flow enough air through the tiny single inlet port. This

The biggest danger when installing larger valves in stock heads is the appearance of cracks between the exhaust valve and the spark plug hole, as seen here. These cracks can lead to the valve seat moving and eventually dropping out altogether.

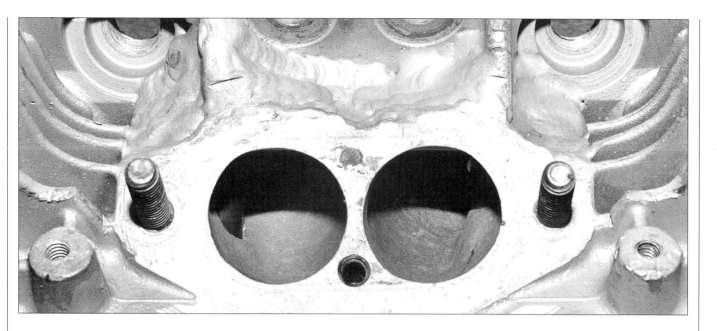

To make the most of large valves, it is necessary to perform some extensive work on the ports – especially the inlet. Here, a stock dual-port head has been welded around the inlet to allow custom porting to be carried out.

When boring any VW head for larger cylinders – especially 94mm – you can expect to break through at the edges of the sealing surface, like this. This will not affect compression as the sides of the chamber do not act as a seal.

Whenever a head has been welded, the port shape should be marked out using engineer's blue (such as Dychem) and a template. Most cylinder head specialists will carry a range of templates to suit various applications.

is the reason why Okrasa and Denzel developed their own heads with dual inlet ports.

Next to appear on the scene were the 113 101 351A through F single-port heads used on the 34bhp (USA 40hp) engines. The first of these, with the suffixes A, B or C, while more efficient than their predecessors, were poor heads with inherent problems relating to the rocker arm studs, which would work loose or pull out of the head altogether. The 'C' heads featured slightly enlarged inlet ports and reshaped combustion chambers. The later 'D' and 'E' heads were an improvement on the previous castings, with extra cooling area and a more efficient combustion chamber design, and

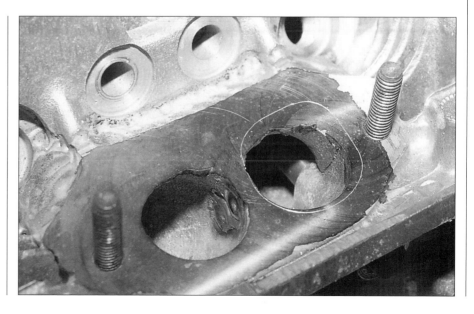

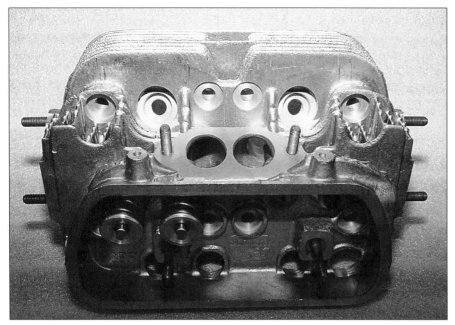

The factory 040 casting is one of the most common and is used as the basis for many excellent performance heads. Similar in appearance to the original 311 dual-ports introduced on the Type 3, the 040 has 35.5mm inlet and 32mm exhaust valves as stock.

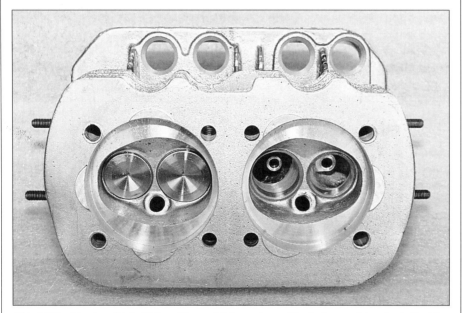

This 040 head has been fitted with large 40mm x 35.5mm valves and has had some mild porting to blend the new seats into the ports. When flycut for increased compression, it may be necessary to mill the top face of the head flat to clear the cylinder fins.

were probably the best 1200 heads offered by the factory. The 'F' head was the universal replacement supplied by Volkswagen for all 34bhp engines. All 1200 heads came with 31.5mm inlet and 30mm exhaust valves.

When Volkswagen introduced the 1300 Beetle, late in 1965, the engine came with new heads marked 113 101 353B which had 33mm inlet and 30mm exhaust valves. The most obvious visual difference between these and the 1200 heads is the angled mounting flange for the inlet manifold which allows better gas flow to the valve. These are good heads as far as single-port castings go but cannot really be considered adequate for performance use. The same holds true for the similar 1500 single-port heads, with their 31.5mm inlet and 30mm exhaust valves used on the Type 2 models from 1962 until 1965. These carry the part number 211 101 351A and 211 101 353.

The Type 3 range was introduced in 1962, with heads that were similar to the 1200 Type 1 head, but bored out to accept the larger 85.5mm cylinders. These heads, part number 311 101 351A, featured larger 35.5mm inlet and 32mm exhaust valves for improved breathing. They were followed by 'B' and 'C' variations which had angled inlet ports like those used on the 1300 Type 1. Later still, the Type 3 came with 311 101 353 heads, which were a further improvement and designed to work with the 1500S model's high-compression pistons.

The best single-port heads of all were those used on the 1500 and 1600 engines up to 1970 - note that US-specification Beetles came with 1600 engines equipped with single-port heads from the 1968 model year on, while European Beetles were not fitted with anything larger than the 1500 engine until the 1971 model year. These heads are very similar to the 1300 casting but have a larger inlet port which flows more efficiently. They carry the part number 311 101 353A and come with 35.5mm inlet and 32mm exhaust valves.

Introduced in 1968 for the Type 3 models, the dual-port heads first appeared with the part number 311 101 355D and have the 35.5mm inlet and 32mm exhaust valves. These are excellent heads which far outflow any single-port casting, regardless of the amount of modification work that might have been carried out. They also appeared on the Type 1, under part numbers 113 101 355 and 355A, in slightly modified form, without a valve guide boss protruding into the inlet port, and with a widened exhaust port, both in an effort to improve efficiency. There is also a step built into the outer edge of the combustion chamber to reduce the compression ratio slightly as part of VW's attempts to meet the new pollution laws. This step may be easily machined out with a flycutting tool to raise the compression ratio. Note that all dual-port heads need shorter top center studs to clear the inlet manifold.

In June 1973, VW fitted sodium-filled exhaust valves with 9mm stems to the dual-port heads in place of the usual 8mm-stemmed parts. This was in an effort to combat valve problems brought about by ever more stringent emission regulations and the use of unleaded fuel. Up until then, all valves had 8mm stems apart from the old 25bhp and 30bhp engines which came with 7mm valve stems.

Since the early 1970s, there have been many Volkswagen-produced heads which carry part numbers beginning with something other than 113, 211 or 311. These heads are largely produced in Brazil, for use in a variety of domestically-produced VWs, such as the SP-2, which uses a version of the Type 1 engine. Rarely seen outside their South American habitat, these vehicles helped to ensure further development of the air-cooled engine at a time when the German factories had their minds on other things. We will take a look at some of these heads later on in this chapter.

Modified heads

The stock VW heads are fine for their intended purpose, but are woefully inadequate for high-performance use. Certainly, in the old days, the advent of the dual-port head turned the VW drag race scene upside down as racers discovered a whole new world of gas flow, but today there are many off-the-shelf alternatives which offer far more potential. However, having said that, there are many VW performance specialists who use the late factory dual-port heads as a starting point for the production of some very efficient heads.

On the matter of suitability for use with unleaded fuel, Gene Berg Enterprises (GBE) points out that all factory heads produced since 1968 are fine. The inlet valve seats are made of steel while the exhaust seats are a hardened steel alloy. The exhaust valves are tri-metal and both inlet and exhaust valves have hardened chrome stems running in brass guides. Most aftermarket heads are suitable for unleaded fuel, too, but beware that some of the less expensive castings may be fitted with cast-iron seats, which may only be used with leaded fuel. If in

The 041 head (bottom) is similar in appearance to the 040 (top) but has a slightly different fin design. The 041 also comes from the factory with larger 39mm inlets but still has 32mm exhaust valves. They require a lot of work to perform well, including moving the spark plug to prevent cracks forming.

doubt, ask for some kind of proof either way. Most aftermarket heads are supplied fitted with stainless steel valves which are fine for most applications, although GBE feels that they are too soft and can stretch, requiring constant valve readjustment. Note that not all stainless steel valves are the same - some are manufactured from very poor quality material. In the long run, it pays to stay with a known make, such as Manley. Titanium valves, of which Del West are the best known, need only be considered where an all-out race engine is concerned but are undeniably light, resist damaging the seats when an engine is over-revved and do not 'float' like a heavier steel valve at high rpm. As a consequence, they do not need such a heavy valve spring to keep them on their seats, thereby reducing the load on the valve train, but their cost is several times that of an equivalent steel valve.

Looking at various of the so-called factory 'performance' heads, the '040' casting is a worthy starting point for a mild performance engine. It is a factory casting with 35.5mm inlet and 32mm exhaust valves and is suitable for some fairly extensive reworking - welding the area round the inlet manifold flange allows the inlet port to be straightened and enlarged but, when the head is flycut for extra compression, it can become thin round the edge of the chamber, requiring further welding to add some strength. With their extensive finning, these heads run cool in street applications.

One of the most popular aftermarket heads is the so-called '041', which is a factory casting from South America with 39mm inlet and 32mm exhaust valves. This dual-port head is available at a very reasonable price, from many sources, but in stock form probably flows no better

There have been several different 041 head castings, and the ones to look for are those with either D01, D02 or D03 markings. These can be found here, adjacent to the inlet ports, or underneath the head, close to the valve cover.

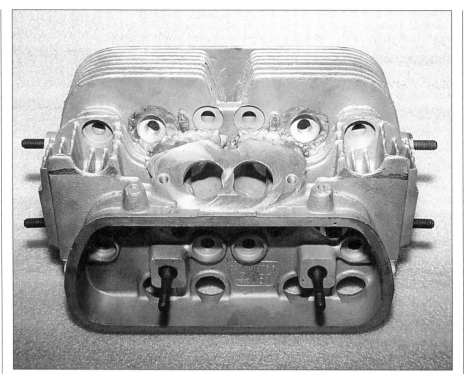

This 041 head is shown in the course of being extensively reworked by Jeff Denham, of Jeff's Speed & Fab in Anaheim, California. Welding round the inlet ports allows for radical reshaping to allow the use of larger valves.

than a conventional dual-port factory head. The main drawback with the 041 is that, while the inlet valve may be larger, the inlet port is no different to stock. To work effectively, the 041 needs extensive modification, including moving the spark plug location away from the inlet valve to prevent cracks appearing between the plug and the valve seat.

With some effort, the 041 can be made into a pretty good head for mild street use but don't expect this to be the ultimate. The heads to look out for are those which carry the marks D01, D02 and D03, as they are better quality castings - this mark can be found adjacent to the valve cover seating surface on the outside of the head.

The '042' head is a development of the 041, produced for CB Performance, and features 40mm inlet and 35.5mm exhaust valves. The 042 comes with reshaped ports, smaller valve guide bosses and, perhaps most importantly, substantially more metal above the combustion chamber to allow for deeper flycutting without the risk of breaking through. These heads will handle machining for up to a 94mm cylinder and flycut to a depth of 0.100in without problem, something neither the 040 nor the 041 will comfortably allow. They are supplied as standard with a 54cc combustion chamber and machined for

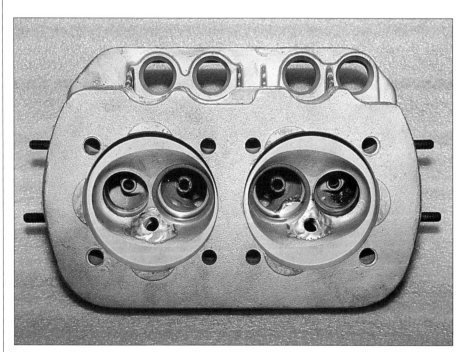

The same head shown from the combustion chamber side shows how it has been welded around the spark plug holes. These have then been redrilled and tapped to accept smaller 12mm spark plugs to help prevent cracking.

85.5mm cylinders and are marketed under a variety of names by various companies.

The next step up from the 042 is the '044' casting, which is also a product of South America and distributed by CB Performance. This head is a marked

improvement over the 041 in that it comes with larger ports and considerably more material round the combustion chamber to allow deep flycutting and other custom machine work. The 044 uses long-reach spark plugs (³/4in instead

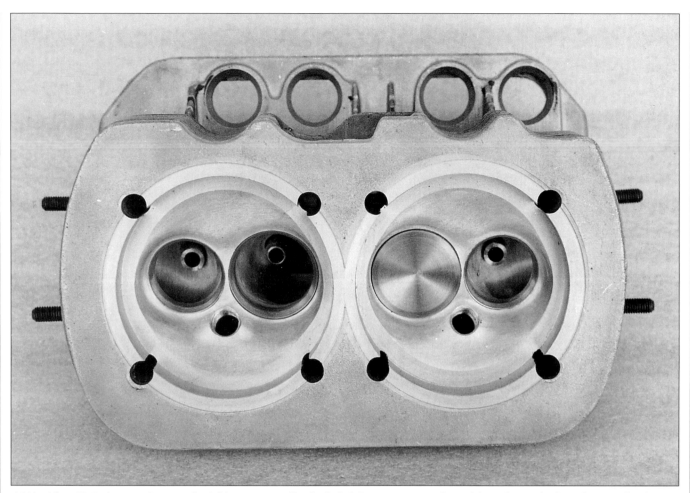

044 head from CB Performance of Farmersville, California, is an excellent head which features extra material around the combustion chamber and ports to allow for extensive reworking. Spark plug location is still not ideal and needs to be moved away from valves slightly.

To make the most of the 044, it is necessary to weld the area above the inlet port. One of the best features of the 044 is the use of long reach 3/4in spark plugs, as opposed to regular 1/2in. This makes the head less prone to cracking.

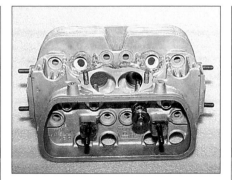

This fully reworked head from Jeff Denham shows what can be done with the 044 casting. Note relatively straight inlet ports, which allow better gas flow, and smaller 12mm sparking plugs. A good head for hot street or mild competition use.

This 044 has been flycut for increased compression and to allow the use of larger cylinders. Note how the head surface has been milled flat and the fin removed between the cylinders. Note also the radically reprofiled combustion chambers.

of the regular 1/2in), in an effort to prevent cracks forming between the plug and the valve seats, and comes supplied with 40mm inlet and 35.5mm exhaust valves. Two versions are available: the Super Sport, which has cast-finish ports,

and the Magnum 44, which is fully ported and polished and can be used straight from the box if so desired. The 044 is a popular head for high-performance engines as it is a good starting point, with plenty of material and

larger ports. However, many feel that the spark plug location is incorrect and that it still needs to be moved further away from the inlet valve. The area above the inlet port will need to be welded before any extensive porting can be carried out.

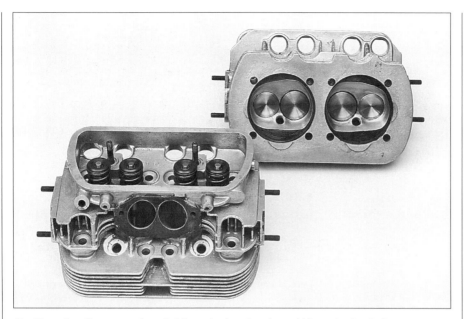

Scat Enterprises offers a range of reworked factory heads, such as these, which are aimed at the hot street market. Heads like this will make a considerable difference to the performance capabilities of your VW.

There are several variations on the above heads available off the shelf from a number of VW performance shops and a good example of these are the heads listed by Scat Enterprises. Scat markets a range of modified VW heads based on the 041 castings which are ported to its own specification, starting with the basic 'Mini-D' heads which have reworked D-shaped inlet ports but are not welded. Supplied with 40mm inlet and 37.5mm exhaust valves, these particular Scat heads are intended for high-performance street use and come equipped with dual springs, chrome-moly retainers and silicon-bronze valve guides and are ready cut for 92mm cylinders. Also available is the Scat 'Round-Port' head, which is also based on the 041 casting but has less radical port work, although the exhaust ports are enlarged to 1.625in. With the same size valves as the Mini-D heads, the Round-Ports are available off-the-shelf, bored for 85.5mm cylinders, and are intended for mild street or off-road applications.

The Scat 'Wedge-Port' head is also based on the 041 casting but features extensively welded inlet ports and relocated 12mm spark plugs for greater strength. The exhaust ports are enlarged to match up with a 1.625in exhaust header. With 42mm inlet and 37.5mm exhaust valves as standard, the Wedge-Ports are equipped with dual valve

springs, chrome-moly retainers and stainless steel valves. They are supplied ready cut for 92mm cylinders and are designed for high rpm applications on the street .

Gene Berg Enterprises offers a range of modified heads based on factory castings, including a modified single-port

head for use on 1500 and US-spec 1600 engines. These, part number GB850, come complete with heavy-duty single springs and a three-angle cut on the valve seat for better flow. However, most people these days would automatically upgrade to the far superior dual-ports rather than play with the less-efficient singles and the GB840 is a good starting point. This is a stock head which has been given a good valve job, shimmed stock springs (to increase the seat pressure) and, where necessary, cut for 90.5mm cylinders. All these heads are also available with Berg's 'Semi-Hemi' modification which lowers the compression ratio and, it is claimed, improves the flame travel in the combustion chamber for more efficient burning of the fuel.

Next up in the Berg range is a series of dual-port heads with either heavy-duty single (GB852) or dual valve springs (GB854), factory-spec unleaded valves, spring shims, hardened valve collets (keepers) and chrome-moly valve retainers. Once again, these heads are available with the Semi-Hemi modification and machined for larger cylinders. The GB854 head can also be supplied with full porting and polishing,

Scat's Wedge-Port head is based on the 041 casting but features smaller 12mm spark plugs, 42mm inlet and 37.5mm exhaust valves and enlarged exhaust ports for use with a 1.625in header. Note extensive welding around inlet port.

along with reshaped combustion chambers, and is listed under part number GB855.

The GB860 is a large-valve head with 40mm inlet and either 35.5mm or 37.5mm exhaust valves, as well as the dual springs, porting etc of the GB855 head; these heads are not welded. Next up from this is the GB865 which features welding above and below the intake ports to allow more radical port reshaping. In GB865C form, they come fitted with heavier Chevy-style springs. It is recommended that both these heads be used with at least an 1.625in exhaust system and dual carburetors.

For competition applications, Gene Berg offers the GB870, which is a fully-welded head with relocated spark plug holes and a choice of either 42mm or 43.7mm intake valves and 37.5mm exhausts. These heads have the larger diameter Chevy-style springs fitted as standard, which require the valve spring pockets to be machined and, as a consequence, have had the small bump in the intake port welded to regain lost strength. The area around the valve guide boss has also been welded and machined to accurately locate the valve springs. One

GB865 features welding above the inlet port, along with 40mm inlet and 37.5mm exhaust valves. Head comes with dual valve springs, Manley valves and all associated hardware. GB865C version uses Chevy-style springs.

other modification is the relocation of the pushrod tube holes to take into account the use of high-ratio rocker arms. Aimed at the racer who will be using dual carburettors and a radical camshaft, these heads should be used with at least a 1.625in, or ideally a 1.75in, exhaust header.

For the ultimate in racing heads from Gene Berg Enterprises, there is the GB872, which is similar to the GB870 but comes with 44.45mm inlet and 38.10mm exhaust valves. These heads are assembled with titanium valves and retainers and have the top cooling fin welded and milled flat for extra strength when used in a high-compression motor. As with all Berg's modified cylinder heads, matching inlet manifolds are available to order to suit the customer's carburetors.

Pauter Machine offers two different modified VW heads, one of which is aimed at the street-driven VW that is likely to see some extensive use, the other being a head intended for all-out street or race use. Neither is available off-the-shelf, as Pauter feels that there are too many variables associated with building an engine, such as camshaft choice, carburation, intended rpm range etc, for any head to be a stock item. The first head is referred to as the Pauter 'A' and consists of a brand new factory 040 casting which has had the spark plug boss welded to accept a smaller 12mm, long-reach plug to reduce the risk of cracks adjacent to the inlet valve seat. These heads come with either 40mm or 42mm inlet valves and 35.5mm exhausts, along with single heavy-duty springs and chrome-moly retainers. Although

Gene Berg Enterprises offers a vast range of cylinder heads, including this GB855 which is a mildly-reworked head for use on street engines. Based on the original factory casting, it is ported and polished and comes with reshaped combustion chambers.

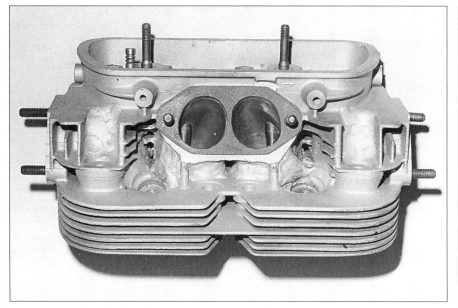

GBE can provide heads for all applications. The GB870 is an all-out competition head which includes either 42mm or 43.7mm inlet valves and 37.5mm exhausts. Smaller 12mm spark plugs are also used, along with Chevy-style springs and retainers.

extensively ported, they are not welded and are primarily aimed at the street and off-road market, where a broad spread of power is required.

For high-performance street and all-out competition use, the Pauter 'B' head is the recommended choice. This is a fully welded 040 casting with extensive porting work carried out to both inlet and exhaust tracts. The 'B' head comes with either 42mm or 44mm inlet valves and 37mm exhausts and dual valve springs. Extra heavy-duty Vasco springs are available at extra cost, as are titanium valves and retainers. Again, as with the 'A' head, the spark plug boss has been welded to accept a 12mm, long-reach plug. Both Pauter heads can be ordered with any cylinder bore, up to 94mm, and combustion chamber volume to suit the customer's requirements.

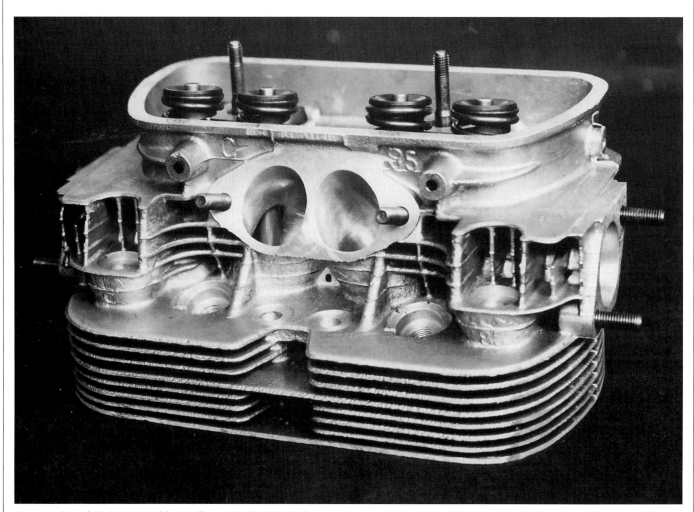

Pauter Machine of Chula Vista, California, offers two head based on the factory 040 casting. The first is this, the Pauter 'A' head, which comes with 40mm or 42mm inlet valves, 35.5mm exhausts and 12mm spark plugs. Theses heads are not welded and are aimed primarily at the street market.

The Pauter 'B' head is meant for hot street or competition use and is a welded 040 with radically reshaped inlet ports and either 42mm or 44mm inlets with 37mm exhaust valves. An excellent choice for both street and strip applications.

Aftermarket heads

Over the years, there have been many aftermarket cylinder heads produced for the air-cooled Volkswagen engine, starting way back with those Okrasa and Denzel heads we spoke of earlier. In the 1970s, Dean and Ken Lowry, of Deano Dyno-Soar, developed an all-new cylinder head which allowed the use of much larger valves and also came with inlet ports which were far bigger than anything which could be achieved with reworked factory castings. Today, there are many different aftermarket heads to choose from, one of the most popular being the Superflo, or SF-1 and SF-2, heads from Dee Engineering and sold under the Bugpack name. The ancestry of these heads can be traced back to the original DDS design which was produced by Ken Lowry's company, ARPM.

The SF-1 and SF-2 are both radically different to the stock VW head in many different areas, but most notably the inlet ports. These are what are known as Cosworth ports, as their shape follows the design pioneered by the British race engineering company of the same name. They are large and slightly oval - or more correctly, slightly squashed - in shape, this design being considered one of the most efficient. As a consequence of this layout, the SF heads require the use of special inlet manifolds, which are located by three studs rather than the usual two.

Another area in which these heads differ from the factory design is the valve cover - it is a large rectangular casting, held in place with four 6mm studs and nuts. It has to be said that SF heads do have something of a reputation for leaking valve covers, but this is more often than not a consequence of the owner overtightening the nuts. Gene Berg Enterprises markets a valve cover conversion which bolts on to the SF heads and allows the use of a stock VW pressed-steel clip-on valve cover. Although slightly unwieldy in appearance, this conversion does indeed cure oil leaks once and for all.

The major difference between the two heads is in the size of the inlet port: the SF-1 has larger ports than those of the SF-2. When the first Superflo heads were released, they were quickly snapped up by racers eager to capitalise on the advanced port design offered by these new castings. However, there was soon a call from potential customers who were after a broader spread of power and didn't need such large inlet ports. The result was the

Superflo – or S/F – heads are among the best-known of all aftermarket castings. They feature Cosworth-style inlet ports and a distinctive valve cover design. The SF-1 shown here comes with larger inlet ports.

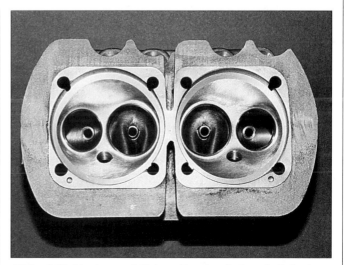

SF-1 and SF-2 heads are available in a wide variety of valve and cylinder sizes. Shown here is an SF-1 which has reworked chambers, has been bored for 94mm cylinders and fitted with 48mm inlet and 38mm exhaust valves.

The SF-2 is very much the same as the SF-1 but comes with smaller inlet ports to allow use on smaller capacity engines. Both SF-1 and SF-2 heads features short 1/2in reach spark plugs and a 3-bolt inlet manifold design.

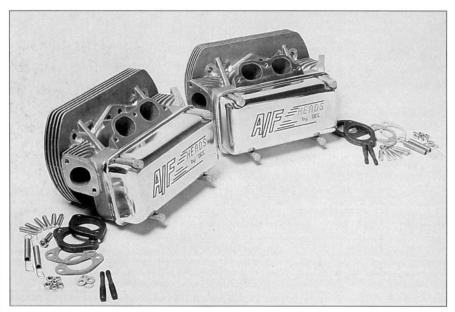

Dee Engineering's A/F (Angle Flow) head features angled exhaust ports for improved gas flow, and requires the use of a special exhaust system to suit. A/F heads are supplied with 48mm inlet and 38mm exhaust valves and have 12mm spark plug holes.

Superflo II (now SF-2) which was designed to offer improved bottom-end performance compared to the SF-1.

Both heads offer redesigned exhaust ports, along with plenty of metal around the combustion chamber walls to allow for deep flycutting and boring for large cylinders. The area under each valve seat is also built up to keep the seats stable, even when used in high-rpm conditions with high valve spring pressures. Some early Superflo heads did appear to suffer from seat movement, although that problem has now been cured.

SF-1 heads are available with either 42mm, 44mm or 48mm inlet valves, while the SF-2 is only available with 42mm or 44mm inlets. Both heads come with 37.5mm exhaust valves (the 48mm inlet SF-1 has 38mm exhausts) and can be purchased ready-cut for 92mm or 94mm cylinders. In general, 48mm is considered to be the maximum valve size that can be used with a 94mm bore but many engine builders feel that 44mm is a more practical limit. This is because the larger the valve, the more the cylinder wall will tend to shroud the port and thus gas flow may be even less than that obtained by using a smaller valve. It should be also recognized that these heads, in common with virtually all aftermarket castings, will still require porting and polishing to achieve the optimum level of flow.

A close 'sister' to the SF heads is the A/F (Angle-Flo), also offered by Dee Engineering under the Bugpack name. This is a similar design but features angled exhaust ports which are designed to give even greater gas flow. As with the SF-1 heads, they come with the larger 1.375in Chevy-style springs and chrome-moly retainers as standard, but are only available with 48mm inlet and 38mm exhaust valves. However, the A/F heads can be supplied cut for the large 4in bore aftermarket cylinders, which are popular with many drag racers, and all feature 12mm spark plugs. The Dee Engineering heads come with stainless steel valves as standard, but may be ordered with lightweight titanium replacements if so desired. Note that the A/F head castings will require a special header system to be used due to the angled exhaust port.

CB Performance offers a very similar head to the Dee Engineering products, called the Competition Eliminator. This features the same Cosworth-style inlet port as the SF but makes use of the conventional factory-style valve cover. The benefit of this design is that there are no leakage problems and no need to purchase an aftermarket valve cover conversion. The Competition Eliminator heads are available with 42mm, 44mm or 48mm inlet valves and with either 37mm, 38mm or 40mm exhausts and are supplied to accept either 92mm or 94mm cylinders.

For people who do not wish to run quite such a radical head as these, there is the option of the Eliminator 2000, also offered by CB Performance, the S/E by Dee Engineering or the Super HO by Performance Technology. All three heads are very similar and resemble the factory castings but have extensive finning around the exhaust port area, in an effort to reduce combustion chamber temperatures and to make the heads better suited to

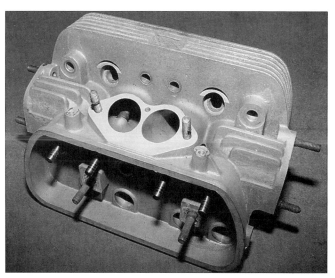

Over the years, Superflo and SF heads have been plagued with leaking valve covers, usually due to people over-tightening the fixing bolts. To combat this, Gene Berg Enterprises markets this valve cover conversion which allows a stock VW part to be used, in conjunction with the original spring clip, or 'bail'.

For those who do not wish to use a head as radical as the SF series, there is the Street Eliminator from CB Performance, Super HO from Performance Technology or the S/E from Dee Engineering. These heads feature heavy finning round the exhaust port but still run a little hot when used for extended periods on the street.

The Street Eliminator head – and its brethren – is available with 40mm, 42mm or 44mm inlet valves and either 35.5mm or 37.5mm exhausts. It is also available machined for 85.5mm, 92m or 94mm cylinders.

The Competition Eliminator from CB Performance is similar in appearance to the SF head, but allows the use of a stock-style clip-on, or aftermarket bolt-on, valve cover to prevent leakage problems without having to use a valve cover conversion.

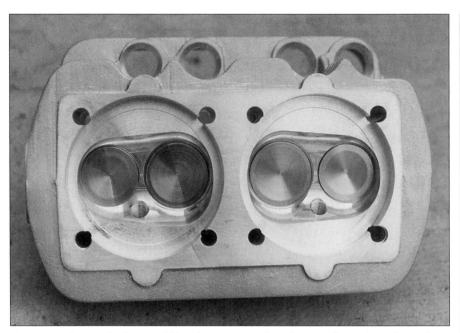

Competition Eliminator heads are available with up to 48mm inlet and 40mm exhaust valves. There is plenty of material around the combustion chamber to allow for some extensive flycutting and reshaping.

high-performance street use. Each of these heads is available with a choice of valves size combinations, ranging from 40mm x 35.5mm through 42mm x 37.5mm and up to 44mm x 37.5mm. They are also available machined to accept anything from 85.5mm stock 1600 cylinders up to 94mm big-bore kits. These heads can be considered an excellent choice for someone wishing to build an all-out street car or one which sees occasional competition use, although there are some cylinder head experts who believe these heads run too hot for regular street use and some castings have been known to be rather soft, allowing the valve seats to move, especially in high-rpm applications or where high spring pressures are used. As with other aftermarket castings, they still require porting to finish. The advantage, however, with this type of head is that they represent excellent value for money and also do not require the use of special cylinder head tinware, unlike the SF-style head.

All-out race heads

For the ultimate in VW performance, there is no substitute for effectively putting the original factory design to one side and starting totally from scratch with a cylinder head which can deliver

Autocraft 910 is the most widely-used aftermarket head in all-out competition applications. Cast from 206 aluminum alloy, the 910 features a large, rigid, bolt-on valve cover which has provision for breather lines. Six mounting bolts help prevent oil leakage from the valve cover.

optimum flow without compromise. There are currently three models of aftermarket head available which are purely aimed at all-out race applications: the Auto-Craft 910, the Pauter Machine Super Pro and the Scat Split-Port. They are soon to be joined, at the time of writing, by another head from the fertile minds of Dean and Ken Lowry, formerly of Deano Dyno-Soar.

The Auto-Craft 910 is, without doubt, the most popular of all the outright race heads currently on the market. Designed and manufactured by

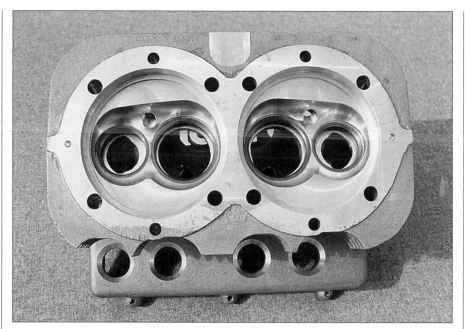

Autocraft head comes ready-drilled to accept two extra head studs per cylinder for use with Autocraft's own aftermarket crankcase. This unfinished head still requires the final porting and shaping of the combustion chamber.

infringe on the valve cover area at all. Auto-Craft uses short studs both top and bottom, as it is a felt that they hold their torque better than the longer studs used on most other heads. There is also the option of using two extra studs per cylinder on full-race, high-compression applications where an aftermarket crankcase is used.

To make the best use of the larger valves that are available, and also to take into account the altered valve train geometry associated with using high-lift camshafts and high-ratio rocker arm assemblies, the Auto-Craft head is available with relocated valve centers with the exhaust valve moved over by as much as 0.100in. The rocker arm supports can also be relocated for specialist applications. The spark plug boss is moved from the stock location and is also designed to accept the popular 12mm ^{3}/$_4$in reach plug.

In engines running very high compression ratios, it may be necessary to add strengthening gussets to keep the head from distorting. This Autocraft 910 head has been extensively modified in this way.

Pauter Machine's radical aftermarket head is called the Super Pro and is designed for use with up to 4.25in cylinders. The heads are substantial castings, with extensive finning and a distinctive valve cover design.

Auto-Craft Machine of La Habra, California, this head is cast from high-specification 206 alloy and is available to accept either 94mm or 101mm cylinders. Exhaust valve sizes range from 37.5mm up to 45mm, while inlet valves can be specified in anything from 48mm up to a massive 55mm! The valves are 5.07in in length (some 0.34in longer than stock), to allow for use of radical high lift camshafts and large 1.44in diameter Chevy-style springs. The valves supplied use the

Chevrolet-style retainers, as Auto-Craft feels that there are too many failures associated with the stock VW three-groove keeper design.

The 910 head is available with either standard VW stud spacing, or with the optional wider pattern (0.070in larger in diameter) to accept the aftermarket 96mm and 101mm cylinders which are commonly used in drag-race applications. An interesting feature of these heads is that the cylinder head studs do not

One of the most striking features of the 910 head is the large inlet port and mounting flange for the inlet manifold. The latter is held in place with four bolts and located with a pair of dowels to ensure perfect alignment every time. Manifolds are available for either the popular 48IDA or IDF-series Weber carburetors, or Auto-Craft's own fuel-injection system. With their distinctive bolt-on valve covers, the Auto-Craft 910 heads are some of the finest heads

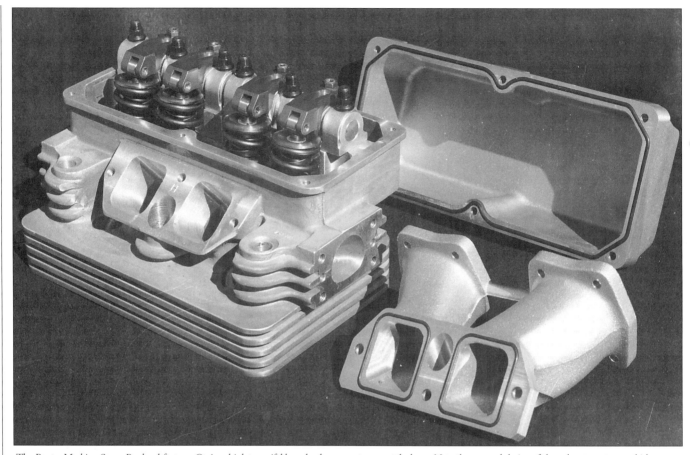

The Pauter Machine Super Pro head features O-ringed inlet manifolds and valve covers to prevent leakage. Note the unusual design of the exhaust port area which requires a special header system. Inlet ports are unique in shape and layout.

The rocker shafts are supported by no fewer than six bolts, unlike the stock head's two, thus preventing any possible problems caused by extremely strong valve springs and high engine rpm.

currently on the market and come supplied with stainless steel valves, chrome-moly retainers (titanium is an option in both cases) and silicon-bronze valve guides as standard.

One of the more recent products on the market is the Super Pro cylinder head which is manufactured by Pauter Machine of Chula Vista, California. This head was designed with two principal aims in mind:

to withstand extremely high valve spring pressures and to allow the use of the 4.25in cylinders which could be used with Pauter's own aftermarket crankcase.

The heads are truly massive castings, with distinctive styling which makes them stand out from all other aftermarket heads. The O-ringed inlet manifolds are held in place by three bolts, while the heads can be supplied to fit stock Type 1 or Type 4 crankcases, or Pauter's own case, with cylinder head stud location varied to suit. The latter application uses six 1/2in cylinder head studs. Other aftermarket cases are also catered for, such as the Auto-Craft and Scat cases, which require six 10mm studs per cylinder, and the Bugpack/ARPM case which features six 12mm and four 8mm studs per side. Worthy of note are the large, six-bolt exhaust flanges which allow exhaust headers of 2.0in, and larger, in diameter to be used.

Beneath the cavernous valve covers, each head features a version of Pauter's

7075 T-6 aluminum billet roller-tip rocker assemblies, those used in this application being unique to the Super Pro head as the rocker shafts are held in place by no fewer than six studs each. Part of the reasoning behind the use of these special rocker assemblies is to allow the fitment of large

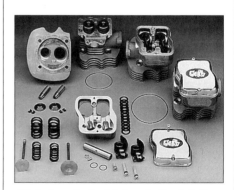

Of all aftermarket head designs, the Scat Split-Port is the most unusual as it is literally two heads in one. Following the lead set by Porsche and many aero-engine manufacturers, Scat Enterprises' design provides each cylinder with its own separate head and rocker arm assembly.

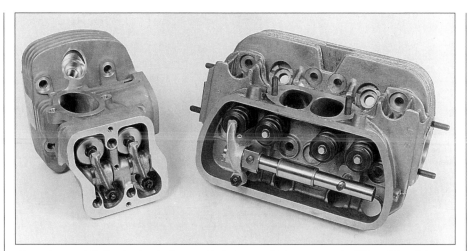

Comparing one Split-Port head and a factory-style dual-port and it is easy to see the difference! Scat design offers massive inlet ports and a well-supported rocker shaft. If any engine damage is suffered on one cylinder, only one chamber needs to be replaced, rather than a whole head.

1.625in O/D valve springs with up to 700lb seat pressure.

Regular valve sizes for these heads are either 52mm inlet and 40mm exhaust or 54mm inlet with 41mm exhaust. In each case, the valves are 0.100in longer than the regular Chevy style, making them some 0.600in longer than stock Volkswagen valves. The usual choice is either 1.500in or 1.550in diameter Super Vasco Jet valve springs with large 10° Chevy-style valve retainers. Particular attention has been paid to ensuring there is plenty of material above each combustion chamber and around the valve spring/guide area to ensure the head is adequately strong to cope with extreme full-race applications. Large diameter pushrod tube holes can cope with up to 7/16in pushrods.

These heads have become popular with the sand drag fraternity who demand large-displacement, high-horsepower turbo engines to compete against the many V8-powered machines in the open classes. Development is still continuing apace on the Pauter Super Pro heads and future plans include a water-cooled version to cope with extended use during long-distance off-road races.

Almost certainly the most radical of all aftermarket cylinder heads is the Split-Port, manufactured by Scat Enterprises in Redondo Beach, California. Scat looked at the basic Volkswagen head - a single casting which sits on top of two separate cylinders - and felt that this could not be

considered the optimum design, as there was always the risk of inadequate sealing between the combustion chamber and the cylinder as a result of differing rates of expansion. Also, if any damage was suffered by one cylinder (such as a dropped valve or melted piston) then there was a good chance that the whole head would have to be scrapped, even though one combustion chamber remained undamaged.

Taking a look at both the Porsche 911 motor and many aero-engines, Scat felt that the solution lay with having a separate head for each cylinder. This would effectively reduce the risk of

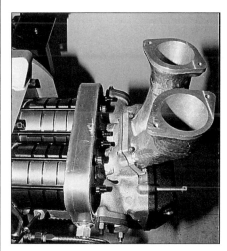

For something completely different – Jack Sacchette of JayCee Enterprises modified this Autocraft 910 head to allow it to be water-cooled. Idea works extremely well but proved to be illegal in American PRA drag racing series.

cylinder leakage and also mean that only one head would have to be replaced if a partial engine failure occurred. These individual heads are cast in three parts from 356 alloy (heat-treated to H-450 specification): the main head with combustion chamber, the rocker box and the valve cover. The combustion chamber section houses the valves, seats, springs and guides, while the bolt-on rocker box features a specially-made rocker assembly with a short, well-supported shaft. The valve cover is held in place with two bolts.

One of the more significant aspects of the design is that the angle and location of the valves are changed with the valves now on a 6° angle to the center line of the cylinder, as opposed to the factory 9.5°. This results in the inlet valve being placed in the center of the cylinder at 0.500in lift, thereby reducing any effect it might have on swirl within the chamber. The valve springs supplied with the heads provide 400lb of seat pressure at 0.700in lift (145lb static).

The Scat Split-Port heads are available with a range of valve sizes according to the chosen cylinder bore. Heads for 92mm cylinders feature 42mm inlet and 37mm exhaust valves, while the 94mm and 96.8mm heads are fitted with 48mm and 38mm valves. The large 101.6mm (4.0in) heads are supplied with 50mm intake and 40mm exhaust valves. The stainless steel valves are 0.200in longer than stock.

Although the heads are two separate castings for each side of the engine, the inlet manifolds are not and simply bolt across each pair of heads. They are available to accept a range of carburettors, including the popular 48IDA and its derivatives, the Dell'Orto DRLA and Weber IDF ranges and Scat's own fuel-injection system, which is based around a Hilborn fuel pump.

By throwing the text book away, Scat has been able to design a head which, in theory at least, offers considerable advantages over the conventional VW design. At present Scat is the only company to offer such a radical departure from the norm as the Split-Port head, and it remains to be seen whether any others will explore this avenue of design in the future.

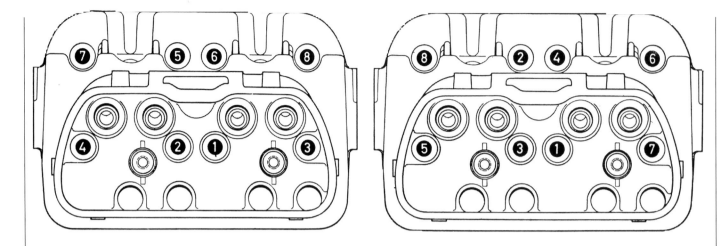

Volkswagen cylinder heads need to be tightened evenly and the nuts torqued to a specific figure. This should be carried out in two stages and following a set sequence, as shown. Begin with 7ftlb (1mkg) and finish with 23ftlb (3.2mkg). For race applications, this can be carried out in three stages: 10ftlb (1.4mkg); 18ftlb (2.5mkg) and 28ftlb (4.0mkg).

VALVE SIZES

Probably the most common error when buying a pair of cylinder heads is over-estimating your requirements. You should consider what you are expecting from your engine and what you are using your car for on a regular basis. A common mistake is to fit heads with valves that are too large for the intended usage - in most applications, a combination of 40mm inlet and 35.5mm exhaust will suit the majority of street engines up to 2-litre, whereas a 42mm x 37mm combination is better suited to a larger capacity engine. However, there are exceptions to every rule and the choice of carburation, camshaft specification and bore/stroke combination can make a significant difference. In general, if you are intending to use your car on a daily basis, it is suggested that you err on the mild side when it comes to valve sizing.

COMPRESSION RATIO

To calculate the compression ratio (CR) of your engine, you need to know three things: combustion chamber volume (head cc), deck height displacement (that's the volume of the area above the piston at the top of the stroke) and the cylinder displacement.

$$\text{Cylinder displacement} = \frac{\text{Bore x Bore x Stroke x 0.003142}}{4}$$

$$\text{Deck height displacement} = \frac{\text{Bore x Bore x Deck Height in mm x 0.003142}}{4}$$

Combustion chamber volume (head cc) is measured using a calibrated syringe or, in the case of many aftermarket heads, this figure can be supplied to you by the cylinder head manufacturer.

$$CR = \frac{\text{Cylinder Displacement + Deck Height Displacement + Head cc}}{\text{Deck Height Displacement + Head cc}}$$

For example:

Bore = 90.5mm; Stroke = 82mm; Deck height = 1.5mm; Head cc = 46cc

$$CR = \frac{521.66cc + 9.65cc + 46cc}{9.65cc + 46cc} = 10.37:1$$

While many carburetted race engines will use compression ratios of up to 14:1 or more, it is generally accepted that a limit of 9.0:1 is acceptable for the street - the main problem today is the poor quality of fuel available. Race engines have to use special high-octane race fuel to prevent the detonation that would be caused by using regular fuel. The factory compressions ratios were always kept very low - regularly below 7.5:1 - in an effort to keep cylinder head temperatures to a minimum. A high-compression engine will always produce more horsepower than an identical low-compression motor, but possibly at the expense of long-term reliability.

RECOMMENDATIONS

Mild Street	Modified VW dual-port; 041; 042; Scat Round Port; Scat Mini-D; Berg GB840; Berg GB850; Berg GB854; Pauter 'A'
Hot Street	Modified 041; 042; 044/Magnum; Scat Mini-D; Scat Wedge Port; Berg GB855; Berg GB865; Pauter 'A'; Pauter 'B'; Eliminator 2000; Bugpack S/E; Super HO; Bugpack SF-1★;Bugpack SF-2★; Bugpack A/F★;CB Competition Eliminator★
Competition	Modified 044/Magnum; modified Eliminator; modified S/E; modified Super HO; Berg GB870; Berg GB872; Bugpack SF-1; Bugpack SF-2; Bugpack A/F; CB Competition Eliminator; Auto-Craft 910; Pauter Super Pro; Scat Split-Port

★These heads, while primarily intended for race use, have been used with success on all-out street cars which see only occasional road use. However, be aware that these heads tend to run hot and may not be suitable for prolonged street use.

CAMSHAFTS & VALVETRAIN

Camshafts, lifters, pushrods, rocker arms, springs and retainers.

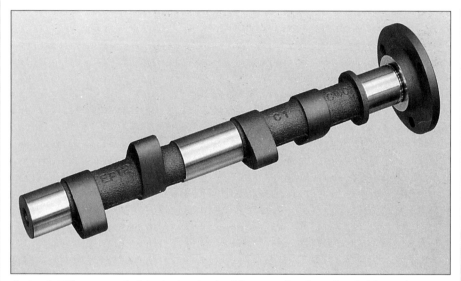

Stock-style Volkswagen camshaft showing how just four lobes serve eight valves – the inlet lobes are the two in the center of the cam. From left: exhaust lobe for numbers 1 and 3 cylinders, inlet lobe for the same, inlet lobe for numbers 2 and 4 and exhaust lobe for the same. Timing gear mounts to flange on end of cam.

Camshafts

Many engine builders feel that the last thing you should change in your engine is the camshaft. Now, while that may seem a rather negative view in a book about performance products, there is a great deal of merit in the statement. A considerable amount of thought went into deciding upon the specification of the camshaft used in the Volkswagen engine and, while it may be a modest affair with short duration and low lift, it perfectly matches the rest of the components used in the engine.

The cylinder heads, valves and inlet manifold, for example, are designed to work efficiently together at low revs, producing maximum torque and horsepower at well under 4,000rpm. The camshaft is designed to bring out the best in this combination, nothing more,

nothing less. By changing the camshaft and leaving the rest of the engine alone, you are going to upset this perfect working relationship and find yourself with an engine which will probably produce less horsepower and torque than the original.

Power output is directly related to engine rpm, so any increase in power is going to require an increase in engine speed. To make the engine turn at higher rpm, it is necessary first of all to allow it to breath more efficiently and that is why the first steps you take in modifying your Volkswagen should be in the direction of improving the induction and exhaust systems (see chapters on cylinder heads, carburetors and exhaust systems). Only then, when the engine is capable of taking deeper breaths, should you think about changing the camshaft to make the most

of this new-found breathing ability.

Anyone who has taken even the most casual look though a camshaft catalogue cannot fail to have noticed the words 'lift', 'duration', 'advertised duration', 'lobe center', etc. They are obviously all important, but quite what they refer to, and how they should influence you when making your camshaft selection, is another matter. Let's first of all take a simple look at what a camshaft does.

In a VW aircooled engine, the camshaft is located below the crankshaft, running in its own set of bearings (although, prior to 1965, the cam ran directly in the crankcase), and is driven by a pair of gears off the end of the crankshaft. Because the camshaft revolves at half the speed of the crank, the timing gear on the cam is twice the size of that on the crankshaft. The cam has four lobes: two of these are the inlet lobes, the other two, the exhaust lobes. Note that opposing cylinders 'share' the cam lobes. As the cam rotates, the lobes push against the cam followers (lifters) which, in turn, push against the pushrods. The pushrods themselves operate the rocker arms which then force the valves open.

From this very simple description, we can see two things: the height of the cam lobe will dictate how far the valve opens and the profile of the cam lobe will affect how long the valve is held off its seat. The first of these is referred to as 'lift', the second as 'duration'. Note that duration is always measured in degrees of crankshaft rotation. Let us take a look at the subject of lift first of all.

This is probably the easiest part of the cam's specification to understand, and the easiest to see. Compare a stock cam with an aftermarket one and the chances are that the lobes will be taller, suggesting the cam will push the valves open further. Cam lift is a measurement of the height of the lobe above the base circle, the imaginary circle drawn to define the non-effective part of the lobe when viewed in profile.

However, the lift at the cam lobe is not the same as how far the valve is lifted off its seat. Most rocker arms have 'ratio' rockers: the stock factory rockers have a ratio of 1.1:1, while aftermarket ones can have ratios of 1.25:1, 1.3:1, 1.4:1, 1.5:1, or more. What this means, in an original factory-spec engine, is that the valve will be lifted off its seat by 1.1 times more than the height of the cam lobe (more in the case of those aftermarket ratio rocker arms). To complicate things further, to obtain an accurate valve lift figure, you have to deduct the valve lash (clearance) - typically 0.006in. This is why it is so important when choosing a cam to ascertain precisely what figures are being quoted by the grinder: are they lift at the cam, lift at the valve (without taking into account any valve lash) or true lift at the valve with 0.006in lash?

Cam lift can be misleading for it is not always a case of more is better. Certainly the higher a valve is lifted off its seat, the more air/fuel mixture can be drawn into the cylinder and, in general terms, increasing cam lift will result in more power. The problem is that the cylinder head has its own limits as to how much mixture can pass through the inlet ports. There is no point in installing a cam which gives 0.550in of valve lift if the head does not flow anything more above 0.450in valve lift because the port design is too restrictive - no matter how far you lift the valve off its seat, the design of the cylinder head will prevent any more air/fuel flowing into the combustion chamber.

Cam duration is a measure of the number of degrees of crankshaft rotation the valve is held off its seat by the cam and valve train. Just as with lift, duration can also be measured at the cam ('advertised duration') or at a chosen (or 'checking') lift - typically 0.050in. The greater the duration, the more potential there is to allow more air/fuel into the

Some aftermarket camshafts are reground from an original VW cam but others, like this from Autocraft, are ground from fresh blanks (at top of picture). Timing gear shown with cams is usually a bolt-on where aftermarket cams are concerned.

cylinder which, as long as the engine can burn it, means more power. In practice, camshafts with short duration, such as the stock factory cam, result in better low-rpm performance while long duration cams will give better top-end horsepower.

Another expression which is frequently used in association with camshaft specification is 'overlap'. This is a measure of how long (once again, in degrees of crankshaft rotation) both inlet and exhaust valves are open at the same time. This may seem at first sight like an odd situation - surely the inlet valve should open and close to let the fuel in and then the exhaust should open and close to let the waste gases out - but it is a necessary function of an efficient engine, as a few degrees of overlap helps to keep the exhaust valves cool (some of the fresh air/fuel mixture will escape past the exhaust valve) and also, as the exhaust gases exit the chamber, they create a partial vacuum which helps to pull the incoming air/fuel charge into the cylinder.

One by-product of large overlap - as a point of reference, the stock Volkswagen cam has only about 1° of overlap while a race cam such as the Engle FK-89 might have 66° or more - is to reduce the cylinder pressures at low rpm. In a motor with a stock camshaft, the valves are not held open at the same time for very long. As a result, the pressure built up in the cylinder on the compression stroke remains high for the whole time the piston is travelling up the bore. Engine rpm will have little effect on cylinder pressure in this instance. However, if a cam with long duration and large overlap is installed in an otherwise identical engine, the cylinder pressure will almost certainly be lower at low rpm - what is happening is that the valves are both open for longer, allowing some of the pressure to bleed off. It is only at the higher rpm at which the camshaft is designed to work efficiently that the pressure builds up - we all recognize this as the point when the engine 'comes on the cam' and starts to produce some real horsepower.

To understand this, imagine placing your thumb over the end of a bicycle pump, partially covering the hole. If you push the handle (piston) slowly, the air will escape past your thumb (valve) and you will be able to push the handle all the way in without much effort. However, if you try to push the handle in very quickly, you will find the pump becomes almost impossible to move as the air cannot escape fast enough through the partially blocked hole. In the engine, the cylinder pressure will continue to increase (and the engine will produce more horsepower as a result) until the point is reached where other factors come into play: the heads or exhaust will not flow any more air, the carburetors are too small, the valves begin to float, etc. Only by addressing these areas can more power then be extracted from your engine.

Lobe Center is a measurement in degrees between the center-line of the inlet lobe and that of the exhaust lobe. Typically it is around 108° for most aftermarket cams, this figure proving to be a good compromise between a low lobe center measurement of 107° or less, which will give better mid-range and low-end power, and a higher figure which will tend to shift the power band further up the rpm range. Every cam grinder has his own feelings on lobe centers and a quick look at the specification chart at the end of this chapter will give you an idea of what is available. Note how some of Auto-Craft Machine's cams feature very shallow lobe centers - this is usually indicative of a cam designed for prolonged high rpm use, such as that used in a midget circle-track race car.

Amongst other aspects of cam design to bear in mind is the shape of the lobes themselves: a fatter lobe not only increases duration, but also causes the valve to open more slowly for a given lift. Extremely high lifts (for example, as might result from using high-ratio rocker arms with cams not designed for use with anything other than a stock 1.1:1 rocker) can cause the valve train to undergo severe strain as the valve is accelerated rapidly off its seat and slammed shut again. Cams that are intended for use with ratio rocker arms generally have a specification which suggests a lower lift for a given duration.

There are two aspects to consider regarding opening a valve more rapidly: on the one hand it can be argued that the valve will be at its maximum opening for a longer length of time, thus allowing greater gas flow into the cylinder (assuming the duration is suitably matched) while, on the other, the faster you ask a valve to lift off its seat, the greater the wear that will be caused in the valve train - guides, springs, lifters and lifter bores will all suffer as a result.

In some applications, such as an all-out drag race motor, this is of relatively little consequence as the engine will almost certainly be freshened up on a regular basis. However, on a regularly-used street engine it is a very real concern. Aside from the poor gas mileage which results from using a cam with a radical profile ('race' cams are not designed to work at low rpm and cause the engine to run inefficiently, with a very rough idle being the first tell-tale sign), greatly increased valve guide wear will soon result in a costly trip to the local cylinder head specialist.

If there is one thing you can be sure of when choosing a camshaft, it's that there is no easy answer! A camshaft which works well in one engine may be totally unsuited to another of the same capacity. There are so many variables that have an effect on how a particular engine responds to a given camshaft that making a bland statement about how this cam is right or that cam is wrong simply is not possible. Certainly every cam grinder will make recommendations about his products, but be aware that they cannot be treated as hard and fast rules.

For example, a well-respected camshaft such as Engle's 110 would be a fine choice for a relatively mild 1700cc street engine with dual 40IDF Weber carbs, modest headwork and an extractor exhaust system, giving plenty of usable mid-range performance along with a greatly improved top end. Put that same cam in a 2.2-liter motor with dual 48IDA carburetors, a set of wild heads with 12:1 compression and 44mm x 38mm valves, and the engine will be crying out for more. By the same token, a 10:1 compression 2.1-litre race engine with dual 48IDAs and a good set of heads

would thrive on an established grind such as Engle's FK-89 but one of the latest 2.8-litre, 14:1 compression Pro-Stock engines with a pair of 62mm JayCee Terminator carbs and 50mm x 40mm valves would feel strangled.

Cam selection is something that can only be done after you have asked yourself some searching questions. What is the car to be used for? Daily driving to and from work? Weekend bracket racing? All-out competition? Do you need to worry about a loss of bottom-end torque? Do you mind having to have the heads rebuilt on a regular basis? Do you mind poor gas mileage? Some cam suppliers (note we say suppliers rather than grinders - most grinders are far more switched on than many of those who sell their products) will simply give you a cam which they claim is a 'hot street cam giving loads of power throughout the range' without asking you pertinent questions about the specification of your engine. A good example of how things should be done is the Gene Berg Enterprises catalogue, in which there are several cams listed. Rather than making simple statements about whether the cams are for street, race or off-road, there are detailed recommendations. For example, 'GB302: For the more radical engine. The larger the displacement and the more head work, the better the performance and the smoother it runs. Commonly used in hot street cars with 1900cc or larger motors with dual dual-throat carbs and head work. Requires GB273A dual springs shimmed to 0.070in from coil bind and if used for higher rpm purposes, use GB269. 2,500rpm-6,500rpm range with dual dual-throat carbs and proper head work. 308° duration, 0.405in lift at cam'.

From this description, you learn that the cam is not for the smaller, single-carb engine which is used in heavy traffic. 'Larger displacement', 'dual dual-throat carbs' and 'head work' all point to the fact that this cam is intended for a heavily modified engine. '2,500-6,500rpm range' shows that the cam won't allow the car to lug along in traffic at low rpm without protesting. The final specification lets it be known that the figures are measured at the camshaft rather than at a checking figure of, say, 0.050in lift. There are also reminders that any significant change in cam specification will result in the need for heavier valve springs due to the greater loads imposed as a result of a combination of high valve lift and high engine rpm.

So, where does this leave the enthusiast engine builder who wishes to buy a cam as part of a project, the aim of which is to produce a reliable, high-horsepower street car? Let us summarize our findings: increasing valve lift will increase horsepower without any major effect on low-rpm performance. However, ultimate power output will be limited by other factors, such as cylinder head flow capabilities. In general terms, an increase in duration will also bring about an increase in horsepower, but at the expense of bottom-end performance. An increase in valve overlap - itself a result of increased duration - will cause the power band to be moved higher up the rpm range, once again at the expense of low-end power, and result in a rough idle. Widening the lobe center angle will move the power band up the rpm range, while decreasing the lobe center angle will give better mid- and low-range power. The figure of 108° is accepted as being a good compromise. Cams with steep opening and closing ramps (the 'sides' of the cam lobe) will open and shut the valves more quickly but at the expense of greatly increased valve train wear.

If there is one golden rule on camshaft selection it is to err on the side of caution. Unless you are running a high-rpm, large capacity race engine, stay away from cams which have long duration and excessively high lift. It could be argued that something like the Engle FK-87 (320° duration and 0.401in cam lift) is as radical as you would want to use on the street, and then only in a large displacement engine (2000cc and above) with heavily modified heads and matching induction and exhaust systems. Generally, for a mild street engine, keeping duration below 290° and valve lift under 0.450in will result in a smooth-running, fuel-efficient engine with a useful increase in horsepower and torque, the ultimate output of which will, naturally, be dependent on the choice of carburation and cylinder head. This is why a cam like

Fitting a new camshaft will mean you need to fit a new set of lifters. You may also need to change the valve springs if your engine is to turn at higher rpm and this will require new retainers and valve collets. Some manufacturers offer complete cam kits, such as this from Scat.

Engle's 110 has proved to be so popular over the years - it is a 'good all round cam', if such a thing really exists. And for all-out race applications? With advertised durations of over 330° and valve lifts approaching 0.650in, the sky (or should that be the piston crown?) is probably the limit!

Lifters

The stock, so-called 'flat-tappet', lifters are very good quality items which rarely fail except as a result of missed oil changes or extremely high mileages. The exceptions to this were the two-piece lifters used in the first 34bhp (US 40hp) 1200s up until 1961. Once these had been replaced in 1962 by superior one-piece lifters, the problems went away. Like all VW lifters, the stock part has a shallow radius ground across its face, the intention of which is to cause the lifter to rotate in its bore, thereby spreading the wear pattern evenly.

Factory lifters are fine for use with the stock camshaft, the materials used to produce the two components being perfectly compatible. By this, we mean that one part is not harder than the other, a situation which would lead to accelerated wear of the softer of the two parts. When installing an aftermarket camshaft, there is no guarantee that there will be this material compatibility if stock

lifters are used and, for this reason, even when a very mild, low-lift, low-duration cam is installed, it is imperative that a matching set of lifters from the same manufacturer should be fitted at the same time if there is any doubt at all about the materials used.

There are several aftermarket lifters available to the VW engine builder, ranging from ones which appear to be exact replicas of the stock Volkswagen part, to lightweight components aimed at the drag racer. All the major cam manufacturers offer lifters for the VW engine and all recommend that only their

There is a wide variety of lifters on the market, including these lightweight racing components from Bugpack. When changing your camshaft, make sure you fit a set of lifters that are manufactured from a compatible material.

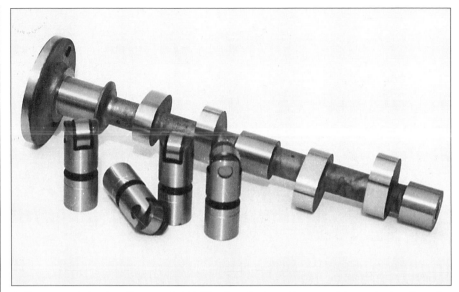

Roller cams are designed to offer extremely high lift or long duration without any of the associated problems of increased lifter bore wear or wear between the lifter and cam lobe. Note the unique profile of the cam lobe of this roller cam from Pauter Machine compared with a that of a regular 'flat tappet' cam shown elsewhere.

lifters be used with their cams. Bugpack lists two styles of lifter, a heavy-duty one for use with their aftermarket cams and a lightweight design sold under the Tayco brand name. These lightweight lifters are shorter than stock and also have a smaller diameter head - the aim is to help reduce the load on the valve train which would otherwise sap power.

Engle and CB Performance, along with a number of others, market what is called a wide-base lifter for the VW engine. The thinking behind this is to spread the load applied by high-lift, long-duration cams across the face of the lifter to prevent scuffing and premature camshaft wear. Gene Berg Enterprises, however, feels that the use of wide-base lifters is unnecessary in any VW engine and does not list them in its catalog.

While an individual engine builder's opinion of the merits of each type of lifter may vary, there is almost universal agreement that the VW oiling system does the lifters few favors. They receive their supply of oil last in the line, so to speak, and their seizure in the lifter bores in the crankcase is not an unknown problem. To alleviate this, GBE suggests a simple modification which involves grinding a couple of small grooves between the oilways in the side of each lifter to help spread the lubricant around more easily.

Although commonplace as far as other engines are concerned, one relatively unusual product on the VW market is the hydraulic camshaft kit for the aircooled engine. Offered by both Mofoco and Bernie Bergmann (and formerly by CB Performance), the conversion consists of a camshaft and a set of special hydraulic lifters, the idea being that, once installed, there is no further need for the owner to carry out valve clearance adjustments. They are simple in concept: the hydraulic lifter is basically an oil reservoir with a check valve included. The lifter follows the profile of the cam at all times (hence the valves are adjusted for zero lash, or clearance) but as the cam rotates and the lobe begins to push on the lifter, the pressure inside it rises to over 1500psi and causes the check valve to close. The lifter then becomes solid and operates the valve train as normal. As the cam rotates further, the lifter slides down the other side of the lobe and the pressure inside it drops off again as the check valve reopens.

Hydraulic lifters require the use of cams ground especially for the application, and CB Performance, Bernie Bergmann and Weber Cams each produce cams suited for use in such circumstances. In general these cams are not radical grinds aimed at the racer as hydraulic cams are best suited to street applications.

It is also important to note that any hydraulic camshaft installation requires a plentiful supply of good, clean oil otherwise the check valves in the lifters will become blocked. At the very least, a full-flow external oil filter system is required, preferably along with a deep sump and a high-volume oil pump.

For the driver wishing to use his car on a regular basis but who doesn't wish to have the hassle of adjusting valve clearances on a routine basis, hydraulic camshaft kits would appear to be the perfect answer. They are also very quiet in operation as they automatically adjust to take into account the expansion of the VW engine as it gets hotter.

Other camshaft variations include roller-cams. The major problem with flat tappet cams is that there is always going to be a problem with frictional loss (and increased wear) between the lifter and the cam lobe, especially where extreme cam profiles are used. As the cam rotates, the lobe will apply some side-loading to the lifter before it starts to move in its bore. The situation becomes worse the more radical the cam design. Also, to ensure the lifter remains in contact with the cam lobe at all times and that the valves do not float at high rpm, valve spring pressure must be increased significantly. This imposes further demands on the flat tappet arrangement by increasing the friction between cam and lifter.

These problems can be addressed by using lifters which have small rollers built into the ends of them (the matching camshafts are thus referred to as 'roller cams'). These follow the profile of the cam lobe with ease and do not suffer from the same problems of side-load and frictional loss. They allow the engine builder to use much higher spring pressures, along with extreme cam profiles, in high rpm situations. The major disadvantage of the roller set-up is the increased cost as the special lifters are considerably more expensive to manufacture than conventional solid lifters. However, Pauter Machine, the current leader in roller-cam technology for the VW engine, considers that any disadvantages are considerably outweighed by the benefits, at least as far as the race engine builder is concerned.

Pushrods

Wherever a high-lift cam or stronger valve springs are used, it is imperative that the stock pushrods are changed for something more substantial. The stock aluminum pushrods are prone to flexing at the best of times and especially so when subjected to the greater stresses of a heavy-duty valve train. There are two alternatives as far as material for aftermarket pushrods is concerned: aluminum and chrome-moly. While carbon fibre has been used experimentally in race applications in an effort to reduce weight, the main problem with this material is its inability to expand and contract at a rate to match the VW engine, resulting in constantly changing valve clearances.

Aluminum pushrods are best suited to mild street applications which rarely see high rpm and do not feature radical cam profiles requiring heavy-duty valve

The stock pushrod tubes can foul the pushrods in situations where a high lift camshaft is used. Pauter Machine and some other companies manufacture special large-diameter tubes which prevent this from happening. These tubes are adjustable in length to cater for varying engine widths.

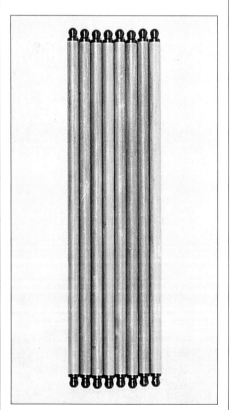

Any change in valve spring strength and cam profile, or an increase in maximum engine rpm, will necessitate changing the stock aluminum pushrods for something far stronger. These pushrods from Manton are manufactured from 4340 chrome-moly and have ball-ends to accommodate greater rocker arm movement.

To establish the required length of any new pushrod, it is necessary to use a dummy adjustable pushrod. This can either be purchased from one of the several aftermarket suppliers, or made from an old stock pushrod and a piece of threaded stud – the lighter colored pushrod shown here was home-made.

springs. While it is possible to buy aluminum pushrods which are somewhat more substantial than their stock counterparts, their use is not to be recommended in any high performance engine.

Chrome-moly pushrods are available from a variety of manufacturers, and in a variety of diameters to cope with even the strongest of valve springs and most extreme cam profiles. GBE manufactures its $^3/8$in diameter rods out of 0.035in-wall 80,000psi chrome-moly and recommends their use for all engines which turn as

high as 8,500rpm with dual or triple valve springs. For more extreme applications, and engines which use heavier Chevy-type springs, GBE offers its 160,00psi chrome-moly pushrods. These have ball-shaped ends which take into account the action of the rocker arms when using high-lift cams.

Scat Enterprises and Bugpack both offer a range of pushrods to suit virtually all applications, as does CB Performance. However, CB also lists something rather unusual: adjustable pushrods. Acknowledging that many V8 engines come with pushrods that can be altered in length to suit any valve-train combination, CB Performance designed and manufactured a similar system for the VW. However, as far as is known, CB's remains the only such pushrod for the Volkswagen engine and is not a product which has gained wide acceptance in VW performance circles.

Similarly unique among aftermarket pushrods are the tapered chrome-moly rods manufactured by JayCee Enterprises. These are $3/8$in in diameter at one end, and $5/16$in at the other, the idea being to increase the clearance between the pushrod and the pushrod tube/cylinder head when a high-lift cam is used.

The majority of aftermarket pushrods are available either in a variety of preset lengths, or may be cut to length by the customer. This is necessary because, whenever there is a significant change in engine specification, such as increased stroke (which can result in a wider engine) or altered valve train geometry due to a change in cam or rocker gear, the required pushrod length will change. If cylinder heads are flycut, the pushrods would need to be shorter than stock. Simply fitting shims under the rocker arms will not always solve the problem of how to restore the correct geometry.

Valve gear

Once the lifters have converted the rotational movement of the camshaft into the linear motion of the pushrod, the task of then opening the valves is handled by the rocker arms. The stock rockers have a ratio of either 1.0:1 (on 1200 models) or 1.1:1 (on all others). The latter means that if the cam raises the pushrod by 4mm, the valve will open 4.4mm (assuming no valve lash). The factory rocker arms are very good quality forgings but they are poorly located on the rocker shaft by spring clips which are prone to breakage when used at high-rpm or with high-lift camshafts. The solution here is to replace the shaft and clips with an aftermarket bolt-together set-up which prevents the rockers from moving sideways away from the valve head.

In the stock engine, the pushrod locates in a socket machined into one end of the rocker arm, while an adjusting

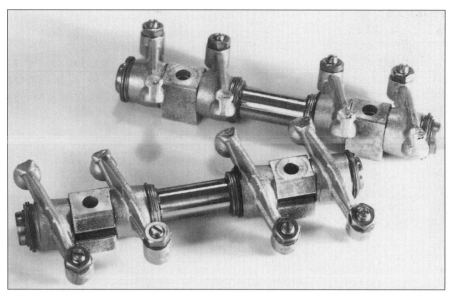

Stock rocker assembly has either a 1.0:1 ratio for 1200 engines or 1.1:1 ratio for all others. The inherent weak points are the spring clips which locate the rocker arms on the shaft – Pauter Machine cures this with new C-clips in place of originals.

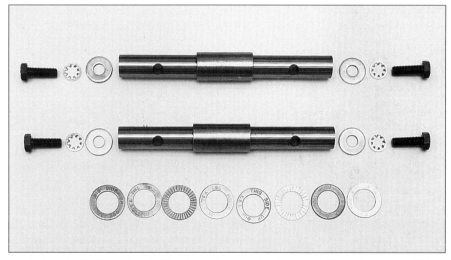

The best way to solve the problem of failing stock rocker arm springs is to use a bolt-up rocker shaft kit. This prevents any future problems with the stock design and is a worthwhile, but relatively inexpensive, modification to make to any mild VW engine.

screw at the other end operates directly onto the tip of the valve. This is fine for a low rpm engine with a modest cam profile, but results in excessive wear on the valve tip as the adjusting (tappet) screw sweeps across the head when a high-lift camshaft is used. To combat this, virtually all aftermarket high-ratio rocker arms - including the popular Autocraft and Gene Berg assemblies and the original EMPI design - have the adjusting screw at the pushrod end, with a radiused pad at the other which opens the valve without damaging the tip. Pauter

Machine and Autocraft also both offer roller-rockers, which have a hardened steel roller secured by a pin which rolls across the top of the valve, reducing wear and tear even when extreme cam profiles are used.

The Pauter Machine roller-rocker assemblies are unique in that the rocker arms themselves are machined from billet aluminium for light weight and greater strength. In common with many aftermarket assemblies, they feature needle-roller bearings between the rocker arms and the rocker shafts in an effort to

There are many different rocker assemblies on offer, from a variety of manufacturers. Auto-Craft Machine makes three types, one of which is a roller-tip design. All use bolt-up rocker shafts and have the adjusters at the pushrod end of the rocker arm.

prevent galling and potential seizure. This used to be a problem on the old Sig Erson rockers which would often break when the rocker arms tried to weld themselves to the shaft due to a lack of adequate lubrication. However, as long as there is adequate provision to ensure a plentiful oil supply and the bearings are of the correct material, there is no reason why a plain-bearing rocker assembly should not survive the rigors of use in a high-performance VW engine.

The main reason most people change their rocker assemblies is to install high-ratio rocker arms. It is possible to buy a set of 1.25:1 rockers to fit onto the stock rocker shaft, but this is not really the best way to improve the output of your engine unless you are keeping the stock camshaft, or using one of the very few aftermarket cams specially ground for use with them. Most new cams are designed for use with either stock 1.1:1 rockers or aftermarket 1.4:1 or 1.5:1 assemblies.

Some of the most impressive rocker assemblies are those manufactured by Pauter Machine. They are machined from billet 7075-T6 aluminum and feature roller tips. The shaft is a two-piece design which is integral with the rocker pedestals for greater strength. Needle roller bearings are used in the rocker arms.

Auto-Craft Machine's roller-tip rocker arms are designed to reduce wear and tear on the tip of the valve when a high-lift cam is used. Note that most aftermarket rocker assemblies come with new, longer rocker studs.

street up to full-race. Of these, the most widely used in all-out competition applications are those from Autocraft, Pauter Machine and Gene Berg Enterprises. While others may be acceptable, these three makes dominate the aftermarket, having proved their durability over the years.

Fitting any high-lift camshaft or high-ratio rockers will cause more rapid wear of the valve tip as a result of the rocker arm sweeping across the end of the valve in a wider arc than would normally be the case. This wear can be prevented - or rectified - by fitting lash caps to the end of the valve stem. These are small, hardened caps which slot onto the end of the valve, the rocker arm now acting against this cap rather than the valve itself. Lashcaps are available in a variety of thicknesses to allow the engine builder to equalize the height of the valve stems to ensure accurate valve-train geometry.

One way to help prevent premature valve tip wear when stock-style rocker

The original Sig Erson high-ratio rocker assemblies are no longer available and were prone to failure due to the rocker arms seizing on the shaft. A greatly improved version is now available from Bugpack.

Gene Berg Enterprises were among the first to offer high-ratio rocker arms, these being similar to the original EMPI design. The arms are available with either 1.40:1, 1.45:1 or 1.54:1 ratio to suit a variety of applications.

Note that you should not use high ratio rocker arms with a cam that has not been designed with them in mind, otherwise the valve will be accelerated open and slammed shut too quickly, damaging the valve-train, valve and seat. However, it is acceptable to use lower ratio rockers than the cam was designed for if it proves necessary to soften the cam specification for any reason (for example, where a bracket race car is used regularly on the road as a daily driver - a swap to high-ratio rocker arms would quickly restore the cam specification ready for competition).

There are several high-quality aftermarket ratio rocker assemblies available today, each of which would be acceptable for any application, from hot

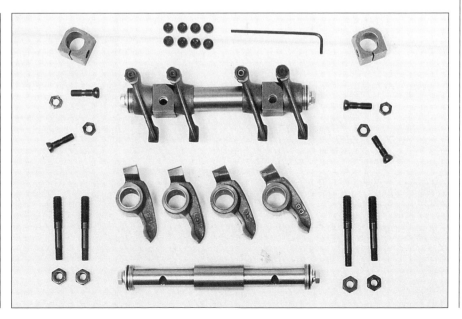

A Gene Berg Enterprises rocker arm in detail. These use a plain bushing, rather than a needle roller bearing, as GBE feels that the latter are not suitable for this type of application.

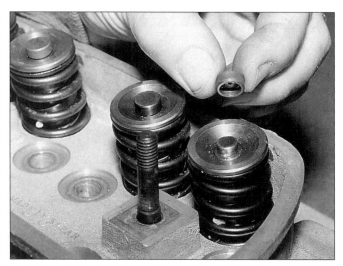

High lift camshafts and high-ratio rocker assemblies can bring about premature wear of the valve tip due to the increased movement of the rocker arm against the end of the valve. To combat this, lash caps should be fitted – they are available in a variety of thicknesses to take into account differing valve height.

If the stock rocker arms are to be retained, the original adjusting screws should be replaced with swivel-feet adjusters. Those shown here are the so-called Ford Courier or Mazda type which feature a small ball-bearing with a flat surface machined onto it.

arms are retained is to use a set of swivel-feet adjusting screws. These were first put to use on Porsches as a way to allow a high-lift camshaft to be used with VW-style rockers. Swivel-feet adjusting screws are just that: replacement tappet screws, the ends of which are allowed to swivel and remain in full contact with the tip of the valve stem. Two styles are available, one being a Porsche 911-style with a complete swivelling end, the other featuring a small ball-bearing with a flat surface machined onto it. This latter design is commonly referred to as the Ford Courier or Mazda style and can make it more difficult to use a feeler gauge to set valve lash (the ball revolves, tending to cause the flat part of it to disappear from view). Swivel feet adjusting screws preclude the use of lash caps except where adjustments to valve length have to be made.

Valves & valve springs

Aftermarket valves are available in either stainless steel or titanium, the latter being the choice of the racer as they not only reduce the weight of the valve-train but also allow lighter valve springs to be used. Stronger springs are normally necessary to prevent 'valve float' at high rpm - this is where a weak spring cannot return the valve to its seat fast enough to keep up with the profile of the camshaft. Stainless steel valves are widely available in a

The second type of swivel-feet adjuster is the Porsche 911-style. As with most aftermarket adjusters, these from Gene Berg Enterprises require the use of a small Allen key to set the valve lash.

Stainless steel valves are the most popular choice as they are available in a wide variety of diameters and lengths at an affordable price. Beware of poor-quality 'no-name' valves which may stretch after relatively little use.

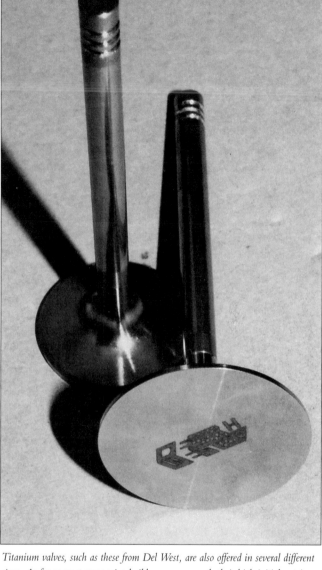

Titanium valves, such as these from Del West, are also offered in several different sizes. As far as most race engine builders are concerned, their high initial cost is offset by their reduced weight, which allows a lighter valve spring to be used without the risk of valve float at high rpm.

variety of dimensions, but it should be noted that some are better than others when it comes to the matter of material. Many aftermarket stainless valves are soft and can stretch, especially when used in an engine which sees regular high-rpm use. Beware of inexpensive, no-brand, aftermarket valves - it is better to stay with a known make, such as Manley, even if the cost is a little higher. Titanium valves are available in virtually all diameters to suit every application, and a variety of lengths to suit specialist cylinder head/valve-train combinations. Longer

valves allow the use of larger, heavier valve springs such as those referred to as 'Chevy-style' - valve springs which were originally intended for use with larger V8 Chevrolet engines. Aftermarket valves are available with either the factory 8mm stems or Chevrolet 11/32in stems. The latter are only really necessary in high-rpm competition applications.

The stock VW springs are very weak and are unsuited to any performance application. Even when the stock camshaft is retained, if the engine is run to higher rpm than originally intended,

the valve springs will need to be changed if the lifters are to track the cam lobe properly. Single heavy-duty springs are available from every aftermarket specialist, and measure the stock 1.225in in diameter. Heavy-duty dual valve springs (which feature a second, damper, coil wound inside the outer spring) are available in either stock diameter or the larger, 1.437in, Chevy style. Triple springs are also available, for high-rpm use on engines which feature very radical camshaft profiles. You should not use a heavier spring than is absolutely necessary,

Valve springs are available in several different styles – single springs are perfectly acceptable for situations where an engine is not going to see high rpm, but should not be considered in high-performance applications. Valve spring retainers are available in a range of materials, from aluminum (not recommended) to titanium.

It is important that the manufacturer's recommendations be followed regarding the installed height of a valve spring. To this end, most manufacturers offer valve spring shims which can be used to adjust the spring height, and therefore static valve seat pressure.

Vasco-Jet springs are available from a variety of sources and include both dual and triple designs – the latter are Chevy dimension. The triple spring features a flat damper coil between the main outer and the smaller inner spring. This helps reduce harmonics setting in at high rpm.

otherwise this may result in unnecessary wear in the valve-train, bent pushrods and possible lifter/cam failure.

The largest range of valve springs is available from GBE which lists no fewer than five different spring sets to suit any condition. The GB 271 is a single heavy-duty spring which provides 125lb of valve seat pressure at 1.500in installed height (that's the height from the base of the valve seat pocket in the head to the bottom of the valve spring retainer) up to 225lb at 1.00in. The dual GB273A gives between 150-160lb at 1.500in and 280-290lb at 1in. Triple GB269 springs are rated at 160lb at 1.500in but a massive 320-340lb at 1.00in. These springs are all stock VW diameter.

The larger Chevy springs begin with number GB272A, which provides 195lb at 1.500in and 440-450lb at 0.980in. For the racer who demands the highest valve spring pressures available, GBE offers the GB272AR which gives 240lb at 1.500in and a colossal 490lb at 1.00in. It almost goes without saying that valve spring pressures of this magnitude demand very strong pushrods and high-quality valve-train components from beginning to end.

One name which is synonymous with high-performance valve springs is Vasco-Jet. These springs are widely used by many engine builders and are listed by Pauter Machine, among others. Vasco-Jet springs are available in both VW and Chevy diameters, the former offering up to 375lb of seat pressure, the latter 440lb, at maximum valve lift.

Note that all dual and triple valve springs will require the valve guide boss on the cylinder head to be machined to allow the spring to seat correctly. This simple machining operation can easily be carried out by a competent machine shop, while most aftermarket cylinder heads will already be so modified.

Using anything other than stock springs will, in almost all cases, require the use of aftermarket valve spring retainers. This is especially true where dual and triple springs are concerned as the stock retainer, designed as it is for use with a single coil, cannot correctly locate the inner springs. Aftermarket retainers are usually manufactured from chrome-moly or aluminum. However, titanium retainers are also available for race applications where reducing the weight of the valve-train is a positive benefit. While chrome-moly retainers are perfectly acceptable for virtually every situation, aluminum ones are not. All too often they are manufactured from material which is too soft and this can cause the valve and its retaining collets to pull through the retainer, potentially wrecking the cylinder head, piston and anything else which may get in the way of a dropped valve. If aluminum retainers are used, they should only be fitted in conjunction with modest single valve springs.

There are two basic styles of valve collet (or keeper) in use: the stock-style three-groove design and the aftermarket single-groove 'Chevy' style. Opinions are divided over the merits of each design, but the stock-style three-groove keeper is still the most widely used and generally

Gene Berg Enterprises manufactures no fewer than five different types of valve spring to cater for virtually any application. Dual springs should always be fitted where higher-than-stock rpm is to used. Those shown are GBE273A and offer between 150 and 160lbs of seat pressure at an installed height of 1.500ins.

Web-Cam offers two different valve springs. One is a single spring which allows up to 0.470in valve lift, while the dual spring shown here handles up to 0.520in lift and 8,000rpm.

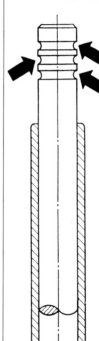

Stock-style valves have three collet (keeper) grooves machined in the end, while some aftermarket valves have one larger, tapered groove, commonly known as 'Chevy style'. The three-groove design is the most widely used.

gives little cause for concern. To get the best from any valve keeper set-up, it is necessary to modify the two halves of each keeper so that, when they are assembled on the valve, they do not touch each other. This ensures that the valve is held as tightly as possible. (In the stock situation, the two collets are in contact with each other, allowing the valve to rotate freely - the aim of this is to prevent rapid valve seat wear.) Aftermarket valve keepers are available from the majority of suppliers - check with the manufacturer to ensure that they are made of a suitably hardened material.

When installing a high-lift camshaft, it is vital to check the clearance between the cam lobe and the lifter. This should be a minimum of 0.040in (1.0mm) otherwise damage may result at high rpm. The lifter bore can be machined to increase this clearance.

INSTALLING A CAMSHAFT

Most aftermarket cams do not come fitted with the timing gear. The gear should be bolted on so that the slot in the camshaft lines up with the small '0' stamped in the outer edge of the gear. If you are using adjustable timing gear, which has elongated holes to allow for a variation in cam timing, do not worry about fitting the washers supplied at this stage. Place the lifters (cam followers) in both halves of the crankcase and then slip the camshaft into first one half then the other and look to see how much clearance there is between the tip of each cam lobe and the corresponding lifter (having made certain the lifters are pushed all the way into their bores). You need to have at least 0.040in (1.0mm) and it may be necessary to have the case machined slightly to achieve this, especially where a very high-lift cam is being used in conjunction with a stock crankcase. Many ready-modified cases, such the Rimco Supercase, will often already have had the lifter bores cut back slightly.

OK, so you're happy with the clearance. So what's next? Carry out a dummy assembly of the bottom end of the engine, taking care to ensure the '0' on the cam gear is aligned with the dot on the crankshaft timing gear. If it isn't then your cam timing will be out by a

rather large amount. The crankshaft and cam should turn over smoothly without feeling tight - any tightness may be due to a variation in cam gear diameter and can often be relieved by lapping in the gears using some fine valve-grinding paste. The factory offered cam gears stamped with anything from +7 to -7, which is a

You will need to use a dial gauge when setting cam timing. A dummy lifter inserted in the case allows the cam lift to be measured. Almost all cam manufacturers suggest using a checking lift of 0.050in when dialling in a camshaft.

reference to their diameter. This was to allow for any deviations in the measurement between the cam bore and the crankshaft center line. Most aftermarket cams come with '0' gears.

To degree the cam, open up the crankcase and remove the lifters. Ideally you should make up a dummy lifter, by welding or brazing a piece of rod or a cut-down bolt into an old lifter where the pushrod would normally sit. The bolt should be long enough to extend out through the case when the follower is installed. Fit this dummy lifter into No1 cylinder inlet cam follower bore and then reassemble the case halves with the crank and camshaft. With a degreed crank pulley fitted to the end of the crankshaft, turn the engine over until you find TDC (top dead center) on number one cylinder. Now, mount a dial-gauge (dial-indicator) so that it is possible to take a reading off the end of that bolt you fixed into the dummy lifter. Zero the dial gauge.

Rotate the engine in the normal direction (clockwise as you look at the pulley) and keep turning until the dial gauge begins to measure some lift. Continue until the reading is 0.050in (1.25mm) and stop at that point. Now

A degreed pulley wheel is a must when setting camshaft timing. However, do not take it for granted that the degree markings are accurate. Check the TDC (top dead centre) mark by comparing it with the true TDC when checked at the number one piston.

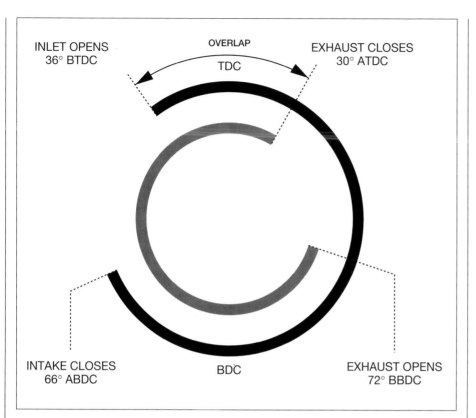

INLET OPENS
36° BTDC

OVERLAP
TDC

EXHAUST CLOSES
30° ATDC

INTAKE CLOSES
66° ABDC

BDC

EXHAUST OPENS
72° BBDC

Typical Cam Card (in this case for an Engle FK-89 camshaft) shows the specification in diagrammatic form. Note how opening and closing figures are given in relation to either Top Dead Center (TDC) or Bottom Dead Center (BDC) on number one cylinder. Overlap refers to length of time in crankshaft degrees that both inlet and exhaust valves are open at the same time. Cam timing needs to be set at 0.050in (1.25mm) lift at cam follower.

The dial gauge can also be used to check the true valve lift and to establish the half-lift point necessary to accurately set pushrod length and valve train geometry. If you build engines on a regular basis and do not possess a dial gauge, buy one!

The valve train geometry will be correct when the angle of the rocker arm with the valve closed mirrors that when the valve is fully open. Minor adjustments can be made with shims under the rocker assemblies but you may need to make up some pushrods of a different length.

take a look at the crank pulley and take a reading from this – we'll call this reading 'A'. Now continue turning the crank – the dial gauge will continue to rise as the cam lobe raises the dummy lifter. Keep going until the reading on the dial gauge starts to drop back down again and stop when it reaches 0.050in (1.25mm) once more. Now read the crank pulley and note the number – reading 'B'. This is the point where the inlet valve is closing.

Let's put some figures to this. An Engle FK-89, an all-out race cam designed for use with large capacity engines, comes with a cam card that says the inlet valve should open at 36° BTDC (Before Top Dead Center) and close at 66° ABDC (After Bottom Dead Center). Now Bottom Dead Center is 180° (or half a turn of the crankshaft) later than Top Dead Center, so the inlet valve is open for 36° + 180° + 66° = 282° which happens to be Engle's factory figure quoted for the FK-89. The advertised

duration, incidentally, is 328° – quite a difference.

If, in our example, the dummy inlet lifter reaches 0.050in at 36° BTDC and closes at 66° ABDC then all is well. You can remove the cam and timing gear and tighten the bolts up, having remembered to fit some washers first! However, it may be that the first reading is 38° and the second is 64°. In this instance, although the overall duration works out the same (38° + 180° + 64° = 282°), the cam will be 2° advanced from the recommended setting - ie, the valves will be opening 2° earlier than intended. Loosen the bolts holding the timing gear to the cam (you can do this through the oil pump hole) and rotate the camshaft slightly clockwise (the cam rotates in the opposite direction to the crank - rotating the cam anti-clockwise will advance it). Tighten the bolts and recheck the timing.

Now it is possible that the figures you get don't precisely match up with those

The stock cam timing gear is cut with the teeth on a helix. This results in reduced gear noise but does cause an increase in load on the thrust face of the cam bearings as the camshaft is pushed back into the case.

Double-thrust cam bearings help to combat increased wear when stock timing gears are used with heavy-duty valve springs. They are available from several sources.

on the cam card, possibly due to machining tolerances etc. Say, for example, reading 'A' is 36° BTDC but reading 'B' is 68° ABDC. What you need to do is split the difference and set the cam so that the inlet reaches 0.050in lift at 37° BTDC and closes at 67° ABDC. OK, so the overall total duration may differ from what you expected, but the timing will be correct for the cam - ie the inlet valve will be fully open at the intended point.

You will find that your aftermarket camshaft gear comes with three sets of washers. One set has the hole drilled in the center, the other two sets have the holes drilled slightly offset. These are to allow for the cam having been advanced or retarded in relation to the timing gear.

Once you have established the correct timing for your cam, you'll find one or other set of the washers will fit in place without disturbing the overall setting. Advancing the camshaft (ie, fitting the cam gear so that the cam is turned anti-clockwise in relation to the crank) will generally improve low-rpm power slightly, while retarding the cam will improve high-end power.

REGROUND CAMS

You will often see camshafts advertized as being 'reground'. This means that a stock cam has been reprofiled by machining the lobes to a different shape. As the lift of a cam is a measure of the difference between the base circle dimension and the height of the tip of the lobe, it is possible to produce a high-lift or long-duration camshaft from a stocker by reducing the base circle diameter and/or changing the shape of the cam lobe.

This is an inexpensive way to produce a performance camshaft but the disadvantage is that there are limits to how far the stock cam can be reprofiled and so limits as to the specification. Also, by reducing the base circle diameter of the cam, the lifter will have to protrude further out of its bore which could lead to increased wear of the crankcase. Web-Cam, along with other companies, also offers a service whereby the stock cam can be welded (called 'hard-welding') to

allow it to be machined to a more radical profile than a regular reground cam.

STRAIGHT-CUT GEARS

The stock cam gears are cut on a helix - ie, the teeth are at an angle across the gear. The aim of this is to make the timing gears as quiet as possible. Many builders of performance engines will replace these with straight-cut timing gears, which have the teeth cut straight across rather than at an angle. Part of the thinking behind this is to reduce power loss (helically-cut gears are less efficient than straight-cut gears). The only drawback is that straight-cut gears are significantly noisier than the stock ones and result in a whining sound which rises and falls with engine rpm. On the street, some people will love the sound, others will learn to hate it, especially if they opt to use so-called steel-on-steel gears (normally the cam gear is aluminium while the crank gear is steel. Aluminium straight-cut gears have a tendency to wear very quickly so many people prefer to use steel for both cam and crank gears). It has to be said that, on a street-only engine, the power losses resulting from using the stock-type gear are negligible. However, where straight-cut gears really are of benefit is when extremely strong valve springs are used, along with a radical camshaft profile. This situation leads to such great forces being exerted on the camshaft that the stock-type helically-cut timing gears become forced against the thrust face of the cam bearings. This leads to premature wear, even when double-thrust cam bearings are fitted.

For race use – or where increased noise is not a problem – straight-cut timing gears may be used. These are significantly louder than the stock helically-cut gears but help to reduce frictional losses.

CAMSHAFT AVAILABILITY

(Valve lifts: figures shown are those quoted by manufacturer for either lift at cam or at valve)

AUTO-CRAFT MACHINE

(Duration shown at 0.050in lift; lift at cam)

Part no	Drtn	Lift	Lobe Centers	Application and comments
9500	250°	0.410″	111°	
9505	285°	0.422″	110°	
9506	285°	0.422″	106°	
9515	285°	0.427″	110°	
9523	297°	0.427″	103°	
9525	297°	0.427″	107°	
9599B	297°	0.427″	109°	
9527	297°	0.427″	104°	
9528	297°	0.427″	101°	
9529	292°	0.428″	102°	
9530	292°	0.428″	105°	
9531	292°	0.428″	108°	
9532	292°	0.428″	106°	
9533	292°	0.428″	104°	
9534	292°	0.420″	104°	
9535	297°	0.427″	110°	
9545	280°	0.450″	110°	
9555	280°	0.450″	106°	
9565	285°	0.422″	108°	
9575	285°	0.422″(in)	110°	Dual lobe
	261°	0.380″(ex)	110°	
9585	285°	0.422″	104°	
9595	268°	0.420″	106°	
9596	285°	0.422″(in)	110°	Dual lobe
	257°	0.375″(ex)	110°	
776.7	287°	0.430″	106°	
600B	287°	0.430″	110°	
428HV	280°	0.400″	106°	
SCO	287°	0.430″	104°	
900TX	318°	0.430″	110°	
925	287°	0.430″	112°	
120	261°	0.435″	108°	
125	270°	0.460″	108°	

GENE BERG ENTERPRISES

Cams for use with 1.1:1 rocker arms (Advertised duration; lift at cam)

Part no	Drtn	Lift	Lobe Centres	Application and comments
GB295	276°	0.418″	108°	Small capacity, short course off-road
GB296	276°	0.374″	108°	1300-1700cc single 2-bbl or dual carbs
GB296A	279°	0.433″	108°	1200-1700cc short course or heavy street car
GB297	284°	0.385″	108°	All-round street cam; up to 5800rpm
GB297A	288°	0.425″	108°	Similar but needs head work; 1600cc and up
GB300	294°	0.390″	108°	1700cc and up; 1500-5500rpm; dual carbs
GB300A	292°	0.450″	108°	Similar but wider rpm range; good bottom end
GB301	300°	0.405″	108°	Street engine with dual carbs and head work
GB302	308°	0.405″	108°	1900cc and up; dual carbs and head work
GB302A	309°	0.445″	108°	Similar but wider rpm range; large dual carbs
GB303	313°	0.424″	108°	More top end; less lower end; from 4000rpm up

Cams for use with 1.4, 1.45. 1.54 and up to 1.65:1 rocker arms:

Part no	Drtn	Lift	Lobe	Application and comments
GB307	278°	0.341″	108°	1600cc and up; single 2-bbl or dual 1-bbl carbs
GB308	286°	0.356″	108°	1600cc and up; dual carbs; 1000-5000rpm
GB309	297°	0.335″	108°	Small to mid-size engine; ratio rockers
GB310	304°	0.380″	108°	Street or buggy; large motor; head work; exhaust
GB311	306°	0.378″	108°	Larger engine; head work; 3500-7000rpm
GB315	320°	0.390″	108°	Hot street; large engine; 48IDA carbs; close-ratios
GB316	329°	0.411″	108°	All-out race; very popular drag race cam
GB316B	328°	0.429″	108°	Similar but for more radical heads
GB317	328°	0.436″	108°	Similar but for more radical heads
GB318	332°	0.440″	108°	All-out race; over 2200cc; radical heads
GB319	334°	0.407″	108°	All-out race; even more duration and lift
GB319A	338°	0.410″	108°	All-out race; even more duration and lift
GB319B	333°	0.430″	108°	All-out race; even more lift

BUGPACK

Cams for use with 1.1:1 rocker arms (Advertised duration; lift at valve)

Part no	Drtn	Lift	Lobe Centres	Application and comments
4061-10	270°	0.396″	108°	Small displacement; high torque; bus or off-road
4062-10	284°	0.415″	108°	Good all-round street cam; up to 6500rpm
4063-10	296°	0.430″	108°	Street and strip; heavy idle; up to 7000rpm
4064-11	282°	0.448″(in)	108°	Dual-lobe; off-road competition; head work
	293°	0.578″(ex)	108°	
4065-10	268°	0.364″	108°	Turbo cam; good bottom end; reduced turbo lag

Cams for use with 1.5:1 rocker arms

4064-10	302°	0.633″(in)	108°	Dual lobe; midget competition; high rpm
	304°	0.578″(ex)	108°	
4064-12	328°	0.645″(in)	108°	Dual lobe; drag race competiton; 5500rpm up
	328°	0.624″(ex)	108°	
4065-11	297°	0.515″	108°	Super street; heavy idle; mid to high rpm
4065-12	304°	0.573″	108°	Street and strip; heavy idle; 4500rpm up

CB PERFORMANCE

Cams for use with 1.1:1 rocker arms (★ also for 1.4 & 1.5:1)
(Advertised duration; lift at cam)

Part no	Drtn	Lift	Lobe Centers	Application and comments
2229	262°	0.300″	108°	Street; 1500-4500rpm; mild engine mods
2230	266°	0.302″	108°	Street; 1500-4500rpm; mild engine mods
2231★	274°	0.317″	108°	Street; 1500-4500rpm; mild engine mods
2233	272°	0.370″	108°	Street and bracket race; off-road
2234	274°	0.388″	107°	Super street and off-road; dual carbs; larger cc
2235	273°	0.375″	108°	Street and bracket race; good mileage and bhp
2236★	278°	0.335″	108°	Hot street; head work; dual carbs etc
2237	278°	0.423″	108°	Super street; dual carbs; larger displacement
2238★	280°	0.309″	108°	Hot street; head work; dual carbs etc
2239	282°	0.385″	108°	Street and bracket race; off-road
2240	284°	0.420″	107°	Super street and off-road; dual carbs; larger cc
2241	286°	0.390″	108°	Hot street and off-road; head work; dual carbs etc
2242★	300°	0.392″	108°	Hot street and off-road; head work; dual carbs etc
2245	314°	0.393″	108°	High rpm midget racing etc.
2246	314°	0.436″	108°	All-out competition
2247	322°	0.408″	108°	All-out competition
2248★	325°	0.426″	108°	All-out competition
2250★	290°	0.408″	108°	Off-road; wide power band

Part no	Drtn	Lift	Lobe Centers	Application and comments
2251	273°	0.375″(in)	-	Dual lobe; 109° or 115° lobe centers
	272°	0.370″(ex)		
2252	291°	0.422″(in)	-	Dual lobe; 109° or 115° lobe centers
	280°	0.427″(ex)		
2253	273°	0.374″(in)	-	Dual lobe; 109° or 115° lobe centers
	282°	0.385″(ex)		
2254★	305°	0.375″(in)	-	Dual lobe; 109° or 115° lobe centers
	14°	0.393″(ex)		
2255	317°	0.423″(in)	-	Dual lobe; 109° or 115° lobe centers
	321°	0.412″(ex)		
2256	322°	0.408″(in)	-	Dual lobe; 109° or 115° lobe centers
	325°	0.426″(ex)		
2257	325°	0.426″(in)	-	Dual lobe; 109° or 115° lobe centers
	330°	0.405″(ex)		
2262	328°	0.477″(in)	-	Dual lobe; 109° or 115° lobe centers
	330°	0.492″(ex)		

Cams for use with 1.25 rocker arms (★ also for 1.4)

Part no	Drtn	Lift	Lobe Centers	Application and comments
2208★	254°	0.413″	108°	Street and bracket race; good low and mid-range
2209★	260°	0.395″	108°	Hot street; head work; dual carbs etc
2207	274°	0.418″	108°	Super street; dual carbs; larger displacement
2210	283°	0.446″	108°	Super street; dual carbs; larger displacement
2211	295°	0.448″	108°	Super street; dual carbs; larger displacement
2212	301°	0.446″	108°	All-out competition
2213	308°	0.446″	108°	All-out competition
2214	320°	0.446″	108°	All-out competition
2215	328°	0.478″	108°	High rpm midget racing etc.
2216	330°	0.448″	108°	High rpm midget racing etc.

Cams for use with 1.25,1.4 and 1.5:1 rocker arms

Part no	Drtn	Lift	Lobe Centers	Application and comments
2288	303°	0.385″(in)	108°	Dual lobe; drag race competition
	299°	0.382″(ex)	108°	
2289	314°	0.390″(in)	108°	Dual lobe; drag race competition
	321°	0.404″(ex)	108°	
2298	319°	0.405″(in)	108°	Dual lobe; drag race competition
	323°	0.402″(ex)	108°	
2299	321°	0.440″(in)	108°	Dual lobe; drag race competition
	321°	0.435″(ex)	108°	

Cams for Hydraulic Lifters (1.1:1 rockers or high-ratio)

Part no	Drtn	Lift	Lobe Centers	Application and comments
1466	252°	0.350″	108°	Stock street
1467	263°	0.352″	108°	Street; single or dual carbs
1468	272°	0.360″	108°	Mild street; single or dual carbs
1469	282°	0.365″	108°	Strong mid-range and top end
1470	288°	0.375″	108°	Full-race; dual carbs; good idle
2260	266°	0.393″	108°	Street; strong mid-range; 5000rpm up
2261	278°	0.410″	108°	Hot street; dual carbs
2263	288°	0.440″	108°	Hot street; good mid-range and top end
2264	305°	0.440″	108°	Road race for kit cars; dual carbs; good idle

CHASSIS SHOP

Cams for use with 1.4 or 1.5:1 rocker arms

Part no	Drtn	Lift	Lobe Centers	Application and comments
C15-040	-	-	-	Turbo grind for engine on gasoline
C15-045	-	-	-	Turbo grind for engine on alcohol

CROWER CAMS

Cams may be used with stock or ratio rocker arms
(Advertised duration; lift at valve with 1.1:1 rocker arms)

Part no	Drtn	Lift	Lobe Centers	Application and comments
61002	260°	0.375″(in)	110°	Dual lobe; stock replacement; 1000-5000rpm
	268°	0.381″(ex)	110°	
61000	268°	0.354″	110°	Lower- to mid-range; torque; 1800-6000+rpm
61003	276°	0.401″(in)	107°	Dual lobe; 1600cc and up; 2000-7000+rpm
	284°	0.429″(ex)	107°	
61004	284°	0.429″(in)	107°	Dual lobe; up to 2180cc; 2000-7000+rpm
	290°	0.452″(ex)	107°	
61005	290°	0.452″(in)	107°	Dual lobe; up to 1800cc; 2500-7500+rpm
	298°	0.468″(ex)	107°	
61006	298°	0.468″(in)	107°	Dual lobe; increased CR; 3000-8000+rpm
	306°	0.489″(ex)	107°	
61007	306°	0.489″(in)	107°	Dual lobe; 2000cc and up; 3500-8500+rpm
	312°	0.506″(ex)	107°	

ENGLE RACING CAMS

Cams for use with 1.1:1 rocker arms (Advertised duration; lift at cam)

Part no	Drtn	Lift	Lobe Centers	Application and comments
VZ-14	274°	0.420″	108°	Small displacement off-road closed course
VZ-15	279°	0.435″	108°	Medium displacement off-road closed course
VZ-25	286°	0.429″	108°	Midget circle track; bracket race; off-road comp
VZ-30	298°	0.461″	108°	Off-road and drag race competition
VZ-35	309°	0.448″	108°	Off-road and drag race competition

Cams for use with 1.1 or 1.25:1 rocker arms

Part no	Drtn	Lift	Lobe Centers	Application and comments
W-100	276°	0.383″	108°	Street and buggy, sand rail, vans, small capacity
W-110	284°	0.392″	108°	Hot street and off-road; good low and mid-range
W-120	294°	0.397″	108°	Hot street; large displacement; off-road comp
W-125	301°	0.418″	108°	Drag racing and off-road competition
W-130	308°	0.419″	108°	Drag racing and off-road competition
W-140	313°	0.424″	108°	Drag racing competition only
TCS-10	284°	0.430″(in)	112°	Turbo cam; street and strip; good idle; low CR
	276°	0.420″(ex)	112°	
TCS-20	294°	0.435″(in)	112°	Turbo cam; drag race only; large cc; low CR
	284°	0.530″(ex)	112°	

Cams for use with 1.4 or 1.5:1 rocker arms

Part no	Drtn	Lift	Lobe Centers	Application and comments
FK-65	280°	0.342″	108°	Small displacement; off-road closed course
FK-7	288°	0.357″	108°	Medium displacement; off-road closed course
FK-8	298°	0.382″	108°	Large displacement street and strip or off-road
FK-10	310°	0.385″	108°	Off-road and drag race competitio
FK-87	320°	0.401″	108°	Off-road and drag race competition
FK-89	328°	0.416″	108°	Drag racing competition only
FK-97	328°	0.443″	108°	Drag racing only; wide base lifters; 1.4:1 rockers
FK-98	332°	0.446″	108°	Drag racing only; wide base lifters; 1.4:1 rockers

FAT PERFORMANCE

Cams for use with 1.1:1 rocker arms (Advertised duration; lift at valve)

Part no	Drtn	Lift	Lobe Centers	Application and comments
FC400	274°	0.424″	108°	Mild street; small displacement; low compression
FC410	284°	0.430″	108°	Street; single or dual carb; up to 2000cc
FC411	284°	0.442″(in)	108°	Dual lobe; off-road; Class 9 competition
	274°	0.424″(ex)	108°	
FC415	290°	0.450″(in)	108°	Dual lobe; off-road comp; Class 1/2 and 5/1600
	284°	0.430″(ex)	108°	
FC420	294°	0.434″	108°	Off-road; 1600cc and up; head work
FC425	301°	0.442″	108°	Off-road; large displacement; single or dual carb
FC430	309°	0.444″	108°	Off-road; large displacement; head work; carbs etc

PAUTER MACHINE

Cams for use with 1.1, 1.3, 1.4 or 1.5:1 rocker arms (Advertised duration; lift at cam)

Part no	Drtn	Lift	Lobe Centers	Application and comments
B4E7	262°	0.372″	107°	Mild street; under 2000cc
F6B6E7	274°	0.424″(in)	107°	Dual lobe; off-road
	264°	0.409″(ex)	107°	
F8E7	276°	0.366″	107°	
K8E8	288°	0.384″	108°	Strong mid-range
O8E8	296°	0.465″	108°	Off-road; 2000cc plus
P3E8	297°	0.429″	108°	
T1E8	307°	0.350″	108°	
T3E8	307°	0.437″	108°	Off-road; light vehicle; large displacement
T8E8	307°	0.451″	108°	
V5E8	314°	0.451″	108°	
X3E0	321°	0.417″	110°	Drag race competition; high rpm
X5E0	321°	0.475″	110°	Drag race competition; high rpm
X6E0	324°	0.372″	110°	
P4E8	298°	0.371″	108°	Hot street
V9E0	315°	0.367″	108°	Off-road; large displacement

Cams for use with roller-lifters

Part no	Drtn	Lift	Lobe Centers	Application and comments
VN025	293°	0.406″	108°	Dune buggy; off-road; large motor
VN011	312°	0.452″	108°	Hot off-road; turbo dune buggy etc
VN130	314°	0.438″	108°	Drag race (turbo or carb); midget race

SCAT ENTERPRISES

Cams for use with 1.1:1 rocker arms (★ or 1.4:1 rockers)
(Duration at 0.050” checking clearance; lift at valve)

Part no	Drtn	Lift	Lobe Centers	Application and comments
C20★	278°	0.338″	108°	Street; mild cam; good with 1.4:1 rockers
C25	275°	0.385″	108°	Bus and off-road, small cc; 5000rpm maximum
C35	286°	0.410″	108°	Street and off-road; good power spread; 6000rpm
C45	296°	0.418″	108°	Street and strip; heavy idle; 4500-6500rpm
C55	312°	0.428″	108°	Circle track; good mid-range; 4500-6500rpm
C65	318°	0.440″	108°	Super Vee etc; variable rpm application
C75	342°	0.445″	108°	Drag race competition; heavy car; 5000-7000rpm
C95	286°	0.475″	108°	All-round competition; large displacement

Cams for use with 1.4★ and 1.5:1★★ rocker arms

Part no	Drtn	Lift	Lobe Centers	Application and comments
C85★	330°	0.574″	108°	5500-8500rpm; competition only
C89★★	325°	0.618″	108°	Drag race competition

WEB-CAM

Cams for use with 1.1:1 rocker arms (★ reground)
(Advertised duration; lift at valve)

Part no	Drtn	Lift	Lobe Centers	Application and comments
00-000★	-	-	-	Stock 1600
00-010★	-	-	-	Stock 30bhp (US 36hp)
00-032	270°	0.358″	108°	Street and off-road
00-042	276°	0.422″	108°	Street and off-road; broad power band; turbo
00-382	280°	0.455″	108°	Street or turbo
00-052	283°	0.402″	108°	Street; good mid-range and top end
00-212	284°	0.422″	108°	Hot street; wide power band
00-062	284°	0.435″	108°	Hot street and off-road; strong mid- and high rpm
00-442	287°	0.465″(in)	108°	Dual lobe; off-road competition; Class 1/2 1600
	276°	0.422″(ex)		
00-072	287°	0.465″	108°	Hot street and off-road
00-312	288°	0.506″(in)	108°	Dual lobe; large displacement
	288°	0.478″(ex)		
00-092	298°	0.490″	108°	Hot street and of-road; large displacement
00-222	312°	0.492″	108°	Hot street; large displacement; mid- to high rpm

Cams for use with 1.4 or 1.5:1 rocker arms (lift shown with 1.5:1)

Part no	Drtn	Lift	Lobe Centers	Application and comments
00-082	290°	0.502″	108°	Hot street and off-road
00-102	300°	0.575″	108°	Hot street and strip; large displacement; high rpm
00-112	310°	0.585″	108°	Drag race competition; high rpm
00-302	304°	0.610″	108°	Drag race competition; good mid- to high rpm
00-392	324°	0.630″	108°	Drag race competition; Pro-sedan and dragster
00-192	320°	0.660″	108°	Drag race competition; Pro-sedan and dragster

WEBER CAM

Cams for use with hydraulic lifters
(Advertised duration; lift at cam)

Part no	Drtn	Lift	Lobe Centers	Application and comments
529-521H	274°	0.350″(in)	-	Dual lobe street cam
	268°	0.330″(ex	-	
56TH	282°	0.338″(in)	-	Dual lobe street cam
	270°	0.330″(ex)	-	
58TH	294°	0.342″(in)	-	Dual lobe hot street cam
	282°	0.338″(ex)	-	
60TH	308°	0.370″(in)	-	Dual lobe hot street cam
	304°	0.360″(ex)	-	
76	270°	0.323″	-	Low end torque; street or van
91	275°	0.382″	-	Street or off-road
142	282°	0.395″	-	Mid-range and good top end
91	286°	0.336″	-	For use with ratio rockers
148	294°	0.395″	-	Hot street; off-road; circle track
WC-1	299°	0.460″	-	Hot street; sand buggy; top end power
151	316°	0.450″	-	Drag race only; use 1.25 rockers
153	314°	0.461″(in)	-	Dual lobe; turbo drag race
	308°	0.458″(ex)	-	

CRANKCASES

From 1131cc to 3 liters - now anything is possible

Stock crankcases

The Volkswagen crankcase is a costly item to manufacture, with high-quality materials used to produce a complex casting. To the casual observer, its design has changed little over the years but in reality there have been several versions, some of which are of use to the performance engine builder while others are not.

It is a two-piece casting (later versions were, strictly speaking, three-piece), split vertically along the center-line of the crankshaft. The crankshaft runs in four main bearings, while the camshaft, located directly beneath the crank, originally ran directly in the case until the design was modified, in 1965, to allow the camshaft to run in its own bearings. The oil system revolves around a series of galleries drilled in the left-hand case half (as viewed from the crankshaft pulley), while the oil itself is contained in a small sump which forms the lower part of the crankcase.

The first crankcases were produced from a magnesium-aluminum alloy which was replaced in January 1951 by a material called Elektron. These early cases carried the part number 101 021 (later renumbered 111 101 025) and were used on the 25bhp engine until its replacement in January 1954. The new engine, the 30bhp (US 36hp), used essentially the same crankcase, this time with part number 101 021A (later renumbered 111 101 025A). These cases are instantly recognizable by their cast-in generator mounting and they are more compact than their successors.

In May 1959, the Type 2 range was offered with a new engine, the 34bhp

The original 1131cc 25bhp and 1192cc 30bhp (US 36hp) engines featured crankcases which were in two parts, the generator mounting (below the generator pulley in photograph) being integral with the right side casing.

The VW crankcase is split vertically along the center-line of the crank and camshaft, the cam being located below the crank (the hole in the center of the photograph is the camshaft bore). Note the drilled and tapped oilways.

1200 (US 40hp), which would see service in the Type 1 from August 1960. These first 34bhp crankcases carried the part number 111 101 025C when used in the Type 2 and 113 101 025A when introduced on the Type 1. This new design is recognizable by the separate generator mounting which is located by four bolts. Late in 1961, the Type 3 range was launched along with another new crankcase, part number 311 101 025A. This case differed from the Type 1 and 2 cases in that there was no dipstick in the normal sense. Instead, the Type 3 engine featured a long dipstick which was located in a tube which bolted in place on the right-hand side of the sump, facing to the rear of the car. As the Type 3 engine is located under the floor of the rear storage compartment, this enabled the owner to take an oil reading without having to disturb his luggage. A simple bolt-on conversion kit is available from most aftermarket suppliers which enables a Type 1 dipstick to be used on a Type 3 case. Later Type 3 crankcases also had provision for a rear engine mounting as the transmission was no longer supported at the bell-housing.

In August 1965, the crankcase was modified so that the camshaft ran in three

All Type 3 crankcases, and Universal models, have provision for a bolt-on dipstick located on the end of the sump. When the case is used in a Type 1 or Type 2, this can be sealed off with a blanking plate.

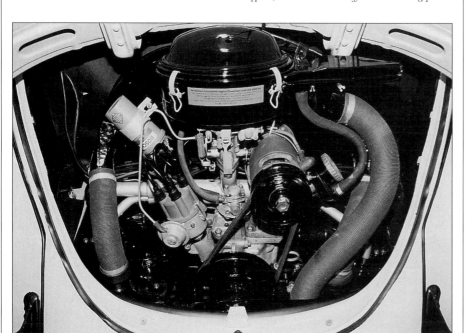

Later cases used on all 1192cc 34bhp (US 40hp), and larger, engines were three-piece castings, the generator mounting (visible just below the generator pulley) being separate to the two main engine cases.

removable bearing shells rather than directly in the case halves. This allowed the crankcase to be easily reused in the event of an oil system failure which might have otherwise resulted in irreparable damage. Today, companies such as Rimco of Santa Ana, California, can machine the older style crankcase to accept the later cam bearings. In September 1966, the case was further modified to make use of small rubber O-ring seals round the base of each main bearing stud, in place of the previously used nuts with integral seals.

The single biggest advance was made when the so-called dual-relief valve crankcase was introduced in August 1969. This case (part number 113 101 025F, later superseded in November 1970 by part number 211 101 025C), featured a

pressure relief valve adjacent to the oil pump, as previously, along with a second by the flywheel. The first of these is set to divert cold, thick oil away from the oil cooler and pass it directly to the bearings. Once the oil has warmed up and the pressure has dropped slightly, the valve closes and passes oil through to the cooler. This is to prevent high-pressure cold oil from damaging the oil cooler. The second relief valve is set to open when oil pressure exceeds 28psi, at which point lubricant is allowed to drain back to the sump, thus allowing the pressure to drop to what VW considered normal levels.

In September 1972, Volkswagen made the change from using 10mm cylinder head studs, screwed directly into the crankcase, to smaller 8mm studs which screwed into steel inserts which were fitted by the factory. The insert for the top stud by number 3 cylinder, closest to the flywheel, was also sunk deep into the case, requiring the use of a longer stud (the same length, in fact, as the lower four studs on each side). The thinking behind this was to help prevent the head studs from pulling out of the case, a common failing, especially on engines fitted to Type 2 vehicles. Today, fitting these inserts - commonly know as 'case savers' - to earlier cases is common practice and is considered a 'must' for all high-performance applications. It is also possible to have case savers fitted which accept the larger 10mm studs and many

In September 1972, Volkswagen began using threaded inserts to hold the cylinder head studs. At the same time, the factory swapped the 10mm studs for smaller 8mm items. many racers prefer to use the earlier style studs, but have inserts fitted to the case anyway. When this modification is carried out, it is imperative that the case be 'spot-faced' to guarantee a flat sealing surface for the cylinders, as shown here.

The threaded inserts, also known as 'case-savers', are available from most aftermarket suppliers and can be used to repair a crankcase which has had the cylinder head studs pull out due to overheating or over-tightening.

The so-called Universal crankcase now sold by Volkswagen comes ready drilled and tapped for a rear engine mounting so that it can be used in a Type 2 or Type 3 without modification.

On the side of each crankcase – and occasionally adjacent to the flywheel – there will be the casting details. This case has been manufactured from AS41 material. Many consider the later AS21 material to be a better choice for performance use.

It is generally believed that the best crankcases of all were those made in Germany, but today you are unlikely to find a new German case, most coming from South America. 'Hecho En Mexico': Made In Mexico.

racers feel this is the best way to go. However, be aware that if your case is machined to accept larger cylinders (especially 94mm), the case savers run very close to the edge of the cylinder bore. It is imperative, therefore, that only a competent machine shop should carry out this work.

On the subject of cylinder heads studs, there are various aftermarket kits available in both 8mm and 10mm diameter. Rimco makes 10mm studs which are 'waisted' - ie, reduced to a smaller diameter in the center - to allow their use on a Type 1 engine which is fitted with 94mm cylinders and pistons. Most aftermarket studs are manufactured from chrome-moly for greater strength, although Gene Berg Enterprises (GBE) advises that these studs do not have the right rate of expansion to suit the VW

engine, and their use can lead to pulled studs. However, many engine builders do use these studs in race applications without any apparent problems.

Another conversion which is sometimes carried out to the stock case was pioneered by GBE - the use of 15mm-headed (instead of 13mm) nuts on the 8mm studs which hold the crankcase together. The thinking behind this is to allow these studs to be torqued to a higher reading (19-20ftlb) than the stock 14ftlb. As far as the six main crankcase studs are concerned, these should be torqued to 29-30ftlb for high-performance street use and up to 33-35ftlb for race applications.

At present, there are only three Type 1 cases listed by Volkswagen on their dealer microfiche. They have the following part numbers: 111 101 025H

(34bhp 1200); 043 101 025D (the AF-series Type 1 1600 from August 1970) and 043 101 025, which is the so-called Universal Case, suited for use in all Type 1, 2 and 3 1300 and 1600 models. This case has been drilled and tapped for a rear engine mount as used in Type 2 and 3. These cases come with lifter bores which have thicker walls so that they may be machined at the factory to accept the hydraulic lifters now fitted to South American VWs. As supplied, however, they are machined for use with stock solid lifters.

One of the biggest areas of debate is the matter of material used in the late-model VW crankcases. On the side of the sump of each case (or adjacent to the flywheel) is a code which will read either AS21 or AS41. This is a reference to the material used in the casting process.

Volkswagen made the change to the AS41 material in August 1970 as it was felt that it offered better heat resistance, heat being the number one enemy of any aircooled engine. In 1975, with the introduction of the fuel-injected engines primarily for the American market, the factory began using a case marked with the legend 'AS21' - fuel-injection cases can be readily identified by their lack of provision for the factory fuel pump. AS41 is a softer material than AS21 and, for that reason, there are many - most notably GBE - who feel that the latter is the better choice. Berg made some investigations into the two materials and discovered that the factory considered AS41 cases to be non-rebuildable, ie, if they suffered any damage that would normally have been put right by machining, then the case would have to be scrapped. Berg also discovered that the AS21 material resisted heat-related problems far better. Today, although in theory superseded by the AS21 case, the AS41 casting is still available and has been used in many performance applications without problems. Although AS21 is undoubtedly a better material, it can be argued that, as most high-performance engines do not see very high mileages or prolonged freeway use, there is little cause for concern regarding the long-term drawbacks of the AS41 cases.

The subject of re-machining a crankcase is also one likely to provoke argument in some quarters. For example, there are some who maintain that the VW crankcase cannot be line-bored. Line-boring is the process by which the main-bearing saddles are re-machined to an oversize to take into account wear that has been caused by high mileages or extended high-rpm use. GBE feels that if a case has become so worn that line-boring is necessary to restore oil pressure (a worn case will allow oil to seep past the bearings), then it is beyond further use. However, there are others who will argue long and hard that this is not so and that line-boring is a perfectly acceptable machining process that will extend the service life of a crankcase without any drawbacks. Obviously, there are limits to how far a case can be line-bored, but oversize bearings are available in 0.25mm

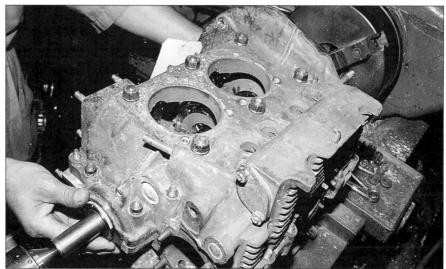

Line-boring a crankcase is thought to be a no-no as far as some people are concerned, but has been successfully used to recover cases which have pounded the main bearings. A boring bar is inserted into the case and the case torqued up on the main case studs. The boring tool is then mounted in a lathe and used to cut the main bearing saddles to an oversize. This operation removes any wear and ensures the bearings are perfectly aligned.

The main bearing saddles (this is the number two – or center-main – bearing) can take a considerable pounding due to high mileage or high engine rpm. Check for wear – you may need to have the case line-bored. Note the dowel hole to locate the bearing shell and the oil-way below it.

increments up to 1mm maximum oversize on the outside diameter.

The stock crankcase is well-suited to high-performance applications, despite its rather humble origins (with the exception of the 1200 case which requires too much modification to make it a worthwhile starting point). However, there are some weaknesses that need to be borne in mind when considering using a case in any high-horsepower situation. With extended use, the VW case can become worn on the number one main bearing saddle, as it is this bearing which takes the

thrust forces from the flywheel as the crank tries to move back and forth in its bearings. Repeated pounding of the thrust surface causes wear in the case, which leads to excessive crankshaft end-float. When a case is line-bored, it is usual to recut the thrust face at the rear of the case which, in turn, requires a new number one bearing shell to be machined to the correct width to fit the bearing saddle.

There is also the possibility of cracks occurring behind the flywheel, adjacent to number three cylinder. These cracks

are usually the result of excessive temperatures or the case having been poorly machined for larger cylinders. Although a cracked case can be rewelded in this area, it is debatable whether it might be wiser to invest in a new one. There have been cases offered with this area welded up to add more strength and, in fact, Volkswagen even offered a case with a thicker section at this point for the fuel-injection engines. This is another feature, the merits of which have given rise to debate. Let us just say that by far the greater number of crankcases in use today, in every application from stock to all-out turbo race motors, have not been welded behind the flywheel, nor do they rely on the factory 'thick wall' case.

Other problems which beset the stock case include the two halves 'shuffling' against each other at high rpm, causing wear on the main bearing saddle surfaces, and a tendency for the cylinders to wear into the case, creating oil leaks and lost compression. These problems, and many others, can be rectified or prevented by a company, such as Rimco, who can, for example, machine the case to take 'shuffle pins'. These are steel sleeves around the number two main bearing saddle studs which locate in a recess machined in the other case half. This modification prevents the case halves from shuffling against each other at high rpm by firmly locating them together.

Inside the VW crankcase are a number of casting marks which should be removed, partly to allow oil to flow more freely back to the sump and partly to relieve stress build up. Note how the cylinder head studs protrude to the inside of the case.

Another thing to check with any stock case is that the oil pick-up tube is a tight fit in the oil gallery. If the tube is loose, then you can use some epoxy glue to help secure it.

To provide a more stable seating surface for the cylinders, Rimco also recommends spot facing the case around the cylinder bores. This is especially important after a set of case-savers has been installed, as the inserts may stand slightly proud of the surface, thus preventing the cylinder from seating correctly.

There are many high-performance engines in use today which rely solely on the VW crankcase, either in stock form or one that has been given the 'works' by a company such as Rimco. Even though the stock case was only ever intended to take a 69mm-stroke crankshaft, it is possible to fit a long-stroke crank with relatively minor modification. With the correct choice of con-rod, the stock case can accept up to 74mm stroke cranks without modification, while the popular 78mm stroke can be used with a small amount of clearancing around the bottom of the cylinder openings and, depending on the rod used, at the top of the case.

Things start to get a little more difficult when cranks of 84mm and above are used, for here we can begin to experience clearance problems between the rods and the camshaft. However, Gene Berg Enterprises points out that its 86mm crank can be made to fit in the same space as a 78mm crank if Porsche-journal rods are used, as the rod bearing dimensions are more compact than those

In most instances, when a long-stroke crankshaft is used, the crankcase will need to be clearanced to accommodate the extra stroke. Here we can see how Rimco does it: note the machining marks at the top of the case, and adjacent to the cylinder bores, to clear the con-rods.

The stock case should also be drilled and tapped to accept an external oil system. This can be carried out by a skilled machine shop. Note also that the main oil gallery (lower) has been drilled and tapped so that the case can be cleaned more effectively at rebuild time. A threaded plug is used to seal the gallery.

Rimco adds shuffle-pins to the center-main bearing studs – these hollow sleeves are pressed into one half of the crankcase and locate in the other, preventing the two halves of the case from moving at high rpm.

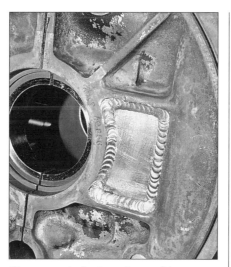

To prevent cracks forming at the rear of the crankcase, some people like to have this area welded for extra strength. The late fuel-injection case came from the factory with this section already filled.

of a VW rod. GBE is also at pains to show that a crank as large as its 88mm or a 90mm strokers can be used in a VW case if the clearancing is carried out correctly. The main problem here is that the stock-type cylinders do not extend far enough into the case to adequately support the piston at the bottom of the stroke.

Aftermarket crankcases

There will always be instances where the stock casting cannot cope with the demands made upon it, for example, long-stroke, large cylinder bore combinations which go beyond the machining limits of the stock crankcase. With this in mind, the brothers Lowry, Ken and Dean of Deano Dyno-Soar, developed the first aftermarket crankcase for the Volkswagen Type 1 engine in the

The original ARPM two-piece crankcase was the first aftermarket case to be offered for the Volkswagen. Very similar in overall appearance to the stock casting, the ARPM product was designed to accept long-stroke cranks with the minimum of clearancing. Note the integral sump.

1970s. This case resembled a VW casting at first glance, but had far greater strength built into it, as well as sufficient space to allow a long stroke crank to turn without clearancing. Early examples did have a problem with oil not being able to return to the sump quickly enough, although this was subsequently cured.

This case was marketed under Ken Lowry's ARPM name and eventually taken up by Dee Engineering and sold under the Bugpack name. The first examples were two-piece designs, but subsequent retooling saw a new three-piece case find its way onto the market. The case, now marketed as the Race Case, is cast from 356 T-6 aluminum and comes ready clearanced for up to a 90mm stroke crank, as long as Bugpack's own Race Rods, or similar, are used. The three-piece case was developed with a separate front cover, which houses the timing (cam) gears and allows accurate changes to be made to the cam timing without splitting the crankcase.

The Race Case has far stronger main bearing saddles than a stock casting and a far thicker deck surface - the area under the cylinders - so that there is less likelihood of problems in high-compression applications. To prevent the two case halves from moving apart at high rpm, the Race Case features 'through bolts' which pass right through the case from one side to the other, unlike the

stock case where the two halves are held together by studs which screw into one half.

The Bugpack case is supplied ready machined for a choice of 92mm, 94mm or 96mm cylinders and can also be ordered with the camshaft bore dropped by 0.100in in relation to the crank center line - this is to allow a larger stroke crank to be fitted without having to clearance the camshaft itself. This requires the use of special, larger diameter, timing gears.

The Race Case is intended to be run with a dry-sump oiling system but it is possible to purchase a separate bolt-on oil sump for applications where a dry sump system is not considered necessary. The wet sump conversion holds a full 4.5 US qts (5.6 Imp pts/3.2 liters) and comes equipped with a dipstick to check the oil level.

In 1977, Scat Enterprises of California released details of its new aftermarket crankcase - or more correctly, aftermarket engine - for the Volkswagen. This was based around a radical five-piece case with a separate flange to mount the

engine to the transmission and a two-piece timing cover. The case was cast from 356 T-6 aluminum and, like the Dee Engineering case, was through-bolted for strength. Clearanced internally to accept up to an 86mm crankshaft without further work, this early Scat case's most unique feature was the gear-drive arrangement for the distributor and fuel-pump, the latter to cater for a Hilborn fuel-injection system. The drive gears for this set-up were located behind the front half of the timing cover and were run off the end of the crankshaft. This system made no provision for a crankshaft pulley of any kind and suggested that the engine was aimed predominantly at the aircraft or midget-racing markets.

Supplied in three levels of completion (Phases 1, 2 and 3), the Scat aircooled 'Killer' engine, as it became known, was available either as a 2514cc unit, with a 100mm bore and 80mm stroke, or as a USAC Midget class-legal engine with a capacity of 2294cc which could be achieved one of two ways: 92mm bore x 86mm stroke or 100mm bore x 73mm

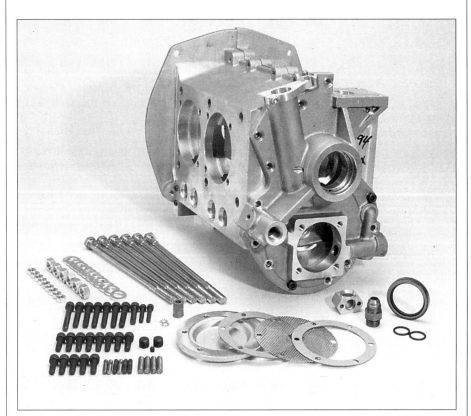

The Bugpack Race Case, from Dee Engineering, is a development of the later three-piece ARPM design and has been used with great success in Volkswagen drag racing by a number of people. Note long through-bolts used to secure the two main halves together.

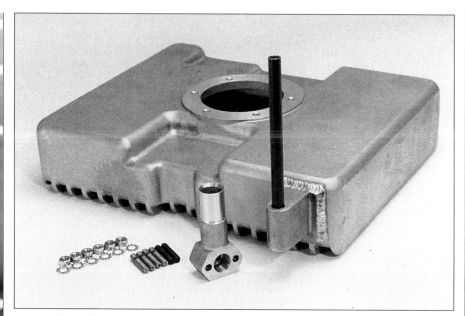

For those who prefer to use a wet-sump oiling system, Bugpack offers this bolt-on sump casting which includes provision for a dipstick. Wide, shallow design allows plenty of ground clearance with maximum capacity.

stroke, according to preference. Development of this concept did not stop there, however, for Scat also produced a watercooled version with special cylinders and heads. This was initially aimed at the aviation industry but later at the automotive market as, by a strange quirk of the rules, the USAC Midget classes allowed a 2425cc watercooled race car to compete with smaller (but more successful) 2294cc aircooled vehicles.

Scat Enterprises currently markets a three-piece aftermarket crankcase - still referred to as the Killer - which is also cast from 356 T-6 aluminum. This case is less radical in design and features a conventional timing gear arrangement, which can still be accessed without splitting the case halves. Solid main bearing webs add much-needed strength and no fewer than six hollow dowels

The original Scat aftermarket crankcase was this spectacular-looking five-piece design. The separate, two-piece front cover housed the timing gears and also the drives for the distributor, oil pump and fuel-injection pump for the Hilborn injection system. At the rear, a separate mounting flange allowed the case to be mounted to a VW transaxle.

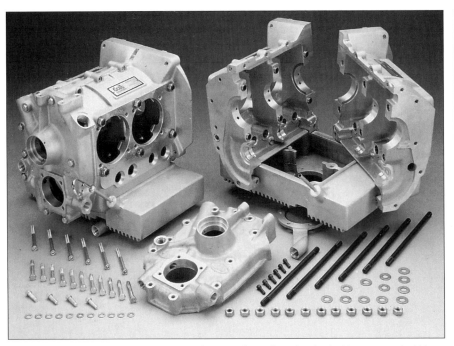

The current crankcase from Scat Enterprises is a three-piece design (four when fitted with a wet-sump) which has found favor with many drag racers. The removable front cover allows changes to be made to cam timing without splitting the case halves.

around the 7/16in diameter 4130 chrome-moly through-bolts locate the case halves and act as shuffle pins. Either 10mm or 12mm cylinder head studs can be specified. Main bearing saddles are machined to accept either Type 1 or Type 4 bearings, according to customer preference, while the case can be supplied to suit either a conventional dowelled crankshaft, Scat's own flanged type or any other custom installation which the customer demands.

The case is machined with 1/2in oil galleries and accepts one of Scat's own dry-sump oil pump units, as a dry-sump system is recommended. However, a wet-sump conversion is also available for those who prefer to stay with tradition and so a conventional oil pump can also be used with this case. In fact, one of the major selling points of this case is that it will readily accept off-the-shelf components, thus helping to keep the overall cost of engine-building to a reasonable level. Baffles cast into the bottom half of the case help to control the movement of oil and prevent crankshaft windage - this is where oil is picked up by the crankshaft and thrown around inside the engine, especially at high rpm. This might lead to problems with excessive amounts of oil being thrown into the base of numbers three and four cylinders. An oil seal is also fitted to the front of the timing case to prevent seepage past the crank pulley.

The Killer crankcase can be supplied to accept a range of cylinder bores, including 90.5mm, 92mm, 94mm, 96.5mm, 100mm and 101.6mm. Internally it is clearanced to accept a crank of up to 90mm stroke, thus allowing an engine of up to 2919cc to be built around the Scat case. This case has proved to be one of the most successful aftermarket castings ever, having seen regular use in everything from aero-engines to drag race VWs and midget racers.

Auto-Craft Machine of La Habra,

For applications which demand a cooling system, or a wet sump, Scat offers this finned sump and special fan-housing with generator mount. Quality of the Scat casting is very high.

Shown here in dry-sump form, the Scat Killer case includes pre-drilled oil galleries for use with an external oil system. The separate mounting flange can be machined to fit a variety of transmissions if necessary.

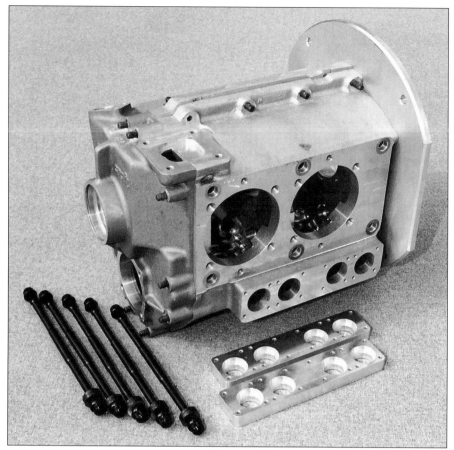

The Auto-Craft Machine aftermarket crankcase differs from the Scat and Bugpack products in that it has provision for no less than six cylinder head studs per cylinder. Through-bolts are used to secure the case halves.

halves apart. The rear mounting flange is located by dowels and held in place by nine socket-head set screws and a pair of O-rings prevent leakage from both the main oil gallery and the camshaft bore.

There are two areas where the Auto-Craft case differs from rival products. One of these is in the provision of no less than six cylinder head studs per cylinder, as opposed to the usual four. The extra studs are located above and below the center line of each cylinder and help to prevent the heads from lifting when used in high-boost turbo or ultra-high compression applications. The matching Auto-Craft cylinder heads are drilled to suit. The other feature which is unique to the Auto-Craft crankcase is the pair of bolt-on pushrod tube seal plates, one on each side of the engine case, which are O-ringed and intended to help prevent leakage from what is often a troublesome area of a VW engine.

The Auto-Craft case has become one of the most widely-used aftermarket VW castings in competition applications. It is available to accept a wide range of cylinders up to 101.6mm in diameter and crankshaft strokes of up to 88mm, giving a possible capacity of 2854cc. In drag

California, also produces an aftermarket case - christened the Pro-Series case - which has been successfully adopted by both the drag race and midget racing fraternities. This four-piece case is also cast from 356 T-6 aluminum. Auto-Craft boasts that its castings are flawless, having achieved zero porosity, and has been granted an aviation specification as a result. The four parts of the case comprise the two case halves, a front timing cover and a separate rear engine plate. The case halves are located with six ground dowel pins to prevent shuffling at high rpm, while 7/16in through-bolts hold the two halves firmly together.

As with other aftermarket cases, particular attention has been paid to providing a rigid seating surface for the cylinders and the main bearing webs are far thicker than stock to add much needed rigidity. Also, in line with other such cases, the removable timing cover allows changes to be made to the camshaft timing without having to split the case

As with the Scat crankcase, the Auto-Craft Machine Pro-Series case features a separate rear engine plate which is located with two dowels and a number of high-tensile bolts. Case design also incorporates separate plates to retain the pushrod tubes.

Pauter Machine's impressive aftermarket engine (heads, case, cylinders, crank and rods are all manufactured by Pauter): everything about it is truly massive! Although heavier than a Type 1-based engine, it is a remarkably strong design which is proving popular with sand drag racers.

Even the engine mounting plate is substantial – it can be supplied to accommodate a multi-disc clutch set-up, like this, or flat for use with a conventional single-plate clutch assembly.

racing it has long been the choice of people who run high-horsepower turbocharged, alcohol-burning dragsters and the like. At the time of writing, at least two VW world records are held by vehicles using an Auto-Craft Pro-Series case.

Without doubt, the most radical of all aftermarket Volkswagen crankcases is that manufactured by Pauter Machine of Chula Vista, California. Pauter started with a blank sheet of paper and designed a crankcase that would appear to be virtually indestructible. It is a unique product that consists of five principal castings: a main engine block, a top cover, a dry sump, a timing cover and a rear mounting flange.

The main block is cast from 356 T-6 aluminum and features massive main bearing journals complete with four-bolt main bearing caps, just like a conventional V8 engine. The camshaft is also located in its own separate bearing caps. The crank is inserted in the case from the top and held in place by the main bearing caps, which can be accessed once the top cover plate is removed. This has the advantage that the bearing shells can be inspected

The beast laid bare! The main block of the Pauter engine is cast from 356 T-6 aluminum and can be supplied with either Ford 351 main bearings or VW Type 4, according to customer preference. Pauter recommends the Ford bearing due to its greater strength.

without having to disassemble the engine. Similarly, the camshaft can be accessed from beneath the engine and can even be removed without extensive disassembly. This would allow a racer to test a number of different camshafts at the track without having to return to the workshop to split the motor.

The main bearing caps are manufactured from 6061 T-6 aluminum and are held in place by 7/16in ARP Chevrolet cylinder head studs. These bearing caps are designed to be used with large 2.75in (69.85mm) diameter Ford 351 Cleveland bearings which are almost 15mm larger in diameter than a stock VW! This obviously means that you need to have a crank specially ground (and Pauter can do that for you...) but the advantages are enormous, for the crankshaft will be far stronger than a regular VW type and, in theory at least, better able to cope with extreme engine conditions without flexing at high rpm. There is another advantage: Ford 351 Cleveland engine bearings are available, in the USA at least, for less money than an equivalent set of VW Type 4 bearings, which have previously been favored by

many racers. There is also an added bonus in that you end up with a spare bearing in every set! However, if you don't wish to go this route, or you already own a good VW-based crank which you would prefer to use, then that is no problem, for the Pauter big-block, as it has become nicknamed, can also be machined to accept virtually any type of main bearing.

The Pauter case has been designed with the camshaft dropped by a massive 0.235in from its stock location, meaning that a 96mm crankshaft can be fitted without any clearance problems, even if stock VW rods were to be used. A typical drag racer's combination of an 88m stroke crank with a set of Pauter's billet aluminum rods can be used without the need for any extra clearancing. Other interesting possibilities include the ability to use a Chevrolet roller lifter set-up with a special Pauter roller camshaft. The 'stock' oil system is a dry-sump arrangement, but a wet sump is available for those who prefer not to run the extra oil lines and oil tank required by the dry-sump system.

In addition to the ability to use a long-stroke crank without problem, the

Pauter case can also accept cylinders ranging in size from 90.5mm right up to 4.125in (105.4mm), although Pauter recommend the use of standard Chevrolet 4in or 4.030in cylinders and pistons which are readily available off the shelf. Combined with a 96mm crankshaft, there is the opportunity to have a Pauter-based engine with a capacity of 3188cc!

If there is a drawback to the Pauter case it is that it is quite heavy but that 'disadvantage', if you can call it such, is almost certainly offset by the bullet-proof nature of the design. Although initially intended for use in drag race or, more particularly, sand drag applications, the case is now finding favor among off-road racers. As a result, there is currently under development a cooling system which will fit the Pauter engine - and we can refer to it as a Pauter engine, for it is possible to build a totally non-VW Volkswagen engine using Pauter parts! - which opens up all kinds of possibilities for the future.

So, starting way back over 50 years ago as an 1131cc VW engine, it is now possible to build a motor which displaces almost three times that capacity. One has to ask, where will it all end?

The main bearings are retained by cross-bolted bearing caps, just like on a high-performance V8 engine. The caps are a close fit in the case and require the use of a special slide hammer to remove them once installed. Bearings can be accessed with the engine in the car by removing the top cover-plate. The camshaft can also be accessed from below the engine.

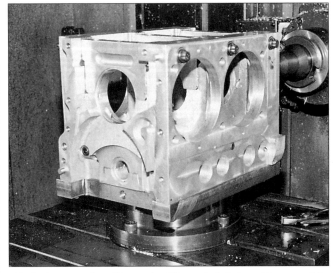

Clearly this is a crankcase like no other. The seemingly indestructible nature of the design is evident in this photograph of an unfinished Pauter case undergoing some final machining.

CRANKCASE CODE LETTERS
(implemented 8/65)

A	1200	Type 1	up to 7/65	(1192cc 30bhp)
B	1600	Type 2	8/67 - 7/70	
		Type 1	8/68 - 7/70	(USA)
C	1600	Type 2	8/67 - 7/70	(M240)
D	1200	Type 2	from 5/59	(1192cc 34bhp)
		Type 1	from 8/65	(1192cc 34bhp)
E	1300	Type 1	8/65 - 7/70	
F	1300	Type 1	8/65 - 7/70	
G	1500	Type 2	up to 7/65	
H	1500	Type 2	8/65 - 7/68	
		Type 1	8/65 - 7/70	
		Type 181	8/69 - 2/71	
K	1500	Type 3	8/65 - 10/73	
L	1500	Type 2	from 11/65	
		Type 1	8/66 - 7/70	(M240)
M	1500	Type 3	8/65 - 7/73	
N	1500	Type 3	8/65 - 7/73	(M240)
P	1600	Type 3	8/65 - 7/73	(M240)
R	1500	Type 3	8/63 - 7/65	(1500S)
T	1600	Type 3	8/65 - 7/73	
U	1600	Type 3	from 8/65	(fuel-injection)
UO	1600	Type 3	8/67 - 7/73	
AB	1300	Type 1	8/70 - 7/73	
AC	1300	Type 1	8/70 - 7/75	(M240)
AD	1600	Type 1	8/70 - 7/73	
		Type 2	8/70 - 7/73	
AE	1600	Type 1	8/70 - 7/71	(USA)
AF	1600	Type 1	8/70 - 1/80	(M240)
		Type 2	8/70 - 7/79	(M240)
		Type 181	1/74 - 1/82	(M240)
AG	1600	Type 181	8/70 - 7/76	
AH	1600	Type 1	8/71 - 1/76	(USA)
AJ	1600	Type 1	8/74 - 12/80	(USA & Japan fuel-injection)
AK	1600	Type 1	8/72 - 7/73	(USA)
AL	1600	Type 181	3/73 - 7/79	
AR	1300	Type 1	8/73 - 7/75	
AS	1600	Type 1	8/73 - 7/80	
		Type 2	8/73 - 7/79	

(Note: M240 = Optional Low Compression Engine)

RECOMMENDATIONS

Mild Street	Stock single or dual-relief valve case; Rimco Super Case★; GBE VWB403-101-025C★★; 8mm or 10mm studs
Hot Street	Rimco Super Case★; GBE VWB403-101-025C★★; 8mm or 10mm studs with case savers
Competition	Rimco Super Case★; GBE VWB403-101-025C★★; 8mm or 10mm studs with case savers; Bugpack Race Case; Scat Killer; Autocraft Pro Series; Pauter Super Pro

★ Stock case machined to accept stroker crank/larger cylinders to customer choice. Other options include fitting shuffle pins, modified oil system etc. Similar cases also offered by many of the major suppliers.

★★ Stock case which is modified to suit customer application by Gene Berg Enterprises, including machining for stroker crank/larger cylinders etc.

CYLINDERS & PISTONS

Cylinders, pistons, piston rings, wrist-pins and wrist-pin retainers

When Volkswagen first decided to increase the capacity of the Beetle engine, it increased the size of the cylinders and pistons from 75mm to 77mm. With this simple modification, the engine size was increased from 1131cc to 1192cc and the power output from 25bhp to 30bhp (US 36hp). VW realized that this was the easiest, most cost-effective way to extract more power from the tiny flat-four and that fact has not escaped the notice of the VW performance industry ever since.

The first Volkswagen pistons were beautifully cast aluminum items (part number 111 107 101), which were available in various weights to ensure a matched set should one piston have to be replaced on its own. To this end, each piston was given a color-key (blue, pink or green) according to its weight. Pistons for the original 1131cc engine were available in six different sizes to match rebored cylinders: 75mm; 75.5mm; 76mm; 77mm; 77.5mm and 78mm. Three different pistons for the 30bhp engine of varying weight and oversize were also available (77mm; 77.5mm and 78mm), with the stock piston being part number 111 107 111.

When the 34bhp engine was introduced (from engine number 5 000 001), a new piston was used, part number 113 107 111. No fewer than 12 different versions of this piston were listed, ranging in diameter from the stock 77mm up to a maximum of 78mm, with four different weights in each diameter. With the introduction of the 1500cc engine in the Type 2, the number of pistons offered by Volkswagen increased yet again. The new 83mm piston (part number 311 107 101AA) was also available in a low

Stock Volkswagen engine uses cast aluminum pistons in separate cast iron cylinders. The 22mm wrist pin is held in place with simple wire circlips. The cylinders are held in place by the cylinder head and use no head gasket.

compression version (part number 311 107 101AD) for vehicles destined for markets where fuel quality was questionable. Including the low compression versions, no fewer than 12 different 83mm pistons were offered by VW for the first of the new Type 2 engines.

With the introduction of the Type 3 range in 1962, there were three more different types of 83mm piston listed in the first year of production alone (each also available in three different weights and four oversizes), these beginning with part number 311 107 101C, followed by

311 107 101F and 101J. When the 1600cc Type 2 engine came into service, the VW parts department shelves must have started to wilt under the strain of yet another 18 different variations of the new 85.5mm piston, beginning with part number 311 107 112F (standard compression) or 311 107 112J (low compression).

It used to be popular to upgrade the 1192cc 34bhp (US 40hp) engine by fitting a set of machined-down 83mm (1500) or 85.5mm (1600) cylinders and pistons. These conversions gave a capacity of 1390cc or 1470cc respectively and were

Mahle/CIMA aftermarket barrels and pistons are the most popular for street and mild competition applications as they are readily available and relatively inexpensive. Stock 85.5mm (1600cc) and 87mm (1641cc) pistons are cast, all others are forged.

an inexpensive way to increase the capacity of the basic Beetle engine. However, the base of the cylinders became so thin that they soon distorted, leading to piston ring problems and ultimate failure of the engine. The 1200 rods also needed to be modified to accomodate the larger 22mm wrist-pins (gudgeon pins) of the new pistons.

Today it is generally accepted that the 1192cc engines are not worth upgrading and most people prefer to use at least a 1300, or preferably a 1600, engine as a basis. The main variation between these engines is that the cylinder heads are different, the 1300 having smaller valves and smaller spigots for the cylinders. These 1300 heads can, however, be machined to accept larger cylinders, although a 'bolt-on' 85.5mm (1600) conversion is available which features thin-wall cylinders and requires no machining. Similarly, there is a bolt-on 88mm conversion for the 1600 engine, giving 1679cc. These conversions are just adequate for low compression engines which will only see modest daily-driver use, but should not be considered for anything else. A better option is the slightly smaller 87mm (1641cc) conversion which is fine for regular use, if

not for true high-performance applications.

There is no simple way to increase the capacity of the VW engine without recourse to machining the crankcase. Few people would consider installing a long-stroke crankshaft in an otherwise stock engine, as opposed to fitting larger cylinders and pistons. Even though the latter requires the crankcase to be machined, the overall cost of the

When a stroker crankshaft is used with stock or certain aftermarket cylinders and pistons, spacers can be fitted under the cylinders to effectively increase their length. By using different thicknesses of spacer, it is possible to accurately set the deck height above the piston and therefore adjust the compression ratio.

conversion would be considerably less than that of a new stroker crank. All machine-fit cylinders require similar machine work to install, from the smallest 88mm up to the larger 94mm conversions. The 88mm (1679cc) conversion is an excellent choice for someone on a budget who wishes to build an inexpensive, reliable engine which has a little extra get-up-and-go compared to the stock 1600. The conversion, manufactured by KolbenSchmidt or Mahle, features cast aluminum pistons in cast-iron cylinders and should give little or no cause for concern. EMPI used to offer a superb 'slipper skirt' 88mm conversion which was the favorite of drag racers in the 1960s but sadly, like so much of the early speed equipment, it is no longer available.

The first progression from the 88mm conversion is the 90.5mm cylinder and piston combination, which gives 1776cc when used with a stock 69mm crankshaft. This is an excellent choice as the cylinder walls are thick to result in better sealing against the cylinder head and less tendency to go out of round and cause piston ring problems. Originally derived from 3 9/16in Chevrolet Corvair pistons, these 90.5mm conversions are available from Mahle in two forms: 'A' and 'B'. The former is for use with stock stroke crankshaft, the latter with stroker cranks of 82mm and above. The difference between the two is in the pin hight (the distance from the center of the wrist-pin to the crown of the piston) and the length of the skirt (the area below the wrist-pin). By reducing the pin height, it is possible to build an 82mm stroke engine without any spacers under the cylinders. Any stroke above this amount will need spacers to be inserted between the cylinders and crankcase to take into account the greater distance travelled by the piston up the cylinder. By reducing the skirt of the piston, there is less likelihood of the piston coming into contact with the webs of the crankshaft, or part of the crankcase, at the bottom of the stroke.

Next in line is the 92mm conversion (derived from a Dodge 3 5/8in piston), giving 1835cc with a stock crank. This combination is very popular but frowned upon by many in the performance

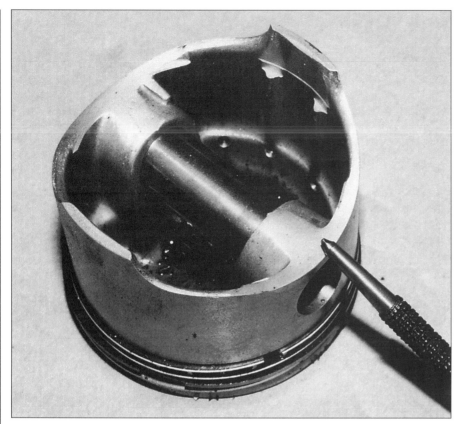

When a stock-stroke piston is used in a long-stroke engine, it is often necessary to clearance the bottom of the piston to clear the crankshaft webs at bottom dead center. This Mahle piston has been modified for use in an 84mm stroke engine which had short Porsche 912 con-rods.

crankshaft, there is a 94mm conversion available which results in a swept volume of 1915cc. This also requires the heads and case to be machined, and this may cause some concern in certain quarters, especially where 10mm case savers have been fitted to the crankcase, as the larger diameter of the 94mm cylinders brings them very close to the threaded inserts. The 94mm conversion is also available from Mahle in stock and stroker configuration and, in common with the 90.5mm and 92mm kits, features quality forged pistons. The 94mm pistons have been a source of potential disaster in the recent past, as a result of poor quality control which allowed some examples to be sold which were very weak around the wrist-pin boss. This resulted in catastrophic piston failure as the boss broke up at high rpm. It would appear, however, that this particular shortcoming has now been rectified, but beware if using secondhand parts purchased at a swapmeet.

There are a number of options over and above the Mahle conversions listed above, some of which are suited for road use, others which are not. In general,

industry who feel, with some justification, that the 92s do not seal well against the head, due to their thinner cylinder wall thickness, resulting in 'blow-by' as the burnt gases escape from the combustion chamber past the top of the cylinders. Having said that, there are many Beetles running around (and some Type 2s) which have 1835cc conversions which have given little or no trouble. The secret is to keep the compression ratio to a reasonable level (something less than 8.5:1 on a Type 1 and 7.5:1 on a Type 2) and to ensure the engine is not allowed to run hot. A cylinder head temperature gauge would be a wise investment. The 92mm conversion is also available in 'A' or 'B' form for stock or stroker cranks. As with the 90.5mm kit, the crankcase and cylinder heads both need to be machined to accept these larger cylinders and pistons (the machining specifications are, incidentally, identical for both 90.5mm and 92mm conversions)

For those who want the largest possible capacity with the stock

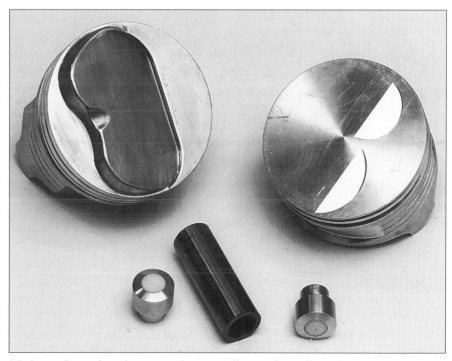

The beauty of using aftermarket pistons is that it is possible to specify virtually any design you want. Piston on left has a raised crown to increase CR while piston on right has notches cut into the crown to clear the valves. Heavy duty wrist pins are necessary in all-out race applications as stock type are prone to deforming under load. Combined aluminum/Teflon wrist pin buttons can be used to locate wrist pin.

VOLKSWAGEN TYPE I AND III PISTON SETS

- Supplied with rings, 64mm x 22mm O.D. 4140 chrome moly wrist pin (wt. 99 gr.). Replacement wrist pin part number S-417S (Set of 4) and CS-22 spiro lox.
- Forged from aluminum alloy to control expansion and allow for tighter piston to wall clearances. Wiseco recommended piston to wall clearance is .004", measured at 1.300" below the oil ring groove.
- IRF 300 piston sets are inventoried with (D) 1mm x 1.2mm x 2.8mm and (E) 2mm x 2mm x 4mm ring grooves.

IRF 300 VOLKSWAGEN PISTON SETS / COMPRESSION HEIGHT 1.373"

Piston Set Part Number	Bore Size	Repl. Piston	Ring Size	Repl. Rings (Set of 4)	Repl. Spiro Lox	Repl. Wrist Pin
K001DS*	3.701"/94mm	6001DS	1mm x 1.2mm x 2.8mm	3701DS	CS-22	S-417S
K001ES*	3.701"/94mm	6001ES	2mm x 2mm x 4mm	3701ES	CS-22	S-417S

Wiseco offers two different forged pistons for the Volkswagen, both being forged 94mm 'slipper skirt' type for race use. Both pistons are available with flat crowns or cut-outs for valve clearance.

unless the vehicle is to be used more for competition than driving on the street, it makes sense to stay with one or other of the above conversions as they are inexpensive, generally reliable and easy to obtain. However, where all-out competition is the name of the game - or ultimate street performance - there is no substitute for using a combination of the Mahle-type cylinders with a lightweight forged aluminum piston from a manufacturer such as Wiseco, J&E or Venolia.

These three companies all make slipper-skirt pistons - the excess skirt has been removed partly to save weight and partly to reduce friction between the piston and the cylinder wall - in a variety of diameters, from 94mm up to a full 101.5mm (4in). They are also available with or without cut-outs in the piston crown for valve clearance.

Wiseco offers four different pistons, all 94mm in diameter, with two choices of piston ring dimension. Part number K001DS uses 1mm x 1.2mm x 2.8mm rings, while the K001ES uses 2mm x 2mm x 4mm rings. A 'V' added to either part number denotes no valve cut-outs. Wiseco pistons are very high quality parts and have been used to good effect by many racers, including the author, without any problems.

Venolia pistons are marketed in the VW scene principally by Jack Sacchette's JayCee Enterprises company. They are available in either 94mm or 101.5mm (4in) diameter and come with either flat or domed crowns and are full-skirt pistons, as opposed to slipper-skirts. They

are also available with a larger 0.927in wrist-pin in place of the weaker 22mm VW style.

J&E pistons are available in several different specifications from three different sources. Auto-Craft Machine offers 92mm, 93mm, 94mm, 96mm and 101mm J&E slipper-skirt forged pistons with a flat or notched crown, while Pauter Machine lists four different versions including: a 101.5mm piston with a 0.990in (Chevrolet) wrist-pin and shallow compression height (1.213in) for use with long-stroke, high-compression engines, and a 101.5mm piston with a

Venolia pistons are a popular choice with the hard-core drag racers, being strong and light. Available from Jack Sacchette at JayCee Enterprises, the Venolia can be supplied in either 94mm or 4.00in diameter.

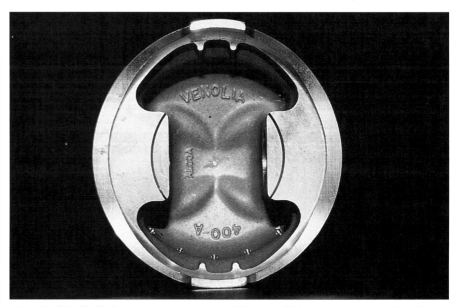

Underside of the Venolia forging shows how extra material has been added under crown to cope with notching for valve clearance. Plenty of material around the wrist-pin bosses ensures adequate strength for even the most extreme engine conditions.

J&E slipper-skirt piston shown here is designed for all-out competition use only. The bearest minimum of skirt cuts down on weight, but can lead to increased wear as the piston is less-well supported in the cylinder. Note how close top piston ring is to the crown.

Pauter Machine offers J&E pistons in four different sizes: 94mm, 4.00in, 4.125in and 4.250in to cater for most popular race combinations. In common with most aftermarket pistons, J&Es have zero-offset wrist-pin bores to reduce wall friction, at the expense of increased noise.

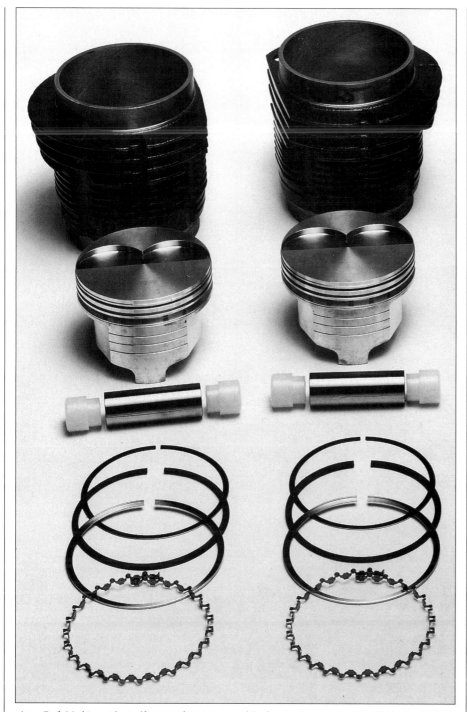

Auto-Craft Machine prides itself in manufacturing some of the finest engine components available. Its cylinders are referred to as 'bullet-proof' and have been used to good effect by many of the top drag racers for several years. Pistons are from J&E.

stock VW 22mm wrist-pin and taller, 1.400in compression height. Finally, Kawell Racing Engines of Tennessee offers a special J&E piston for use with its turbocharged race motors which has a 94mm diameter and a shallow 1.215in compression height to allow a relatively narrow 'stroker motor' to be assembled

without having to use excessive cylinder spacers.

None of these specialist racing pistons have offset wrist-pins, unlike the factory or the Mahle components. The intention behind an offset wrist-pin is to reduce piston/cylinder wear as the piston travels up and down the bore, and also to reduce

mechanical noise. Some engine builders feel that the correct factory wrist-pin offset is vital for a reliable and long-lasting engine, be it for race or road use. However, others feel that, as race engines are usually rebuilt on a regular basis, there is little to be concerned about and some extra mechanical noise (so-called piston

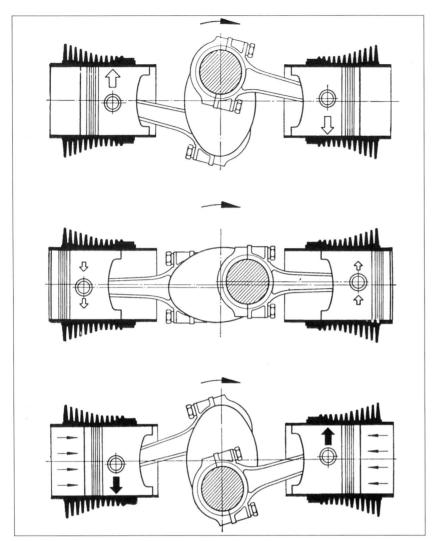

Stock pistons have the wrist-pin offset from the center-line of the cylinder to reduce the amount of 'slap' – the noise that would otherwise be made as the piston rocks from one side of the cylinder to the other as the engine turns over top dead center. VW factory diagram explains the changing side-loads on piston as it reaches TDC.

slap) is hardly likely to be a major problem on an unsilenced race car.

Once a decision has been made about what make or type of piston to use, the next question to be answered is which type of piston rings are right for your particular combination? In most cases, aftermarket pistons of all types come with piston rings already installed, these being selected as a good choice for most general applications. In broad terms, small diameter pistons are frequently fitted with wider, softer rings to effect a good seal against the cylinder wall. As these small-bore pistons are less likely to be used in a high-performance application, the increased friction of the wide rings is of little concern. However, where larger diameter racing pistons are concerned, the rings tend to be narrower to reduce frictional losses and some tuners will opt to use special types of piston ring.

It is common to use a so-called 'gapless' ring, such as a Total Seal, Childs & Albert Z-Gap, a Berg 'TS' or a CB Performance Zero-Gap, particularly on the second, compression, ring of the piston. These rings seal far better against the cylinder wall and reduce the effect of power-sapping blow-by past the piston by relying on a small sealing ring to help bridge the gap between the ends of the otherwise conventional main ring. Another design which is commonly used, especially by serious racers, is the Dykes-style ring which is a narrow L-shaped

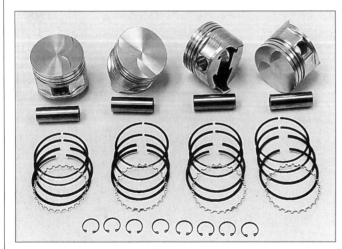

For all-out race use – and high-performance street applications – it is necessary to purchase a set of forged pistons with high-quality piston rings from Total Seal, Childs & Albert etc. Most aftermarket pistons are available with a variety of compression heights to suit different stroke/rod combinations.

Gene Berg Enterprises supplies its cylinder and pistons sets equipped with GB203 internal snap-rings which replace the original wire-type circlips. The snap-rings are far stronger and are suitable for high-rpm race use.

Pauter Machine manufactures cylinders for race use for both Type 1 and its Super-Pro engines. Available in sizes ranging from 94mm to 4.250in, the Pauter cylinders have minimal finning and are intended solely for use on engines which run only for a short time, such as drag race motors.

The original Volkswagen cylinders were made from cast-iron and were extremely hard-wearing. Their only real shortcoming is that they do not lend themselves to over-boring in the same way that you can bore out a conventional engine block of any other type of engine so as to fit larger pistons. However, as the cylinders are entirely separate from the crankcase, they can easily be removed and, as discussed earlier, replaced with larger ones as part of the tuning process. The Mahle range of aftermarket cylinders for the Volkswagen engine are also manufactured from cast-iron and, thin-walled cylinders notwithstanding, are generally extremely robust and resistant to distortion. However, they are only made to a maximum of 94mm bore and to a length which accepts an 82mm stroker crank without using spacers. When larger bores or longer strokes are required, then there is a need to use aftermarket cylinders which have been custom-made to suit your application. Within limits, the Mahle barrels can be used with longer stroke crankshafts (86mm stroke is usually taken as being an acceptable maximum) with extra spacers fitted under the cylinders to effectively increase their length. This allows the piston to travel further up the bore without hitting the cylinder head, but means that the piston is not supported very well at the bottom of the stroke as it is pulled partly out of the cylinder.

piston ring which offers superior sealing and low frictional losses.

All aftermarket pistons come with wrist-pins installed, usually the stock 22mm diameter VW-style. However, in the search for greater strength and lighter weight, it is possible to purchase special wrist-pins which are considerably lighter than the stock type, as well as those of larger diameter (usually 0.927in or 0.990in), which require the use of suitably modified con-rods and matching pistons. In high-rpm, high-compression applications, or where nitrous oxide or turbocharging is used, stronger wrist-pins should be considered a must.

To locate the wrist-pin, there are a number of alternatives. Most inexpensive pistons come with simple wire spring clips which snap into a groove machined round the wrist-pin bore of the piston. These clips are fine for low-performance applications but are prone to coming loose at high rpm. Gene Berg Enterprises offers pistons machined to accept two high-quality snap-rings on each end of the wrist-pin, to make doubly sure they do not pop out at high engine speeds. Several of the race piston manufacturers use Spir-O-Lox clips - spiral-wound flat spring clips which locate firmly in the

groove in the piston. However, for most high-performance applications, the regular choice is to use either Teflon, Nylon or even aluminum buttons in place of any form of spring clips. These may rub lightly against the cylinder wall and incur some frictional loss (albeit negligible, especially in the case of Teflon or Nylon buttons), but they do a better job of locating the wrist pin and cannot fall out of the piston causing damage.

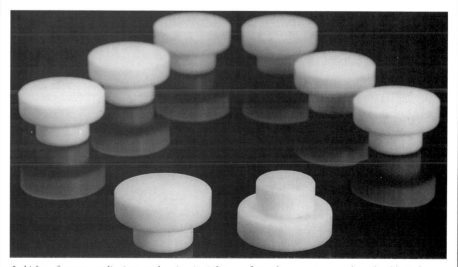

In high-performance applications, stock wrist-pin circlips, or aftermarket snap-rings, can be replaced by Teflon buttons. These slip into end of wrist-pin and locate it by rubbing lightly against the cylinder wall. Teflon material means that frictional losses are negligible.

Pauter also markets this siamesed cylinder for use with its Super-Pro engine case. Steel cylinder sleeves are pressed into a finned cast aluminum casing which adds considerable rigidity to the cylinder walls. Unlike other siamesed cylinder sets, the Pauter Machine design relies solely on the steel sleeve as the structural element.

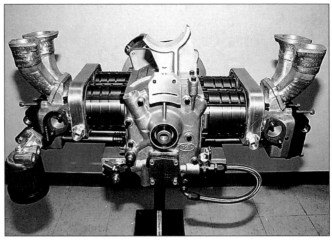

JayCee Enterprises will machine cylinders to suit any bore and stroke combination for Type 1 or aftermarket crankcases. The cylinders are supplied without any cooling fins and are intended for use only in drag racing applications.

Auto-Craft Machine makes cylinders in a variety of lengths and diameters to suit most regular race applications. Manufactured from ductile iron, they have a tensile strength of 60,000psi and are considered to be bullet-proof. They also have full cooling fins, like the original factory parts. The 92mm, 93mm and 94mm barrels may be used with a modified VW crankcase and heads, but the larger 96mm and 101.5mm components require the use of aftermarket case and heads due to the wider stud spacing which is necessary.

JayCee Enterprises also offers custom-made barrels. These do not have any cooling fins at all and can only be used in short-duration applications, such as drag racing. However, they are extremely strong and can be made, almost literally, in any size or length to suit every conceivable engine combination, and have come to be considered the natural choice among many current drag racers.

Finally, Pauter Machine and Bugpack manufacture siamesed cylinders for use with their Pro-Series and Race-Case crankcases. These consist of a pair of cylinder sleeves in a one-piece finned aluminum casing which not only rigidly supports the cylinders but also offers greater cooling than would otherwise be possible in large-bore engines. This concept was first used to good effect by Dean and Ken Lowry on their ARPM aftermarket engine in the 1970s.

The principal difference between the Pauter Machine design and others is that it does not rely on the aluminum casing to act as a structural part of the cylinder assembly in so far as it is the cylinders themselves which seat against the crankcase and the head, rather than the aluminum casing against the crankcase and the liners against the head. This results in a far more stable arrangement as there is no problem regarding differential expansion rates of the aluminum casing and the cylinder liners which might otherwise lead to compression leakage from each cylinder. With this design of cylinder, it is possible to build engines of in excess of 3-liters with relative ease as there need no longer be any problems with cylinder stud spacing and location, thus allowing bores of up to 4.125in (104.7) or even 4.250in (108mm) in diameter. Allied with crankshafts of up to 94mm, or more, the once humble VW engine can now, theoretically, become a 3.5-liter monster!

ENGINE CAPACITY CHART

STROKE (in mm)	BORE (in mm)										
	83	85.5	87	88	90.5	92	94	96.5	101.5	104.7	108
64	1385	1470	1522	1557	1647	1702	1777	1872	2075	2204	2345
69	1493	1585	1641	1679	1776	1835	1915	2019	2237	2376	2528
74	1602	1699	1760	1800	1904	1968	2054	2165	2399	2549	2712
78	1688	1791	1855	1897	2007	2074	2165	2282	2529	2686	2858
82	1775	1883	1950	1995	2110	2180	2276	2399	2659	2824	3005
84	1818	1929	1997	2044	2161	2234	2332	2457	2724	2893	3078
86	1861	1975	2045	2092	2213	2287	2387	2516	2789	2962	3152
88	1905	2021	2093	2141	2264	2340	2443	2574	2854	3031	3225
90	1948	2067	2140	2239	2315	2393	2498	2633	2920	3100	3298
92	1991	2113	2187	2289	2366	2446	2553	2691	2985	3169	3371
94	2034	2159	2234	2338	2417	2499	2608	2749	3050	3238	3445

RECOMMENDATIONS

Street	85.5mm; 87mm; 88mm (machine fit); 90.5mm; forged pistons where available
Hot Street	88mm (machine fit); 90.5mm; 92mm; 94mm; Cima/Mahle cylinders with forged pistons; Teflon wrist-pin buttons or dual circlips; Total Seal or equivalent piston rings
Competition	Up to 108mm cylinders; Wiseco, Venolia, J&E forged pistons; Teflon wrist pin buttons; heavy-duty wrist pins; Total Seal, Childs & Albert Z-Gap, Berg TS or Dykes-style piston rings

CARBURETORS AND FUEL SYSTEMS

Bigger is not always better - but it can be

The Solex 28PCI was used on all Beetle and Type 2 engines from 1952 until 1960, when it was replaced by the 28PICT. These carburetors were of a fixed-choke design and featured an accelerator pump to help reduce flat-spots under acceleration. Note pre-heated inlet manifold on this 30bhp (US 36hp) engine.

By the very nature of its horizontally-opposed (or 'boxer') design, the air-cooled Volkswagen engine would appear to be a natural choice for a dual-carburetor system. However, in an effort to improve torque and restrict rpm for the sake of longevity, Volkswagen saw fit to equip the engine with a centrally-mounted single Solex down-draught carburetor. Only when the Type 3 model was launched, late in 1961, did the factory begin to investigate alternatives, first a single side-draught and then dual down-draughts. Eventually, the Type 3 would even be equipped with the world's first factory-installed electronic fuel-injection system.

The Beetle began life equipped with the Solex 26VFIS, a small removable-choke (venturi) carburetor mounted on a long, tubular inlet manifold with 'hot-spot' pre-heating. This was provided by ducting some of the exhaust gases through a small-bore pipe which ran alongside the inlet manifold. This basic layout was to remain unchanged on the Beetle until the 1990s when VW do Brazil introduced a

By the time the 1970s came around, the Beetle engine looked altogether different. The single Solex carburetor remained but it was a considerably more complex design, with particular attention being paid to smog-control. Large plastic air box tends to dominate the engine bay.

Beetle's predilection for 'running on' when hot (ie, continuing to run even though there is no ignition supply - also know as 'dieseling').

As the Beetle's engine capacity increased and greater demands were made on what was essentially a 40-year-old design, the carburetor size grew, first to 31PICT-3 and eventually to 34PICT-3. As emission laws became ever more stringent, so the design of the Beetle's carburetor became ever more complex. In the 1970s, all manuals carried notes warning owners not to upset the factory settings of the carburetor, and anyone who dared to fine-tune a late-model Beetle carb could soon find himself with a car which ran worse than before. It is no surprise, then, that there has always been a ready market for aftermarket replacement carburetors.

The design of the inlet manifold remained basically unaltered for many years, the principal differences between early and late examples being the change in diameter to suit the larger carburetors and steadily increasing engine capacity. It

dual-carburetor model. In 1952, the original 26VFIS carburetor was replaced by the larger Solex 28PCI, complete with accelerator pump to cure the flat-spots under acceleration which had been a weakness of the old set-up. The 28PCI remained in use on the 30bhp (US 36hp) engine until its replacement in 1960 by the 34bhp (US 40bhp) motor, when it was replaced by a new carburetor, the Solex 28PICT.

This carburetor, which featured an automatic choke, was a fixed-choke design with a 22.5mm venturi, as opposed to the 28PCI's 20mm or 21.5mm, and would remain in production, if slightly modified (to become the 28PICT-1), for many years to come. In 1966, with the introduction of the 1300 and 1500 models, this carburetor was joined by the 30PICT and 30PICT-1. These were also fixed-choke carburetors, not for any other reason than to help reduce production costs. The other feature worthy of note was the inclusion of an electro-magnetic cut-off valve which shut off the supply of fuel to the main jet when the ignition was turned off. This was to overcome the

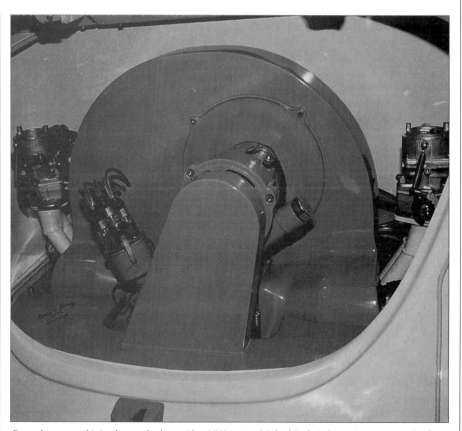

By stark contrast, this is what can be done with a VW engine. Michael Leche's show-winning custom Beetle has one of the cleanest engine bays in town. Dual Solex carburetors help to keep the engine uncluttered.

wasn't until the 1971 model year, when the dual-port cylinder heads were first used on the Beetle, that the manifold was significantly remodelled, with separate cast-aluminum end-pieces which bolted to the heads and connected to a steel center-section with rubber sleeves. Later still, in a further effort to reduce exhaust emissions, twin pre-heat pipes were used on the manifold (the so-called 'twin hot-spot' design).

Ferdinand Porsche was one of the first to appreciate the performance gains which could be made by replacing the stock single carb with a simple dual-carb system, even if that only meant fitting a second Solex carburetor, mounting the two on short, home-built manifolds.

When he launched his own range of sports cars after the war, each was equipped with a dual-carburetor set-up on what was essentially a modified Volkswagen engine. VW, however, never saw the need to follow suit, and steadfastly refused to entertain such ideas.

It was left to the likes of Okrasa and Denzel, along with a host of lesser-known

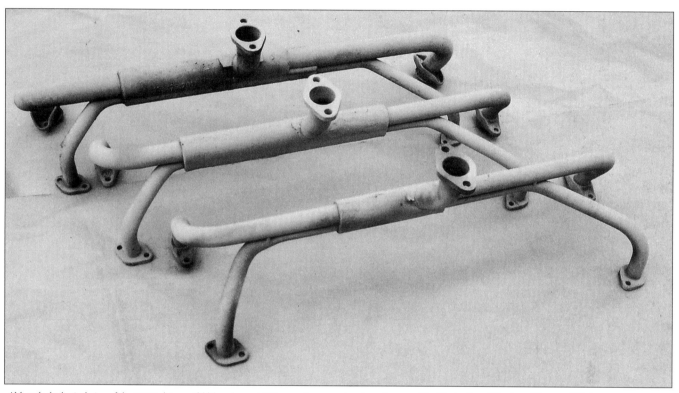

Although the basic design of the VW inlet manifold has changed little over the years, there have been considerable detail modifications. The manifold closest to the camera is that used on the 30bhp (US 36hp) 1200cc engine; next is for a 34bhp (US 40hp) 1200cc motor and finally, the manifold for a 1500cc Type 1. Note the changes in the pre-heat pipe and the larger diameter of the carburetor mounting for the 1500 engine. All these are single-port manifolds.

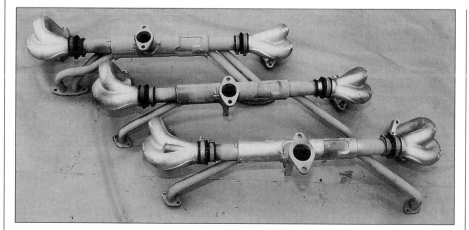

The dual-port cylinder head required a new design of inlet manifold, with separate end-castings and rubber sleeves to connect them to the center-section. Closest to the camera is the 1600cc manifold, followed by the 1300cc manifold and, finally, the late 'twin-hot-spot' manifold used in the mid-1970s – note the dual pre-heat pipes.

To accommodate the larger carburetor used on the 1600cc engine, Volkswagen increased the size of the mounting flange. When searching for a good used manifold at a swap meet, bear this in mind.

Okrasa was just one of many companies who offered a dual carburetor kit for the VW engine in the 1950s. The kit required the use of the Okrasa dual-port cylinder heads and featured a pair of 32PBI Solex carbs.

companies, to prove that the performance of the Beetle could be improved if certain basic tuning principles were followed. One of these dictated that, for improved power output, something would have to be done about the tiny carburetor and overlong inlet manifold of the stock engine. Okrasa's answer was to fit a pair of Solex 32PBI carburetors on special manifolds which were, in turn, bolted to a pair of Okrasa's own dual-port heads. Denzel followed fairly much the same route. The effect was dramatic, for the cruising speed of the old 30bhp Beetle rose by almost 10mph at a stroke, with no loss of fuel economy.

In the 1960s, a variety of aftermarket carburetor kits for the Volkswagen flooded the market. One of the first was the kit marketed by Scat Enterprises, which consisted of a single-choke Holley carburetor, originally destined for a Ford truck, mounted on a custom-made manifold. This carburetor was further developed by Holley itself, specifically for use with the VW, and became known as the Holley Bugspray. Available in two sizes, 200cfm and 300cfm (cfm = cubic feet per minute, a measure of the flow capabilities of the carburetor), the Bugspray was a good carburetor which proved to be well suited to the Beetle engine. The 200cfm and 300cfm Bugsprays came with 23.5mm and 29mm venturis, respectively. When set up correctly, the Bugspray was an excellent carburetor to use on the VW engine,

One of the first true aftermarket carburetor kits (as opposed to a complete engine conversion or simply doubling-up the stock carb) was the Holley Bugspray. This was pioneered by Scat Enterprises and initially used a modified carburetor from a Ford truck.

This Holley Bugspray kit from Gene Berg Enterprises included what was referred to as an 'isolated runner manifold' which featured separate inlet tracts for each head. Tall manifold helped to increase torque.

especially when fitted in conjunction with a well-designed inlet manifold. For most applications, the 200cfm Holley proved to be the better choice.

A similar conversion was also pioneered by Scat: the Zenith 32NDIX. This was a twin-choke carburetor first used on a French Simca and also by Porsche on some of its models. With its 24mm removable venturis, the 32NDIX also proved to be a good conversion and, along with the Bugspray, helped to prove that it was possible to make the Beetle perform in a way which VW would definitely not have approved of. Others also joined the fray, including Carter, which offered the Buggy Deuce, a twin-choke carburetor which began life on early-1950s V8s and the like.

The next logical step was to develop the dual-carburetor system and one of the first of these, following the success of the old Okrasa and Denzel conversions, was the fitting of dual Solex 40P11 twin-choke carburetors on special cast manifolds. This conversion proved to be the mainstay of the early VW drag racing industry and many of the front-running cars of the time, including EMPI's famous 'Inch Pincher', relied on the 40P11 for

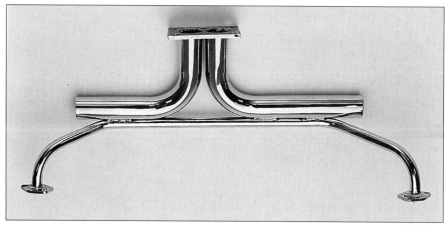

Scat Enterprises' isolated runner manifold for Weber DCNF carburetor. Note that the carburetor is offset to one side – this is to clear the generator. Pre-heat pipe hooks up to stock exhaust system to prevent manifold icing.

power. Today the problem with many of these early carbs is that they have become worn out and, in many cases, rebuilding them is not a cost-effective operation. In some instances, it may no longer be possible to obtain spare parts, or the jets and venturis to enable them to be fine-tuned for use on a modified engine.

One of the most successful dual-carburetor conversions offered for the Volkswagen, a direct descendant of which is still on offer today, was the 40DCN kit - along with the earlier 40DCNL. These

Weber carburetors have been used on a variety of production engines, including sundry Ferraris, and come with removable venturis and a wide selection of jets to ensure perfect matching to virtually any engine combination. Examples of these early Webers frequently come to light at swapmeets, but extreme caution should be taken before making a purchase as many of them will be badly worn. If you come across an inexpensive pair of DCN Webers, one has to ask, if they are that good, why are these carburetors being offered at such a bargain price?

Progressive twin-choke carburetors

Today, there is an incredible range of aftermarket carburetor conversions on offer, ranging from single progressive twin-choke kits up to the mighty 62mm JayCee Terminator racing carburetors. A progressive carburetor is one where the throttle butterflies of each choke open at a different time, allowing the engine to run on a single choke at low rpm and on two at high rpm or when the throttle pedal is pushed to the floor. This has the benefit of improved fuel economy at low engine speeds and greatly improved performance when the driver demands it.

The most common such kit currently available is one which uses the Holley-Weber 32/36, such as Scat Enterprises' 30098HO. This features what Scat refers to as an isolated runner manifold center-section for use with the stock end castings, which is claimed to offer more torque and better throttle response than

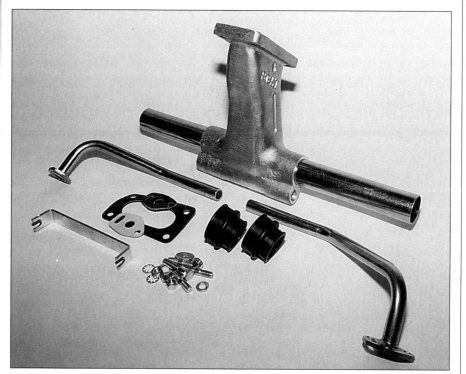

Scat manifold for 32/36 progressive Weber carburetor features cast aluminum centre section with separate pre-heat pipes. Rubber sleeves connect up to stock end castings. Manifold kit comes complete with gaskets and all fittings.

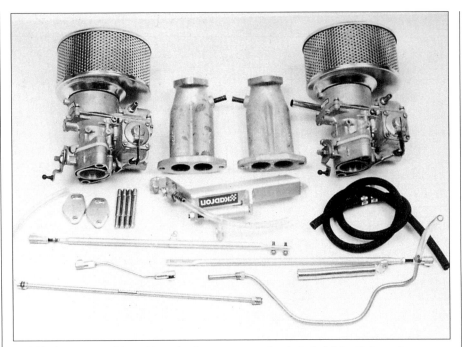

Probably the most successful – and best value for money – conversions is the dual Solex Kadron carburetor kit, the one shown being from Gene Berg Enterprises. The Kadron kit is very complete and includes everything from carburetors, manifolds and linkage, to fuel lines and filters. This is an excellent low-cost conversion for a mild street car.

The 'Baby Del' kit is also available for the Type 3 which has only restricted space under the engine cover. On short manifolds with slim-line air-filters, this kit from CB Performance has been the answer to many a Type 3 owner's dreams.

previous designs. This is an important factor, for many of the early progressive carburetor kits suffered from terrible 'flat-spots' - ie, a hesitation of the engine as the transition is made between running on one choke and running on two. The Scat kit comes with a matching air-filter, throttle linkage which hooks up to the original throttle cable and an electric choke for better cold starting. As a relatively inexpensive conversion for an otherwise near-stock engine, the Holley-Weber 32/36 set-up is well worth considering.

Dual single-choke carburetors

There have been many kits on the market which allow the owner to fit dual single-choke carburetors. For a while, there were even kits which consisted of a pair of manifolds, linkage and a second stock Solex carb, the original being pressed into service to complete the installation. These kits, although offering slightly improved performance over stock, were not really the answer as the factory carburetors were not designed for 'doubling up' like this and it was often necessary to spend a lot of time sorting out the jetting etc.

The factory installed a simple dual-

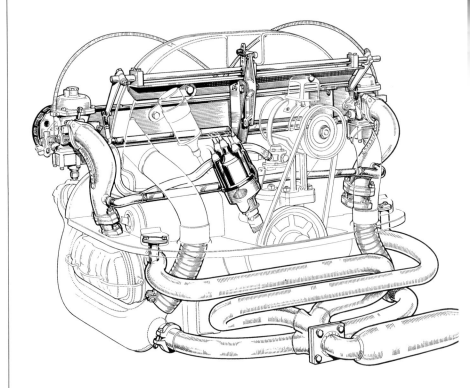

One of the most complex conversions was that developed by Speedwell in the UK and marketed in the USA by EMPI. Consisting of a pair of CD150 Stromberg carburetors, the kit included a substantial mounting bracket, which bolted across the rear of the fan-housing to locate the carbs, and a complex cross-bar throttle linkage. Note the balance pipe between the inlet manifolds to improve low-speed running.

carburetor system on the Type 3, consisting of a pair of Solex 32PDSIT carbs on short manifolds. These were fixed-choke carburetors which came with either 21.5mm, 23mm or 24mm venturis according to engine size (1500 or 1600). These Type 3 carburetors have been used by people on a budget, with some success, on a Type 1 engine, although it should be noted that the Type 3 throttle linkage must be replaced with an aftermarket 'universal' linkage in this instance.

By far the most popular of all dual single-choke conversions is the Solex Kadron kit, manufactured in Brazil, which consists of a pair of Solex H40EI carburetors on either fabricated steel or cast aluminum manifolds. The kit was first marketed in the USA in 1972 by Treuhaft, a now sadly defunct southern California VW performance shop, and proved to be a hit from the word go. With their removable 28mm venturis, the

Kadrons are well-suited to mildly-modified VW engines of almost any capacity. These kits have stood the test of time and, to this day, remain one of the best low-cost conversions you can buy. They are simple to install and come complete with linkage, filters and even steel fuel lines which allow the kit to be installed with the minimum of fuss. There have been some quality problems in the past, most notably with the budget steel inlet manifolds, which often leaked. However, the kits on the market today appear to have those problems solved.

Latterly there have been various dual single-choke conversions, one of the most popular of which was the Dell'Orto 34FRD kit supplied by CB Performance. Frequently referred to as 'Baby Dells', these carbs were marketed primarily as replacements for the often troublesome factory fuel-injection system used on the Type 3 range. However, they are suitable

for use on Type 1 engines and provide a useful increase in performance for those on a budget. Another popular dual single-choke conversion is the Weber 34ICT kit which is sold by several of the aftermarket parts specialists. This kit offers improved performance along with better fuel economy due to the more efficient design compared with the original factory induction system. They are available to fit either single- or dual-port cylinder heads and come complete with manifolds, linkage and air-filters. There is even a kit to fit under the rear luggage compartment of a Type 3. Other dual single-choke conversions in the past have included a 32IMPE Weber kit from Autocavan in England, which was very similar to the 34ICT system, and the old Speedwell-EMPI dual Stromberg CD150 system. Neither of these are any longer available but were excellent conversions in their time.

So-called 'Baby Del' conversion features a pair of single-choke 34FRD Dell'Orto carburetors on cast aluminum manifolds. Marketed by CB Performance in the USA, this kit has proved ideal for smaller street engines, offering flexibility and economy with a worthwhile increase in performance.

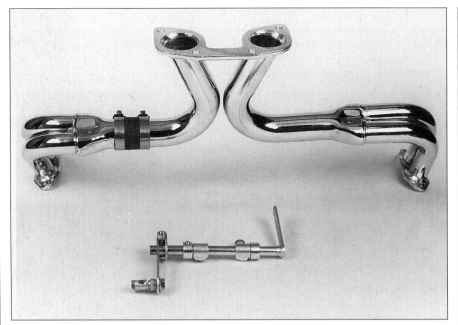

A slightly different type of aftermarket manifold is this one from Scat which is for use with a single 48IDA Weber – not the best of choices for your VW engine. Note how one side of the manifold is welded to the end piece, while the other is connected via a rubber sleeve. The throttle linkage allows the stock cable to be retained.

Single dual-choke carburetors

For those wishing to extract a little more horsepower from their Type 1 engines, but who prefer to stay with a single carburetor system, there are several single dual-choke kits on offer. They each include a carburetor, linkage adaptor to hook up with the stock throttle cable, air filter and a manifold center-section to mate up with either the factory dual-port end castings or aftermarket single-port end pieces.

Among these are kits to fit single 40IDF or 44IDF Weber carburetors, or 36-, 40-, 45-, 48- or even 52DRLA Dell'Orto carburetors. The Weber IDF was an original fitment carburetor on several vehicles, including Alfa Romeos, and has proved to be an excellent carb for use with the VW engine. There is a wide range of venturis and jets available for the IDF, meaning that it is relatively easy to come up with a combination to suit virtually any engine specification. The same holds true with the Dell'Ortos, although it should be noted that the larger 48DRLA and 52DRLA are best suited to large-capacity off-road race engines when used in single carb installations.

Opinions tend to be divided over the relative merits of the Weber IDF or the Dell'Orto DRLA carburetors. There are those who feel that the DRLA is a more modern design than the IDF, with superior flow characteristics, which is easier to set up for use in a variety of applications. Others swear that the IDF is the better carburetor, citing the fact that it has been around for a long time and is well-proven. In the author's experience, having used both 40IDFs and 45DRLAs,

they each have their merits. It can be argued that parts are more readily available for Weber carburetors, although, as Dell'Ortos are so popular, there is no longer any problem with spare parts supply. On the whole, Dell'Ortos tended to be more expensive than the Weber equivalent, which may be a deciding factor. However, Dell'Ortos have become virtually impossible to find in recent times, so the decision may be made for you!

Single dual-choke installations are popular with off-road enthusiasts as the longer inlet manifold tends to help produce more torque than would be the case with dual carbs. However, there are instances where the fuel economy is rather poor with single dual-chokes so, if this is an important factor, it may be preferable to choose a pair of smaller single-choke carburetors, such as the 34FRD Dell'Ortos. In an effort to improve the flexibility of engines using large single dual-choke carb set-ups, some manufacturers add a small balancing port between the individual runners of the manifold - CB Performance referred to this as a 'plenum cross port'. Note that, to get the most out of a single dual-choke system, it is necessary to use a manifold with separate runners (inlet tracts) to each head. A full plenum manifold - ie, one

One of the most popular dual carburetor kits of all time was the Weber 40DCNF conversion. This particular kit from Scat Enterprises included chrome air-filters and a simple 'push-pull' throttle linkage. Today, DCNF kits are relatively rare.

with a single large opening directly under the carburetor - tends to have a softening effect on the carburation and the engine will feel slightly woolly in the mid-range rpm and may even become lean at higher rpm. The only time a plenum manifold should be used on the VW is where a progressive carburetor is installed.

Dual dual-choke carburetors

For outright performance, there is no substitute for using a pair of dual-choke carburetors, thus providing one carburetor venturi per cylinder. If correctly set up, this will always result in improved power output, better throttle response and even, in many instances, improved fuel economy. Dual dual-choke carburetors ensure each cylinder receives precisely the same quantity of air/fuel mixture as the others and allows the owner to fine-tune the carburation in a way that no other induction system can (short of fuel-injection).

Many single carburetor - and indeed some dual single-choke - installations suffer from uneven fuel distribution between cylinders, necessitating a compromise having to be made when it comes to jetting. If there is a tendency for one cylinder to run lean (due to a number of factors, including manifold design) then it means that the carburetor will have to be jetted on the rich side to ensure no damage is done. Obviously this means that other cylinders will be running slightly richer than would be ideal, leading to wasted fuel and diminished power output. By providing one venturi (in effect, one carburetor) per cylinder, such variations are eliminated.

There has been a variety of dual-choke carburetor kits available to the Volkswagen engine builder, principally based around either Weber IDFs, DCNFs and IDAs or Dell'Orto DRLAs. The IDF kits are available from sources such as Bugpack and represent extremely good value for money in terms of all-round performance and ease of installation. These kits come complete with carbs, manifolds, linkage (usually the simple cross-bar type) and air-filters, along with fuel lines and throttle hook-up where necessary. They are available with either 40-, 44- or 48IDF Weber carburetors,

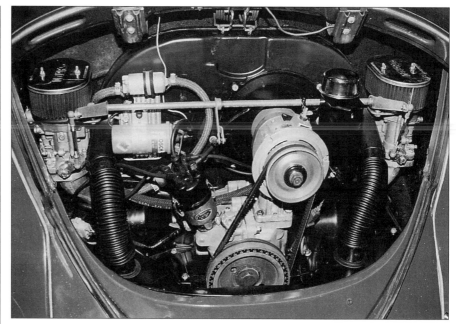

Dual Dell'Orto DRLA conversion is very popular. Available from CB Performance in the USA, the kit is available in a variety of sizes, from 36mm right up to 52mm. DRLAs are also popular for use in single-carb applications but, sadly, Dell'Orto carburetors are becoming hard to find.

according to engine size and application (we will come to advice on choosing carburetor sizes in a moment), and are usually equipped with a fairly 'middle of the road' jetting combination which will, at the very least, enable you to get your car going so you can head to the nearest carburetor specialist to have the fine-tuning carried out there.

The same holds true for the several Dell'Orto carburetor kits which have been on the market. These range from dual 36DRLAs, to 40-, 45 and 48DRLA conversions. All of these are excellent carburetors which appear to be very easy to tune and provide excellent all-round performance for anything from mild to all-out street applications. Many weekend

Dual 40IDF Webers are a good choice for engines over 1600cc and up to 2-liters. The conversion has been around for over twenty years and still proves to be as popular as ever. Scat's kit includes manifolds, linkage and air-filters, as well as all necessary fittings.

AIRCOOLED VW ENGINE INTERCHANGE MANUAL
AIRCOOLED VW ENGINE INTERCHANGE MANUAL

Bugpack 44IDF kit (part number 1086-10) includes these tall K&N air-filters and a high-quality Tayco cross-bar linkage. Dual-port manifolds, fuel hose and all fittings are supplied.

racers prefer to use the 48DRLA Dell'Ortos over the popular IDA Webers as they feel they offer better flexibility and fuel economy with little loss in performance. Championed by CB Performance, the Dell'Orto dual carburetor kits were well-engineered and available to suit an incredible variety of applications, from mild street to all-out off-road. Every kit came complete with manifolds, linkages, air-filters and all the necessary hardware to allow the owner to install it on his engine with little difficulty.

Obviously - and this is true as far as all off-the-shelf carburetor kits are concerned - there is no way that any carburetor supplier can possibly carry kits ready-jetted to suit every engine combination. In general, they tend to err on the conservative side, supplying carb kits with small venturis and slightly over-rich jet combinations to ensure that the customer's engine does not run lean and sustain damage after just a few miles.

The Weber DCNFs are the almost exclusive domain of Gene Berg Enterprises (GBE), which markets the Berg 42mm Weber Specials. This is a dual carb kit consisting of a pair of 42DCNFs which have been modified to make them better suited to use on a Volkswagen engine. This work includes paying particular attention to the fuel flow rate and progression circuits, thereby curing the flat-spots which would result if the DCNFs were used in an unmodified form on the VW engine. GBE does not recommend the use of the 42mm Berg Specials on off-road vehicles or for road-race applications. One of the problems with the DCNFs when used on the VW is that they have to be turned 90° from their intended orientation. The DCN-type carburetors were originally designed to be used in a row of six on a Ferrari engine, with the throttle shaft axis across the car - in a VW, the throttle shaft runs fore-aft resulting in fuel spilling out of the top of the emulsion tubes under hard cornering. However, with GBE's modifications, the 42DCNFs are superb carburetors which are perfect for most hot street applications, providing a blend of performance with drivability and fuel economy which is hard to better. Unfortunately, the source of new 42DCNF carbs has now dried up and GBE is forced to supply all kits with reconditioned carbs that are fully rebuilt

Gene Berg Enterprises is the one company still offering DCNF Weber carbs. Its 42mm 'Berg Special' kit is one of the most widely acclaimed for hot street VWs as GBE has taken a great deal of care to modify the stock DCNF for use on the Volkswagen engine.

Super-clean engine installation includes a pair of 44IDF Webers. Visually the same as the 40IDFs but better suited to engines over 1800cc. Ram pipes, in place of air-filters, offer better performance but at expense of engine longevity. Dust and dirt drawn into carbs can cause rapid wear of piston rings and cylinder walls.

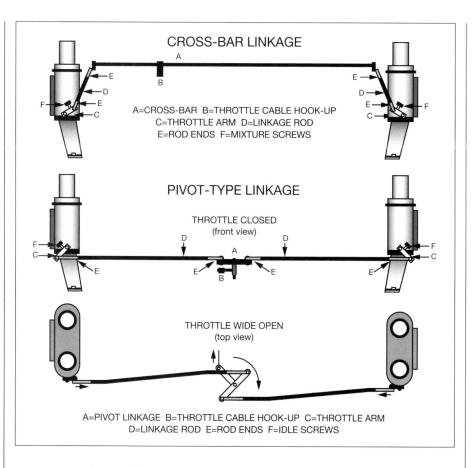

CROSS-BAR LINKAGE

A=CROSS-BAR B=THROTTLE CABLE HOOK-UP
C=THROTTLE ARM D=LINKAGE ROD
E=ROD ENDS F=MIXTURE SCREWS

PIVOT-TYPE LINKAGE

THROTTLE CLOSED
(front view)

THROTTLE WIDE OPEN
(top view)

A=PIVOT LINKAGE B=THROTTLE CABLE HOOK-UP C=THROTTLE ARM
D=LINKAGE ROD E=ROD ENDS F=IDLE SCREWS

The mighty 48IDA Weber is legendary in VW performance circles. First put to good effect by Scat and Gene Berg back in the 1960s, the 48IDA has become the mainstay of the drag racing fraternity. Although it would appear to be far too large a carb to work well on a street engine, experience proves otherwise, as there are many hot street VWs which rely on a pair of these carburetors.

to as-new condition. All jets etc are, however, still available.

The king of the hill, as far as stock Weber carbs are concerned, is the mighty 48IDA. First designed for use on the Ford V8 engines used in the AC Cobra and Ford GT40 race cars, the IDA has long been the drag racer's favorite - and that of the street warriors, too. Many carburetor specialists shake their heads with disbelief when they learn that even VW engines as small as 1776cc can be made to run quite happily on '48s', but it was almost as if this Weber carburetor was made for the Volkswagen engine. Back in the 1960s, Tom Lieb of Scat Enterprises carried out some machining for Carroll Shelby - father of the AC Cobra - and it was this working relationship which brought Lieb into contact with the 48IDA Weber. He recognised its potential for use on the VW engine and the rest, as they say, is history.

Although, on paper at least, the IDA is a race-only carburetor as far as the VW engine is concerned, it can be made to work very well in street applications, especially where large capacity engines are

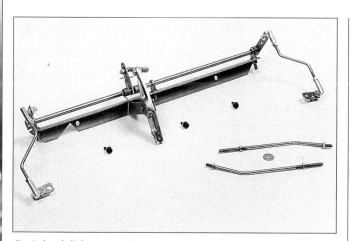

Berg's throttle linkage is superb. Based on the original EMPI-Speedwell design, it offers total adjustability and can be used with a wide variety of carburetors simply by changing the drop links. It is also possible to alter the opening rate of the carbs to suit different applications.

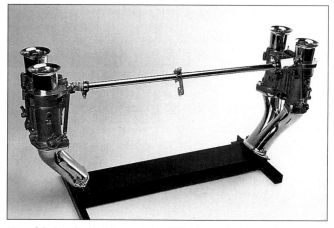

One of the best throttle linkages for the 48IDA is the Tayco design from Bugpack. Fully-adjustable, the linkage is designed for use on race engines which do not run air-filters. This is probably the most widely-used 48IDA linkage around.

There are some instances when even the 48IDA is not big enough and for that reason Gene Berg Enterprises developed its own derivative: the Berg 58mm carburetor. Designed primarily for drag race applications, it uses the same bolt-pattern as the 48IDA, allowing proprietary manifolds to be used.

The JayCee Enterprises Terminator carburetor is a massive 62mm dual-choke which dwarfs the 48IDA, to which it is distantly related. Designed by Jack Sacchette for use with large Pro-Stock drag race engines, the Terminator is now widely used in VW drag racing.

Underside of the Terminator carb shows the large 62mm choke diameter and the accelerator pump linkage. Body is cast from 356 T-6 aluminum while the top cover is machined from a billet of 6061 T-6 using a CNC process.

concerned. With careful venturi and jet selection, it is possible to have an IDA-equipped VW which will happily cruise in traffic at 2,000rpm, or less, and yet scream its way up to 7,000rpm and beyond. The author's own street car, which runs a 2160cc motor with Engle FK-87 cam and dual 48s, will drive like a stocker at low rpm yet provide an adrenalin-inducing rush all the way up to 7,000rpm without any flat-spots or hesitations. Although making full use of the vehicle's performance is no way to

For all-out race applications, JayCee Enterprises manufactures this high-flow float needle valve which allows more fuel to enter the float chamber at high engine rpm and wide-open throttle.

guarantee excellent fuel economy, it is still possible to exceed 20mpg if restraint is shown.

For a while, there was a shortage of 48IDA Webers and racers were forced to start considering life without them. There was also the problem that, as far as many racers were concerned, the 48s were simply not large enough to cope with the demands of the large capacity, large valve, high-rpm competition engines which are now commonplace in VW drag racing. GBE and others offered the facility to bore out the 48IDA to 51 or 51.5mm, with throttle butterflies and venturis to match. This is certainly a useful starting point which provides far greater flow capabilities than the stock IDA, but for some there was still the need go one stage further.

Gene Berg Enterprises cast its own version of the IDA, the Berg 58mm carb, which features chokes a full 10mm larger in diameter than the stock Weber. Using the same bolt-pattern as the 48IDA so that it would bolt onto readily-available manifolds, the Berg 58mm also makes use of the Weber jets and emulsion tubes for ease of tuning. Proprietary 48IDA carburetor linkages also fit the 58s without problem. As far as hooking up fuel lines is concerned, the Berg carburetors come with a choice of two possibilities: either to use the stock 12mmx1.5mm Weber-style banjo fitting, or a 3/8 NPT tapered thread which can accept -6 or -8 braided lines and fittings. These carburetors have been used to great effect by Gary Berg while driving the company's highly-successful black '67 sedan in drag race competition for several years.

There are still some situations where even a 58mm carburetor may not be considered big enough. Jack Sacchette of JayCee Enterprises in Huntington Beach, California, has developed his own brand of carb - the JayCee Terminator, a massive 62mm dual-choke which positively dwarfs the stock IDA to which it is distantly related. The Terminator is an all-new casting which, like the Berg 58mm, makes use of some of the 48IDA internals. However, certain parts, such as venturis, have to be manufactured especially for this product.

Sacchette's own Pro-Stock sedan uses a pair of Terminators on its Auto-Craft engine. Carburetors have been isolated from the heat of the engine by an aluminum shroud to prevent the fuel boiling in the float chambers.

FLOW BENCH TESTS

Weber 48IDA with 44mm venturis	348cfm per venturi	1392cfm total*
Weber 51.5IDA with 47.5mm venturis	395cfm per venturi	1580cfm total*
JayCee 62mm with 55mm venturis	633cfm per venturi	2531cfm total*

(tested by JayCee Enterprises on Superflow 600 flow bench with 25in water)
*using two carburetors

Weber 48IDA with 44mm venturis	311cfm per venturi	1244cfm total*
Weber 51.5IDA with 47.5mm venturis	353cfm per venturi	1413cfm total*
JayCee 62mm with 55mm venturis	565cfm per venturi	2260cfm total*

(tested by JayCee Enterprises on Superflow 600 flow bench with 20in water)
★ Using two carburetors

DYNO TESTS

RPM	With 51.5mm Weber IDAs	With JayCee 62mm carbs
6000	225hp/196.95ftlb torque	248hp/216.9ftlb torque
7000	241.5hp/181ftlb torque	264.25hp/198.26ftlb torque
8000	242hp/158.87ftlb torque	276hp/181.19ftlb torque
8500	237hp/146.42ftlb torque	275hp/169.95ftlb torque

(Testing carried out on JayCee Enterprises-built 2387cc 86mmx94mm Type 1 engine with Autocraft 910 heads, 50mmx39.5mm valves, 13.5:1 compression, Web-Cam 277 cam, 2in headers and JayCee Terminator carburetors with 52mm venturis)

The body is made from 356 T-6 aluminum using an investment casting process, while the top of the carb is machined from a billet of 6061 T-6 aluminum. All machine work is carried out on CNC equipment to ensure 100% accuracy. Venturis are available in sizes ranging from 48mm up to 58mm and come with adjustable main and air corrector jets to facilitate track-side tuning. The flow capabilities of this carburetor are immense, as can be seen from the comparison table (above right):

Fuel injection: stock systems

There are currently two fuel-injection systems on the market for the Type 1 engine, one supplied by CB Performance, the other by Gene Berg Enterprises. In the past, however, the factory has offered two systems, one being fitted to the Type 3 range in the late 1960s and early-1970s (a similar system was also used on the less popular Type 4 models), the other being the often troublesome induction system fitted to US-spec Beetles from 1975. The Type 3 fuel injection was a simple enough system which relied on a high-pressure pump to supply fuel to each of the four injectors. These were triggered in pairs - numbers 1 and 4 cylinders receiving fuel together, as did numbers 2 and 3. The

flow capacity of the injectors remained the same at all times, but the length of time the injectors remained open governed the amount of fuel received by each cylinder. The injectors were controlled by a second set of points in the base of the distributor. A pressure sensor monitored the pressure in the inlet manifold so that, when the throttle was opened to create a change in pressure, a signal was sent to the control system which told the injectors to stay open for longer to introduce more fuel. A cold-start temperature sensor also kept the control system informed of the state of the engine, acting as a choke in cold weather.

For the most part, the Type 3 injection system worked well, the main faults being misfires - or a refusal to start at all - caused by sticking or dirty points in the distributor trigger system, or excessive fuel consumption due to a malfunctioning cold-start system which 'told' the injection that the engine was still cold. This had the same effect as leaving the choke on all the time on a carburetted engine.

The later Air Flow Control (AFC) injection system was produced by Bosch for Volkswagen and saw service in the 1303 Super Beetle range in the USA.

This was an altogether more complicated system which was intended to make the Beetle 'smog legal'. There were four separate circuits to the AFC injection: fuel, electronic, air circulation and exhaust emission. The fuel pump pulled fuel from the tank and supplied it under pressure to a 'ring main' fuel loop which ran round the engine. If fuel pressure exceeded the maximum of 35psi, then the excess was returned to the tank. The four fuel injectors fed off this ring main were triggered on command from an electronic control box. The difference between this and the Type 3 system was that the four injectors opened simultaneously (constant fuel injection) and were triggered once every second time the points were opened. A fifth fuel injector in the main air intake acted as a cold start device.

An airflow meter was placed in the inlet between the air filter and the throttle body (which housed the butterfly valve, similar to that on a carburetor). This monitored the airflow and sent the information to the control box which then richened or weakened the fuel supply accordingly. Signals were also received from cylinder head temperature sensors, the distributor and a throttle position sensor. An auxiliary air regulator controlled the amount of air available to

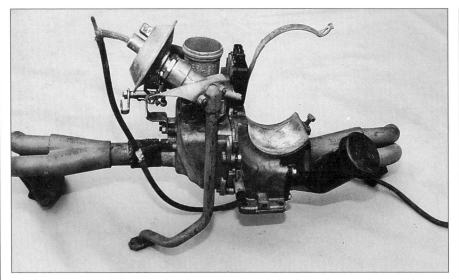

The factory's attempt at fuel-injecting the Volkswagen engine resulted in this cumbersome inlet manifold set-up. As far as performance engines are concerned, the best place for the system is in the scrap bin…

the engine during warm up. Finally, an exhaust gas recirculation system was installed in an effort to reduce emissions, as was a catalytic convertor in some states of the USA.

Unfortunately, these fuel-injection systems were crude by modern standards and, while they functioned well when new, they often proved very troublesome as the vehicle's age and mileage increased. From the performance standpoint, there is little to be gained by retaining the factory systems, as neither of them is particularly 'user-friendly'. The Type 3 system will cope with mild tuning of the engine, but little more than fitting an extractor exhaust system and maybe some modest cylinder head work. The main problem is that the injectors are not capable of

CB Performance markets this electronic fuel-injection system for the Type 1 engine. The dual-choke 48mm throttle body looks for all the world like a simplified carburetor from the outside but is in fact a purpose-made component. Injectors can be seen located on each end casting.

operating above 6,000rpm engine speed. Most people are glad to see the back of the AFC system altogether, however.

Fuel injection: aftermarket systems

CB Performance's own-brand injection system is based around what at first sight appears to be a dual-choke carburetor but is, in fact, a purpose-made throttle body with 48mm bores and simple throttle butterflies. The injectors themselves are mounted in inlet manifolds close to the cylinder heads. Two versions are available, one using a single dual-choke throttle body, the other a pair of them - rather like single or dual carburetors. In fact, the system is designed to accept the regular CB Performance Dell'Orto throttle linkage and air filters which helps to keep manufacturing costs down. The manifolds are similar to those used on carburetted installations but are also purpose-made for the injection system as they include bosses to accept the injectors.

A high-pressure rotary fuel pump delivers fuel at up to 70psi, this being restricted to anything between 34 and 42psi by a special regulator according to throttle position and engine load. An oxygen sensor helps control the 'closed loop' system - this is where the fuel-injection set-up constantly monitors the engine's requirements and automatically adjusts the air/fuel ratio to keep it close to the optimum of 14.7:1. A number of sensors are used throughout the system to monitor throttle position, manifold air pressure, intake air temperature, cylinder head temperature and oxygen level in the exhaust gas. These sensors feed information to a central electronic command module which then controls the injectors.

The CB system is adaptable to virtually any air-cooled Type 1-based VW engine and, although considerably more expensive than an equivalent carburetor set-up, guarantees that the engine receives the correct delivery of air/fuel mixture under all running conditions. This means that there are no flat-spots, even when accelerating in fourth gear from relatively low rpm. With the current shortage of carburetors, systems like this have to be considered the way ahead.

The CB Performance system is also available as a 'dual carb' set-up, so to speak. The twin throttle bodies mount to specially-cast manifolds which feature separate injectors for each cylinder. Sensors adjust the fuel mixture according to engine temperature.

For the serious racer, Bugpack offers this Hilborn-based mechanical fuel-injection system for use with its SF- and A/F-series heads. The throttle bodies require the use of a Hilborn fuel pump which is driven off the oil pump drive – Bugpack can supply a combined oil/fuel pump for this application.

Gene Berg Enterprises certainly thinks so, having tried and tested its fuel injection system on both road and drag cars for a number of years. The Berg system is a fully-programmable set-up which allows the owner, with the aid of a lap-top computer, to programme the control unit to suit all engine loads and throttle positions. Used in conjunction with an exhaust gas analyser, the lap top allows you to monitor the engine rpm and, after checking the analyser's reading, adjust the richness of the air/fuel mixture by simply pressing the up and down control keys. Checks can then be made

under acceleration, idling and steady cruising conditions.

Although best carried out with the engine on a dynamometer, where it is more easily held at constant rpm, this process of calibrating the fuel system using a computer guarantees the perfect set-up for all engine specifications and conditions. The system can cope with all possible combinations, ranging from a stock engine in a Type 2 up to an all-out race engine, as proved by Gary Berg in the family race car. Indeed, so successful was this set-up that rule changes were introduced to prevent certain classes of drag race VWs from using fuel-injection systems.

GBE doesn't sell off-the-shelf, turn-key injection systems as there is the need to programme the control unit for each application. However, there are five basic available options which then need to be set up for - or by - the customer to suit his particular needs. All include provision to select fuel shut-off on deceleration to reduce exhaust emissions, a data logging system to record what the engine is doing at all times, calibrated throttle positioner, programmable accelerator pump to provide extra fuel when the throttle is first

The Judson supercharger was a popular fitment on early VW engines. It was a relatively simple bolt-on conversion which retained the original carburetor, suitably rejetted, but had its own separate oil system which used a glass reservoir mounted to the left of the engine.

opened, progammable warm-up mode, 32 programmable throttle positions every 1,000rpm (switchable to 16 for faster programming) and automatic altitude and temperature monitoring.

The HALF7B kit (the HAL is a reference to the system manufacturer, Haltech) is suitable for use with normally aspirated engines and up to 16,000rpm, while the F7C is for use with turbo or supercharged engines running up to 15psi of boost. This requires programming twice: either on or off boost. The F9 is a further progression from the F7B and F7C systems, designed for either street or strip use and with normally aspirated or turbocharged engines, and includes, amongst other features, a smooth-cut rev limiter. The F9A is a closed loop system which is also suited to street or strip, blown or non-blown applications. This also provides functions for controlling a turbo wastegate and nitrous oxide systems.

Each level of system is available with throttle bodies to fit a variety of manifolds: Weber IDF/Dell'Orto DRLA, Weber IDA and Weber DCNF stud patterns are all catered for. GBE also manufactures what it calls manifold-

throttle bodies. These at first sight appear to be a pair of inlet manifolds with ram pipes (velocity stacks) bolted to them. In fact they each house a pair of throttle butterflies and have provision for the fitting of two injectors. These manifold-

throttle bodies are perfect for race applications as they are extremely efficient and very light. They are also manufactured with extra thick walls to allow for extensive race porting to match the cylinder heads.

The GBE fuel-injection system is so adaptable that it is quite possible to drive what is essentially a full-race engine on the road, with radical camshaft profiles presenting no obstacle to smooth driving. The system monitors the engine's requirements and, when correctly programmed, automatically ensures precisely the correct amount of fuel is delivered to suit the throttle position, load and engine rpm. As is the case with the CB Performance system, this surely points the way to the future.

Supercharging and turbocharging

If 48IDAs or fuel-injection don't offer enough, there is always the option of turbo or supercharging. In the past here have been a number of supercharger kits available for the Beetle, ranging from the Judson and MAG for the old 30bhp motor, through to the later EMPI-Shorrock conversion. However, there is currently just one company which offers a supercharger kit for the VW engine: Dick Landy Industries (DLI). This makes use of

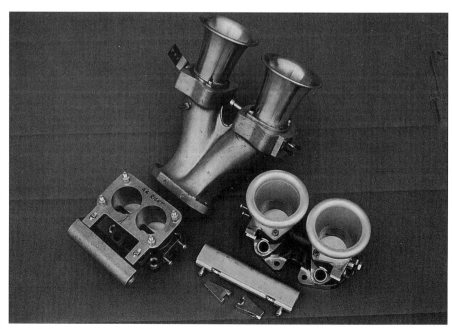

GBE fuel-injection system is available in a variety of configurations, including throttle bodies to fit DCNF (left) and Weber IDF (right) manifolds. In the center is the race-only manifold-throttle body.

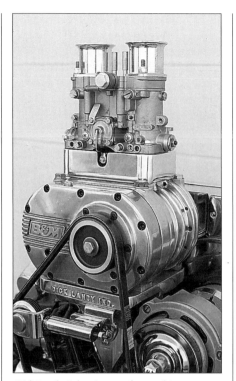

Dick Landy Industries manufactures this supercharger kit for the Type 1 engine which uses a B&M blower mounted on a substantial inlet casting. The kit is available with either a Dell'Orto DRLA or a Holley four-barrel carburetor. Either makes quite a visual statement!

a specially-made B&M dual-rotor supercharger atop a DLI fabricated manifold. Undeniably spectacular in appearance, the DLI kit has not gained favor with the street or drag race crowd, but is beginning to capture the attention of the dune buggy market, at which it was originally aimed. In back-to-back testing carried out by DLI, a 2058cc Type 1 engine, which produced 120hp at 5,000rpm with dual 48DRLA Dell'Ortos, soared to over 180hp at 6,000rpm when fitted with a DLI conversion. For those looking for something unique for a wild custom VW, this could be the answer.

In drag racing circles, the turbocharger has been seen as a successful way to extract almost unbelievable horsepower from the Beetle engine for close to 20 years. It is not unusual to see dyno figures of anything from 400 to 600bhp, or more, achieved from what is essentially a modified version of the half-century-old VW engine. For many years, turbocharger conversions were the domain of specialist businesses catering for

the competition market, with little regard for the street crowd. Although a few companies did offer turbo kits for street cars back in the 1970s, they were not popular and the conversions fairly crude. However, taking note of the development work that has taken place in drag racing circles, there are now some well-engineered conversions on the market which offer reliable horsepower.

CB Performance is one of the pioneers of this relatively new area of VW tuning, with several kits on offer for the Type 1 engine. The kits come 'pre-engineered', as CB puts it, and are intended to be bolt-on conversions. However, as with all such kits, it is important that the engine in question is built to a high standard in the first place - it is not a matter of taking any high-mileage VW and bolting on a turbo system in the hope of finding some outrageous horsepower. As a general rule, the compression ratio needs to be kept to a relatively low level - frequently no more than 7.0:1 in a street application - and it

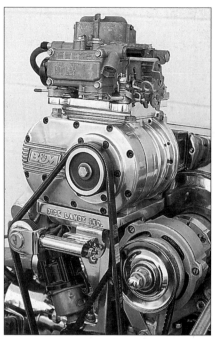

The DLI kit is aimed primarily at the dune buggy market when first launched, but has already picked up some fans among the street crowd. Impressive power outputs are claimed for the conversion, which is superbly engineered.

CB Performance is one of the few companies which makes a bolt-on turbo system for street-driven VWs. This is a 'hide-away' set-up which locates the turbo out of sight below the rear valance. The system shown is a 'blow-through' design which pressurises the dual Dell'Orto carburettors.

For applications where Superflo or SF-1 and SF-2 heads are used with a turbo, Chassis Shop makes these high-quality welded inlet manifold end-pieces. Finished in bright cadmium-plating, they cannot be used with a fan-housing as they are not offset like the factory end-castings.

will be necessary to fit a camshaft that has been designed for turbo use. Too much valve overlap results in wasted fuel and lost horsepower as the air/fuel mixture is forced in through the inlet valve and straight out down the exhaust port.

The CB Performance kits come in various forms, with most being 'blow-though' systems - ie, the turbocharger pressurises air into the carburetor. This often results in improved low-rpm response and better cold starting. Most all-out race conversions, however, are 'draw-through' systems, where the air/fuel is sucked from the carburetor and forced into the engine. The general exception to this is a turbocharged and fuel-injected race engine which functions more efficiently in the 'blow-through' configuration.

CB offers turbo kits with either single or dual dual-choke carburetors - specially-modified Dell'Orto DRLAs - with carb sizes ranging from 40mm to 48mm. One interesting conversion is the 'Dual Hideaway' kit which locates the turbocharger out of sight, below the rear tinware of the engine bay. To the casual observer, the appearance is of a conventional dual-carburetor installation, with only a closer examination revealing that all is not quite what it seems. Other kits are aimed at the dune buggy owner (with mid-engine installations requiring different exhaust headers) and at those on a budget. CB lists an inexpensive side-draught kit, a 'draw-through' design,

which is available for either street or off-road vehicles.

In addition to the turbo kits themselves CB Performance also sells a large range of ancillary equipment necessary to produce a successful custom-made turbo installation, including fuel pressure regulators, wastegates, header systems, turbos and manifolds. If one of CB's own kits isn't what you are after for a hot street car, then the parts are available for you to engineer your own.

If you are looking for an all-out competition system for your race car, then there are several companies which will be able to help, notably Kawell Racing Engines in Tennessee and Ron Lummus and Benchmark in California. Despite scaremongering to the contrary, a well engineered all-out race system need not be a time-bomb waiting to explode which some suggest. Turbocharged race cars are such a large part of the VW performance scene nowadays that this is one ghost which should have been laid to rest long ago. The author's own Kawell-turbocharged sedan competed for over four seasons without a single turbo-related

engine failure - and on the same set of main bearings. Taking the necessary steps to prevent detonation, using a quality oil and calling on the years of experience of one of the acknowledged experts in the turbo scene paid off. After all, what fun is racing if you spend half the time picking up the pieces?

FUEL SYSTEM

There are three areas which are frequently overlooked when people upgrade the induction system on a VW engine: fuel lines, fuel pumps and fuel pressure. Let's look at the first of these. From the factory, the Beetle came with a small capacity engine with a tiny carburetor. The demands on the fuel system were modest and it was only necessary to use a small diameter fuel line from the tank back to the engine bay.

When you install a large capacity engine with dual carburetors which runs to 6,500rpm and beyond, there is, not surprisingly, a greater need for fuel. Now, while the small-bore fuel lines may have been adequate for the original 28PICT carburetor and a 1200cc engine, they

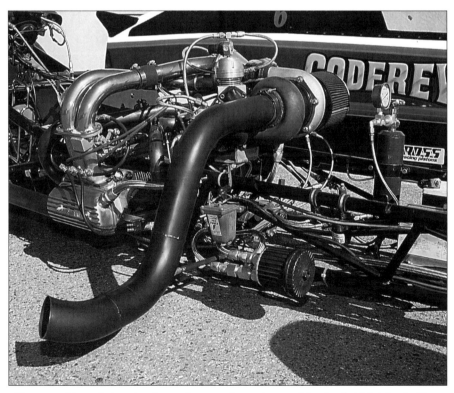

All-out competition turbocharged engines can become pretty complex, especially when fuel-injected and with a dry-sump oil system. Bob Godfrey's 650bhp Auto-Craft engine is used in his record-breaking VW Funny Car. Hilborn mechanical injection system feeds alcohol to this 2.8-liter monster.

The stock fuel pump is not really up to the task of coping with a high-rpm engine running a pair of large dual-choke carburetors. Holley makes a pair of excellent electric pumps – red for up to 5psi, blue for up to 9psi – both of which need to be used in conjunction with a pressure regulator.

simply cannot flow enough fuel to cope with twice the demand. To ensure the engine doesn't run short of fuel at high rpm - possibly causing a dangerously-lean situation - it will be necessary to replace the stock fuel line with one of larger diameter. Using aluminum or steel tubing of at least $1/4$in, and preferably $3/8$in, diameter will go some way to easing the situation. However, it will also be necessary to add a vent to the tank to prevent a vacuum forming as the extra fuel is drawn off. This vent should be of at least the same diameter as the main fuel line, and routed to outside the luggage compartment.

The factory fuel pump is also fine for the job for which it was designed. The stock carburetor makes few demands and only requires a steady supply of fuel at all times. Being a mechanical pump driven off the cam gear, the original pump delivers more fuel as the engine speed rises. When dual carburetors are added, this same fuel pump begins to be less desirable. Many aftermarket carburetors need to be run at fairly carefully governed pressures and require a steady flow of fuel at all times to keep the float chamber topped up. The problem with the stock pump is that it is usually struggling to flow enough fuel to keep up with the increased demand but, in some cases, will even supply fuel at too high a pressure. This can be cured in part by shortening the pump pushrod to reduce delivery.

However, in high-performance street and race applications, there is a need for something better.

Weber carburetors, for instance, prefer to be run at something in the region of 3psi fuel pressure. Above that and excess fuel begins to dribble out of the accelerator pump jets, flooding the engine at idle. However, at high rpm, the stock pump cannot cope with demand and there may be the sensation of the engine 'holding back' as it temporarily runs out of fuel. What is needed is a large-volume electric fuel pump whose output pressure can be regulated to the required level.

By far the most popular aftermarket electric pump is that made by Holley in the USA. Available in either 'red' (up to 7psi and 97 gallons/hour) and 'blue' (up

to 14psi and 102 gallons/hour) specifications, it should always be used in conjunction with a fuel pressure regulator. Gene Berg Enterprises recommends using a red pump with matching red regulator for fast street use, but a blue pump for racing. In this instance, a red regulator should still be used to keep the pressure to an acceptable level, although the blue pump will ensure there is adequate volume at all times. Other fuel pumps currently on the market, which are suited to use on fast street VWs, include the Facet range of interrupter pumps and the same company's smaller solid-state pumps.

Note that, as a general rule, electric pumps should always be mounted below the level of, and close to, the fuel tank. The pump should be wired to switch on and off with the ignition.

WHAT SIZE CARBURETORS?

With sales catalogs suggesting that anything from a pair of 34mm Dell'Ortos up to a pair of 48IDAs will be perfect for your car, there is understandably a good deal of confusion about what size carb is best suited to an engine. There are a couple of simple formulae which allow you to make an initial decision and also establish a starting point for the carburetor jetting. These formulae assume one carburetor venturi per cylinder:

$$\text{Carb size} = \frac{\sqrt{(\text{cc per cylinder} \times \text{maximum rpm})}}{40}$$

$$\text{Choke diameter} = \frac{\text{Carb size} \times 40}{50}$$

Main jet = Choke diameter x 4

For example:
2160cc engine = 540cc per cylinder   Max rpm = 7,000rpm

$$\text{Carburettor size} = \frac{\sqrt{(540 \times 7000)}}{40} = 48.6\text{mm}$$

(A 48 IDA Weber or 48DRLA Dell'Orto would be suitable in this instance)

$$\text{Choke diameter} = \frac{48 \times 40}{50} = 38.4\text{mm (A 38mm choke would be ideal)}$$

Main jet = 38 x 4 = 152

(A 150 or 155 main jet would be a good starting point in this instance)

Note that these are only intended as a rough guide but will certainly point you in the right direction. Do not overestimate your maximum rpm requirements - this will be partially governed by a number of other factors, including camshaft, cylinder head, valve size and quality of engine components, as well as your driving style. Too large a carburetor will only result in a car which is less pleasurable to drive and delivers poor gas mileage.

RECOMMENDATIONS

Street	Holley-Weber 32/36; dual 34ICT Weber; dual 34FRD Dell'Orto; dual Solex Kadron H40EI; single 36DRLA Dell'Orto
Hot Street	Dual Weber IDFs; dual Dell'Orto DRLAs; Berg 42mm Weber DCNFs; dual Weber 48IDAs; CB Performance fuel-injection; Berg Haltech fuel-injection; CB Performance street turbo
Competition	Dual Weber 48IDAs; dual Berg 58mm; dual JayCee Enterprises' Terminators; all-out race turbo system such as Kawell Racing Engines, etc.

EXHAUST SYSTEMS

One of the most effective ways to make horsepower

The stock exhaust system was part of VW's plan to limit the breathing ability of the Beetle engine. Although effective in restricting sound levels, it does little to help the quest for horsepower as it is so restrictive. However, the overall design is very sound, the short exhaust ports of the cylinder head exiting straight into the exhaust system, so removing heat from the head as quickly and efficiently as possible.

The waste gases from cylinders number 1 and number 3 enter the muffler via the long heater boxes (heat exchangers), while those from cylinders number 2 and number 4 enter the muffler almost directly, passing through just a pair of short header pipes. Inside the stock muffler is an expansion, or equalizing, chamber from which the gases find their way out via a pair of baffled tailpipes (vehicles built prior to 1955 used just one unbaffled tailpipe).

The main problem faced by the factory was how to install an effective exhaust system which would fit into the confines of the rear of the car, between the rear valance and the engine. The end result was a masterpiece of packaging but at the expense of efficiency. Good as it is, the stock exhaust system is not suited to use in a performance application.

The single biggest drawback is that the exhaust gases from each cylinder are forced to travel a different distance through the system before exiting via the tailpipes. To some degree, the equalizing chamber in the muffler helps to even out the discrepancy, but there is no substitute for a system which consists of equal-length header pipes for each cylinder. The pipes which bolt to the heads are called

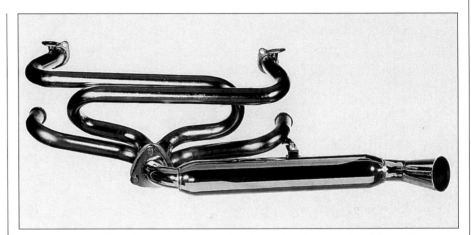

The least expensive aftermarket exhaust systems are those fitted with a glasspack muffler. The roughly equal length headers make a considerable difference compared with the stock system, but the noise level from the muffler may be unacceptable to you – or your neighbors!

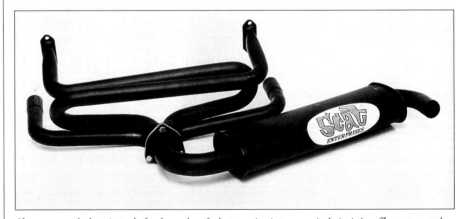

If you are on a budget, instead of a glasspack, a far better option is to use a single 'quiet' muffler system, such as this from Scat Enterprises. The muffler is less restrictive than a glasspack and considerably quieter.. This particulay system is destined for use on a Porsche 356 – note the shape of the exhaust port flanges.

the 'primaries' and the length of these is critical to the way in which an engine produces its power. The shorter the primaries, the higher up the rpm range maximum power will be produced, but at the expense of bottom-end output, while longer primaries will give better low- and mid-range performance at the expense of top-end power. For example, a system with 36in primaries will perform best between 2,500rpm and 5,500rpm, while a system with 28in primaries will work most effectively between 6,000rpm and 10,000rpm.

It is important when buying an aftermarket exhaust system to ensure that the system is designed to produce power at an rpm range which is compatible with the rest of the components used: camshaft, carburetors and cylinder head will all, to some extent, dictate where the engine produces its maximum power and the exhaust system should be chosen accordingly. Now, it has to be said, that most companies who sell exhaust systems either do not publish, or do not have, this information. If you are anxious to get the most from your engine – and you should be – then it will pay to ask some searching questions before making your final decision.

The diameter of the primaries will also have an effect on the engine's power output and here it is important to strike a balance between the free-flowing abilities of a large-bore system and the high gas speed of a small-bore header. In an ideal world, the primary exhaust pipes should be as small in diameter as possible without causing a restriction to the gas flow. This

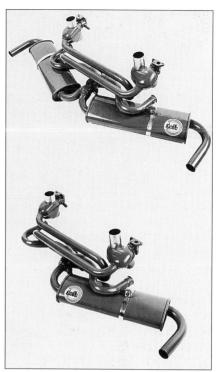

A frequent problem with aftermarket header systems is that they tend to crack around the welds, frequently because the muffler is not properly supported. These systems from Scat show how a quality system should look. Note the support straps round each muffler. Also, note that both these systems have provision for running the original heater system, with factory-style heater connections round numbers two and four headers.

way, the gas velocity will remain high and thus promote better scavenging – this is where the escaping gases from one exhaust stroke create a partial vacuum in the primary pipe and thus help to draw the next lot of gases from the combustion chamber. As the gases expand into the collector or muffler, the vacuum effect will be increased, further aiding this scavenging effect. Too large a primary pipe will result in little or no exhaust scavenging at low rpm as the exhaust gas velocity will be too low. On the other hand, too small a primary will result in a strangling effect at higher rpm. It is all a question of achieving a balance and choosing a system which is, again, matched to the rpm range of your engine.

Most street systems will have primaries of 1.5in or 1.625in in diameter, although a larger 1.75in system may be of benefit on a large capacity hot street engine which sees regular high-rpm use.

In the early days of VW tuning, few people realised the importance of merging the individual exhaust headers so as to improve scavenging of the waste gases. Typical of many an early race system is this used on the original Inch Pincher *race car back in the 1960s. Four megaphone-tip pipes may have looked impressive, but the power output could have been greatly improved had a proper equal-length, merged header system been used.*

Most competition systems will be at least 1.625in in diameter, but anything up to 2in or 2.25in (for example, Berg's GBE938 system) may be the way to go if you are building a large Pro-Stock style motor or one which uses nitrous oxide injection. However, it is important to note that, whenever an engine features larger than stock valves, it will be necessary to remove the stock heater boxes if you are to get the best from your combination. The factory only designed these heater boxes with primary pipes which were large enough to work on a stock VW engine. Change anything, including heads, carburetors or cylinder size, and the heater boxes will cause a restriction which may ultimately damage your engine by making the exhaust valves run too hot due to a lack of adequate scavenging of the exhaust gases. Larger exhaust valves will always require a larger diameter exhaust system to be used.

While reading through a catalog of aftermarket exhaust systems, you will frequently see the word 'merged' being used in connection with a header system. A merged system is one where the exhaust primary pipes enter a longer collector at a slight taper and blend into each other gradually. The gases escaping from one pipe will help scavenge the gases from the next cylinder - the pipes should enter the collector in a rotational order which reflects the firing order of the engine: number 1 primary will be next to number 4 which will be next to number 3 which will be next to number 2, etc. In a regular extractor exhaust system, the four pipes will enter a shorter collector parallel with each other. The scavenging effect will be minimal, although the system will still be almost certainly less restrictive than the stock muffler set-up. A good merged exhaust system will help to make more horsepower for your money than virtually any other component.

When choosing an exhaust system, there are a number of things to consider. First of all, do you require a heater on your car? If the answer is yes, then you should consider one of the systems which has proper provision for connecting up the heater boxes to the outlets from the fan-housing. Cheaper systems require the use of long lengths of flexible hose to do this job, which is a less than satisfactory

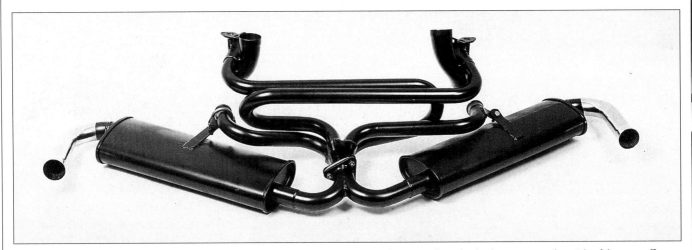

Gene Berg Enterprises GB903DP is a quality dual-muffler system for use on 13/15/1600 sedans. Note that it has brackets to support the weight of the two mufflers and also hook-ups to run a stock heater system.

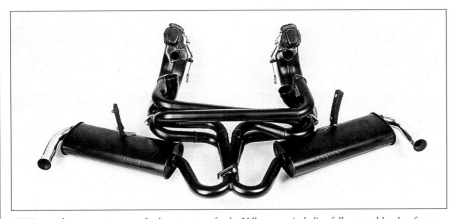

GBE manufactures a vast range of exhaust systems for the Volkswagen, including fully-merged headers for use on hot street cars. Note how the four header pipes merge in a long collector before exiting to the mufflers. This system has been equipped with GB996-KIT, which converts the normal slip joint between the header and the heater box to a leak-free flanged connection. Support straps on the mufflers fix to rear bumper mounts and are flexible to reduce noise levels inside the car.

solution as the hoses frequently come loose or even burn through against the header pipes. Are you using a single carburetor? In which case, do you wish to retain the pre-heat facility on the inlet manifold? Again, check that the extractor exhaust system you are contemplating buying has provision for this.

Are you after all-out performance or a broad spread of power across the rpm range? Is your vehicle a street car or a race car? Do you need mufflers for street use, or will you be running a stinger (unsilenced racing megaphone)? Is the appearance of the bodywork a consideration or do you mind trimming the rear apron to clear a long, large diameter collector on a merged race system? Only by answering questions such as these can you come up with the right system for your needs.

For most people, the choice will be somewhat more simple: single or dual quiet mufflers or a glasspack system. A glasspack consists of a basic tubular muffler which is stuffed full of chopped glassfiber mat around a perforated tube. Noisy and inefficient, glasspacks are gradually falling out of favor, and quite rightly so. So-called 'quiet' mufflers, first installed by Gene Berg, are more akin to traditional chambered mufflers used on other types of car and are generally less noisy and more efficient than either the glasspack or the stock muffler. Dual quiet mufflers - first experimented with by FAT Performance back in the mid-'70s - are more efficient again and offer double the flow capability of a single muffler system. It is worth noting, however, that fitting a dual quiet muffler system to a stock Beetle engine may result in slightly increased noise and a loss in low-end performance as the gas speed through the system will be reduced considerably. Only when a larger, higher-rpm combination is used will a dual-muffler system come into its own.

Other muffler designs are available, although many are probably chosen for aesthetic reasons rather than for their efficiency. Bugpack markets a system called 'Street Tubes', which consists of a pair of chromed rebuildable mufflers located along each side of the engine to exit under the rear valance. S&S offers a similar system, this using dual aluminum mufflers. The main problem with this type of system is the greatly reduced ground clearance which results - most dual-quiet mufflers also suffer badly in this respect. This has led to the development of the 'hide-away' muffler, which consists of one or two quiet-type mufflers tucked up under the rear fenders behind the wheels. Not necessarily the most efficient design in terms of pipe length, these hide-away systems are proving popular among people who are tired of wiping out their regular mufflers on driveways and garage on-ramps. Other designs, such as the GT or Monza four-tip mufflers, are too restrictive for performance applications and should only be considered where

GB932 and GB933 are fully-merged race systems with either 1.500in or 1.625in primary headers. Note the merged collector – essential for optimum performance. Small three-bolt exhaust flange is used on these systems.

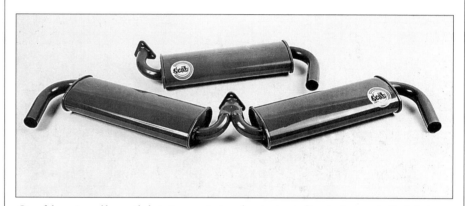

One of the major problems with designing an extractor exhaust system to fit under the rear of a Beetle is the lack of space behind the rear valance. Squeezing one quiet muffler in can be a problem, but two is a challenge. Note how the inlet pipes for these mufflers have been sharply curved so as to tuck the mufflers as far forward as possible. Ground clearance always remains a problem with quiet systems unless a hide-away design is used, which places the muffler up under the rear fender.

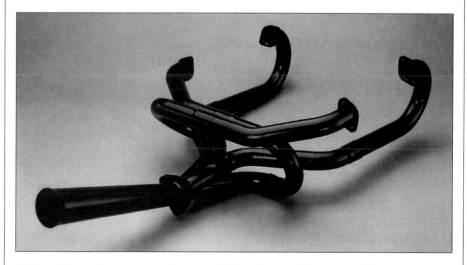

This merged competition system uses a larger three-bolt flange for potentially superior gas flow. However, it is important to note that a larger-diameter exhaust system will not automatically improve power output.

One of the most popular solutions to the problem of how to silence a hot street VW is currently to use a V8-style turbo muffler under the rear valance, like this. Perhaps not the most aesthetically-pleasing solution, but it is effective. Bill Schwimmer's street car runs 12.80s through the muffler!

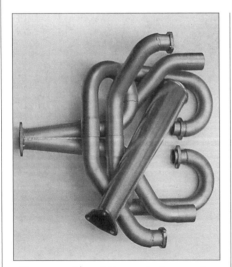

All-out competition vehicles, running large capacity, high rpm engines, will require something special in the way of an exhaust system. This top of the line system from GBE (part number GB936) uses headers which are a full 2.00in in diameter. Large three-bolt flange and a long, large diameter stinger are essential for making horsepower in a modern Pro-Stock type engine. Note the extra-thick header flanges to prevent distortion and leakage.

looks and sound are of primary importance. Remember, function should always dictate form where performance is concerned.

A comparatively recent departure in muffler design is the use of a so-called 'turbo' muffler, normally found on a larger V8-engined vehicle, but adapted for use with a VW header system. Such mufflers are not the most aesthetically-pleasing solution to extracting quiet horsepower from a VW engine as their size usually dictates that they be mounted in full view under the rear valance. It is possible to locate the turbo muffler under one or other bank of cylinders, the main drawback here being that ground clearance is considerably reduced. This may not be a problem with a vehicle which only sees limited road use, but could result in damage to the header system if the muffler regularly makes contact with the road surface.

When choosing a system, take a look at the quality of the finish, especially the

welding. The flanges which bolt to the cylinder head should be securely welded to the header pipes and they should be flat – any distortion will result in the exhaust gasket being blown out in no time at all. A good quality race system will feature thick flanges to prevent distortion due to heat or over-tightening. Many merged systems will have slip joints incorporated into the pipework to allow for use on engines of varying widths. Whenever the stock heater boxes are dispensed with, the replacement J-pipes will almost invariably be a slip-in fit into the main header system, although, if a turbo system is used, it is vital that all joints be bolted together to avoid the exhaust gases escaping and ultimately causing a fall-off in boost pressure.

Several systems are now being sold with an aluminum coating in an effort to prevent rust, while others are available manufactured from stainless steel for the same reason – both Scat in the USA and Autocavan in the United Kingdom offer such systems and, although more costly, are a good long-term investment. Aluminum-coated headers will last far longer than painted ones but are difficult to keep clean as the coating has a slightly rough texture. Gene Berg Enterprises offers a ceramic coating for its header systems which not only prevents the formation of rust inside and out but, it is claimed, adds power due to the heat-retaining properties of the ceramic finish. It has to be said that virtually all proprietary spray-can exhaust paints do not last very long at all, even when applied strictly in accordance with the manufacturers' instructions. The temperature close to the exhaust port reaches in excess of 1200°F (650°C), which is far higher than the paint can cope with. As a result, after only a short time, the system will begin to rust. The only answer is to regularly wire-brush the loose surface rust and re-apply the paint.

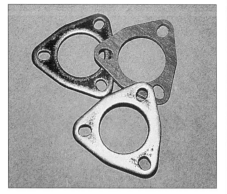

If you decide to build your own exhaust system, or modify an existing one, some companies offer a range of exhaust flanges and gaskets to allow you to produce your ideal design. Flanges are available in a wide variety of diameters to suit all applications.

The header flange at the exhaust port should be slightly larger in diameter than the port itself so as not to restrict the gas flow from the head. However, too large a diameter header will reduce the gas speed in the exhaust system and so affect the scavenging.

RECOMMENDATIONS

Street	Single or dual quiet muffler; 1.5in extractor header system; hide-away muffler (where ground clearance is a problem)
Hot Street	Dual quiet muffler; 1.625in or 1.75in merged header system; turbo muffler where ground clearance not a concern
Competition	Large-bore merged header system up to 2.25in; stinger racing megaphone; thick header flanges

On a street car with a large capacity engine running a pair of 48IDAs, a radical cam and large valve heads, it is important to use an exhaust system that is as free-flowing as possible. This can lead to problems with where to mount a large-diameter muffler. Art Gutierrez's car shows one solution. Note the exhaust tip alongside the rear tire.

IGNITION SYSTEMS

Keeping the fire alive

Distributors

The basic Volkswagen ignition system consists of a distributor, a coil, a set of leads and four spark plugs - as simple as that. The design of the system, though, has changed in detail considerably over the years, with the biggest changes having been made to the specification of the distributor. The first units fitted were all-centrifugal, ie, the ignition timing was advanced automatically as the engine speed increased. The factory eventually realized that, for everyday driving conditions, this was not the perfect situation and introduced a distributor which was also advanced by inlet manifold vacuum. Later still, there were distributors which had no provision for centrifugal advance at all.

The first distributor to see widespread use on the VW engine was the VE4 BRS 383, made for Volkswagen by Bosch. This all-centrifugal unit provided up to 34° of spark advance (all quoted measurements are in degrees of crankshaft rotation = 2 x distributor rotation), this figure being achieved at 2,900rpm. From this point on, Volkswagen introduced a quite bewildering array of distributors, often fitting two different types to the same engine batch during a production run. As new models were added to the range, new distributors were also introduced, meaning that the person who wishes to mix and match ignition components from one model to another stands little chance of finding an ideal combination.

So, where does this leave somebody who wishes to modify his VW engine for more performance? And why would he need to change the stock distributor

Originally fitted to Type 2 models in 1959 and 1960, the Bosch 010 distributor has long been a favorite with Volkswagen engine builders. This all-centrifugal distributor provides between 18°-22° of spark advance, fully in by 1700rpm. Unfortunately good 010s are becoming hard to find.

anyway? Fortunately, the answers to these two questions are relatively straightforward. Taking the second question first, the problem with using either the stock later-style centrifugal/vacuum, or the all-vacuum, distributors is that once you make changes to the engine which affect the vacuum generated in the inlet manifold, then the rate at which the ignition is advanced will change, possibly leading to flat-spots or detonation. Changing the camshaft will have an effect, as will modifying the cylinder heads or changing the valve size. However, by far the greatest effect will be from swapping the stock single carburetor for a pair of aftermarket carbs on individual manifolds.

Although many aftermarket carb kits have provision for connecting the vacuum hose for a stock-type distributor, this should be blanked off and an all-centrifugal distributor fitted instead. This way, there is some guarantee that the timing will be closer to the ideal throughout the rpm range, rather than over- or under-advanced during acceleration from low rpm. On engines with the oil cooler located inside the fan-housing, Volkswagen fitted distributors that had the cam, which operates the points, ground so that the spark to number 3 cylinder is retarded by 3°-4°. This is because this particular cylinder always runs hotter than the rest as the oil cooler obstructs its flow of cooling air. Bearing this in mind, it is important that any VW distributor always be installed following the factory guide-lines, otherwise the wrong cylinder will have the spark retarded.

Of all the various factory-installed (by VW or Porsche) distributors which have been used, there are five which are considered best suited for use on a modified VW engine. Each of these is manufactured by Bosch - the early models in Germany, new ones in South America. The first is one of the most widely respected distributors ever made for the VW engine: the Bosch 010 (the '010' refers to the last three digits of the model number). This was fitted as original equipment on Type 2 models in 1959 and 1960. It is an all-centrifugal unit which can provide a spark advance of between

Today, the Bosch 009 distributor has replaced the 010 as the number one choice. It is a relatively inexpensive all-centrifugal unit which provides up to 24° of spark advance. First used on Porsche 912 engines in 1971, the 009 is a great choice for all but the most extreme hot street and race engines.

18°-22°, this being achieved (or 'fully in') by 1700rpm. The 010 has the in-built retard for number 3 cylinder and has proved itself time and again as being an excellent all-round distributor for mildly modified VW engines. The main drawback today is that 010s are becoming hard to find and many which are in circulation today suffer from excessive wear as a consequence of over 30 years' use.

Another old favorite among VW tuners was the Bosch 019, originally installed on certain 4-cylinder Porsches and Type 2 models prior to 1959. This is also an all-centrifugal unit which offers between 28°-32° of advance which is all in by 3,500rpm. The main difference between this and the 010, apart from the greater amount of advance available, is that the advance curve is different: the spark advance is slightly slower at lower rpm, but faster at high rpm. A common modification to make was to remove one of the two springs which control the internal bob-weights (the centrifugal advance mechanism inside the distributor) so that maximum advance comes in earlier, around 2,000rpm.

Another all-centrifugal distributor which has been popular in the past is the Bosch 031. This starts its advance curve later than most others, not beginning to alter the spark until 1200rpm. By 2,800rpm, it reaches its maximum advance of between 28°-32°. For the VW

Bosch make this high-output coil – called the 'Blue Coil' because of its color – which is often used in conjunction with the 009 to provide a worthwhile improvement over the stock ignition system. Note that coils are voltage dependent and are clearly marked either 6v or 12v.

engine, which requires a maximum spark advance of no more than 32° at the most, this means that the 031 would be set at close to 0° static advance.

Incidentally, except where race engines are concerned, the timing should never be set at more than 32° before top dead center (BTDC) on number 1 cylinder. In fact, with the steadily declining quality of fuel currently available, many engine builders recommend no more than 30°BTDC for road use. Turbo race engines frequently use no more than 24° of total spark advance in deference to the high cylinder pressures and temperatures.

The fourth - and by far the most common - factory-supplied distributor, which is often recommended for use on a modified VW engine, is the Bosch 009. Unlike the distributors mentioned above, this is currently very easy to obtain, as it is still in production - the other units can usually only be picked up at swapmeets. The 009 first saw service on Porsche 912s from 1971 and is also an all-centrifugal unit. With a retarded number 3 spark, the 009 provides up to 20°-24° of maximum advance, all in by about 1800rpm. This distributor has been the mainstay of the VW performance industry for years, and rightly so, for it has proved itself to be reliable and well-matched to the majority of hot street applications. There have been some quality problems in recent years following a shift in production from

Scat Enterprises markets this all-centrifugal distributor, made by Mallory. Providing up to 28° of spark advance, the Scat/Mallory unit is well made. It makes an attractive addition to any performance engine.

Germany to South America, but on the whole the 009 is probably the ideal all-round choice.

The final recommended factory all-centrifugal distributor is the Bosch 050. This features a faster advance rate than the 009 and, for this reason, is not always considered as well suited to a modified VW. Also, it does not feature the spark

The great thing about the Mallory distributor is that it is fully adjustable – set at the factory to give 24° of advance, it can be adjusted to provide anything from 18°-28° of advance. This means it is possible to tailor it to the exact requirements of your engine.

retard for number 3 cylinder. When the 050 first became readily available a few years ago, it was heralded as being the best distributor ever offered for the VW. However the 009 has continued in popular use and still remains the number one choice of many, including Gene Berg Enterprises (GBE) which claims to have tested every distributor currently available on the market and still finds none to beat the 009.

At one time there used to be several aftermarket distributors for the VW on the market but, today, the choice is limited to the Mallory high-performance unit listed by Scat Enterprises, and the billet unit by MSD, of which more later. The Scat/Mallory unit allows the owner to adjust the amount of spark advance from the Mallory setting of 24° to anything between 18° and 28°. This way the ignition system can be tailored to the exact requirements of the engine concerned.

The main drawback with the 009, and other similar distributors, is that above around 5,500rpm, there is the risk of points bounce setting in - this is where the points are no longer able to remain in contact with the cam of the distributor and start to 'float' in a similar fashion to valve springs at high engine speeds. This will result in a misfire which will not disappear until the rpm is reduced again. GBE suggests a simple modification which entails fitting a second spring to the points, using one removed from a scrap set. This allows up to 7,500rpm to be used without points bounce.

Electronic systems

However, the best way to cure this problem is to fit an electronic 'breakerless' system - one which does away with the points altogether. Several such systems are manufactured for use with the VW engine, which not only cure high rpm misfires, but also provide a fatter spark at the plugs to improve combustion. The Stinger S4 system is sold by GBE (part No 629) and consists of a larger distributor body and cap (based on modified Chevrolet Vega parts), rotor with magnetic pick-up in place of points, an ignition module and a wiring harness. The kit is claimed to produce a spark

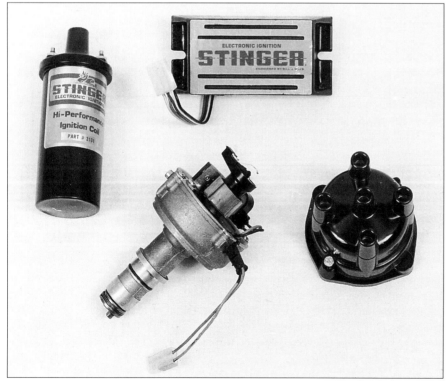

Gene Berg Enterprises markets the Stinger electronic ignition system. The model shown is the S4 system – part number GB629 – which consists of a larger distributor body and cap, rotor with magnetic pick-up, ignition module and wiring harness. GBE claim the unit is up to two and a half times more powerful than any other system.

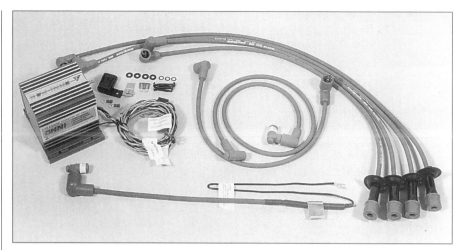

Jacobs Electronics' 'Bug-Pak' kit contains everything you need to change from the conventional coil set-up to a modern electronic ignition system. The 'Omni-Pak' replaces stock coil and can be mounted to firewall. High-energy ignition leads are also part of the package.

CB Performance Magnaspark is a high-energy electronic ignition (HEI) system which does away with the stock points and coil. Kit comes with all necessary components to make the switch, including adaptor to convert distributor to breakerless design.

increase in engine speed. This makes it possible to run much higher spark advance than normal in the mid-range rpm, for more power, yet be safe in the knowledge that the timing will not be over-advanced at high rpm.

A simpler system, which has proved to be perfectly adequate for road use, is the Ignitor breakerless conversion. This fits straight into the stock 009 or 050 distributors in place of the points and provides a stronger spark at low rpm for improved starting and a smoother idle. The manufacturer claims that fuel economy will also be improved. Although not a set-up which is intended for competition use, it is an excellent low-cost conversion for the factory ignition system on a mildly-modified street car.

There are a number of other straightforward ignition conversions for the VW, including the Compu-Fire electronic system, the Crane Cams series, the Magnaspark from CB Performance and the Jacobs Electronics' 'Bug-Pack'. The Compu-Fire is an electronic ignition system which consists of a pair of low resistance, closed-core coils, a control module, rotor and cap for the Bosch 009, and a set of plugs leads. The stock 009 cap, rotor arm and points are replaced by the new control module and ignition sensors - the module looks from the outside like a flat cap which has been fitted over the distributor body. The dual coils are connected to a pair of opposing cylinders and are triggered not only on

some two and a half times more powerful than any other street/race ignition system and has proved reliable in excess of 10,000rpm.

The GBE 629A is a development of the basic Stinger system and includes dual magnetic pick-ups which allows the driver to change between two ignition timing settings at the flick of a switch. This may prove to be useful in a race installation where it is necessary to retard the ignition timing at high rpm, or when using nitrous oxide injection. GBE 629B is somewhat more sophisticated in that it offers an advance curve similar to the Bosch 009 up until 5,500rpm, at which point it begins to automatically retard the ignition by 2° for every 1,000rpm

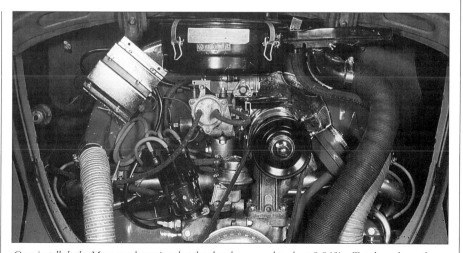

Once installed, the Magnaspark requires that the plugs be regapped to about 0.040in. Tests have shown the system to improve low-speed running, curing the off-idle flat-spots which can be a problem with stock-carbureted late-model VWs.

Crane Cams' XR3000 breakerless ignition system relies on the company's PS91 coil to provide the necessary spark. Easy to fit and relatively inexpensive, the Crane Cams ignition systems have proved to be reliable and effective.

the induction stroke but also the exhaust stroke, thereby helping to clean up emissions. The system has been tested to in excess of 10,000rpm and should provide much improved flexibility and fuel economy.

The Crane Cams range of electronic ignition conversions consists of four different systems to suit all applications from stock to race. Another breakerless conversion, it is suitable for use with either 6v or 12v electrics, so the vintage crowd can also benefit from modern technology. The range begins with the XR700, which is aimed at the daily-driven VW and can be used in conjunction with Bosch coils with internal ballast resistors as standard. The XR3000 is a high-performance version of the XR700 but does not use the stock coil. In its place, the XR3000 should be used with Crane's own, such as the PS91, which does not have a ballast resistor. The HI-6 is a system aimed at the hot street car, while the top of the range HI-6R is a race-only system which includes multiple spark discharge and an adjustable sequential rev-limiting facility. Fitting is very straightforward and the system retains

MSD makes a vast range of ignition products and you would be well advised to obtain a copy of its latest catalog. It is packed full of useful information about high-performance ignition systems and related products. MSD is the number one choice of drag racers throughout the world.

The MSD6A is a high-output ignition system which pumps out some 45,000 volts and is tested to over 10,000rpm. This breakerless system is an excellent choice for high-performance street VWs which see some drag strip use. Used in conjunction with MSD's own Blaster Coil, as shown here, you won't go far wrong with this system.

the factory (or 009-type) distributor.

CB Performance's Magnaspark is described as an HEI - High Energy Ignition - system which is, once again, breakerless, relying on a magnetic pick-up to trigger the spark. The Magnaspark works with the popular 009 distributor and includes a module to replace the points, along with an HEI coil pack which replaces the original coil. The major benefit of this system is that it provides a strong spark all the way up to a claimed 12,000rpm and much improved drivability.

The Jacobs Electronics' Bug-Pack is a somewhat simpler system which retains the 009 distributor, points and all, and consists of a large control box which houses the coil and the electronic ignition components. Although the Jacobs conversion will not cure high-rpm problems like points bounce, it provides a fatter spark for improved economy and smoother driving.

When it comes to the ultimate ignition systems for hot VWs, one name stands above all - MSD (Multiple Spark Discharge). The product range begins with the basic MSD 5, which is a simple add-on to the factory ignition system and is intended to work with either the stock points or a breakerless triggering system. However, of more interest to the performance market is the MSD6A. This is a high-energy electronic system which pumps out 45,000 volts and is tested to over 10,000rpm. The MSD6AL is a similar system but benefits from the added feature of 'soft touch' rpm limiting - ie, the spark is cut to each cylinder at

The ultimate race system is MSD's famed 7AL-2 which is a race-only multiple spark discharge (hence 'MSD') electronic ignition package. The 7AL-2 must be used with the matching Pro Power coil and can be linked to a range of ancillaries, such as two- and three-step rev limiters and ignition timing controls.

random, rather than cut altogether, when the desired rpm limit is reached. This prevents spark plug fouling. The MSD6 and 6AL systems can be used with the normal Bosch distributor but require the use of MSD's own 'Blaster' coil.

The top of the range race system is the MSD7AL-2, which must be used with MSD's own Pro-Power coil and either the MSD billet distributor, a modified large diameter VW distributor (to prevent cross-firing - this is where the spark destined for one cylinder jumps across to the next and causes a misfire at high rpm) or a crank-trigger system, such as that made for the VW race engine by Jack Sacchette of JayCee Enterprises. The 7AL-2 is a race-only system which has a built-in rpm limiting facility controlled by plug-in 'chips', which can be supplemented by a remote adjustable rpm limiter control or even by a two- or

three-step system which allows the driver to control engine rpm during a burnout, on the startline and during the run down the drag strip. Not suitable for use on the street, the MSD7AL-2 package is undoubtedly the best-proven, and most versatile, competition system available.

To get the most out of this, or any ignition system, it is imperative to use high quality plug leads. The original factory-supplied carbon-core leads tend to break down with age and are not suitable for high-performance applications as they can cause severe misfires. Many suppliers sell more suitable 'silicone' leads, which are both inexpensive and perfectly adequate for all but the most sophisticated race ignition systems. Others, like the MSD7AL-2, require the use of special leads such as MSD's own Heli-Core leads. These are multi-layer leads with a central glass inner core surrounded by a wound solid conductor, a high dielectric insulator and a heavy glass braid. Covering all this is a temperature-resistant flexible jacket. MSD, and certain other high-power electronic systems, should never be used with solid-core plug leads or damage to the command module could result. If there is any doubt, check the manufacturer's recommendations before installation. Note that MSD race ignition systems require a wider plug gap - up to 0.035in.

Magneto ignition

Many race - and some hot street - Volkswagens can be seen equipped with magneto ignition systems. The magneto first saw use on the VW industrial engines

The MSD7AL-2 can be used with a distributor and a set of points, but should ideally be used in conjunction with a magnetic pick-up like this crank-trigger set-up manufactured by Jack Sacchette of JayCee Enterprises.

The JayCee crank-trigger system is CNC machined from billet and allows fine adjustments to be made to the timing. The matching crankshaft pulley has timing marks machined into it for use with a strobe lamp.

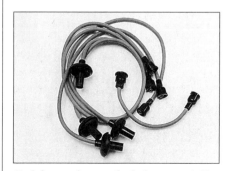

Stock factory carbon-core plug leads are not suitable for high-performance applications and should be replaced with a set of good quality aftermarket leads. Most suppliers stock a range of suitable leads, or check with the manufacturer of your ignition system.

Whenever a magneto is used in a VW engine, it is important to make sure it is rigidly supported with a bracket like this, otherwise the magneto's weight, combined with vibration, will cause damage to the crankcase. Note the crankcase on this engine – a late fuel-injection model without provision for mechanical fuel pump. Vertex magneto is an OAC model.

which are intended to run for many hours at a time at constant rpm - these engines were frequently used as power-plants for mobile generators, water-pumps and heavy machinery. The magneto is particularly well suited to use 'in the field', as it generates its own spark without need for a separate battery. However, from the street or race VW point of view, much of the magneto's appeal lies in the fact that it produces a high-energy spark from relatively low rpm, the strength of which increases with engine speed, and does not make any other demands on the electrical system of the car (some race-type electronic systems can quickly drain the vehicle's battery if no charging system is used). There is also the fact that, for maximum visual impact, there is little to beat a magneto on a hot street engine.

A magneto generates its own primary voltage by way of a magnet whose poles rotate past coils in a stator. As the magnetic field close to these coils is

Vertex Scintilla magnetos frequently show up for sale at swap meets at very attractive prices. Beware of units which have been used on industrial engines or those which have been badly stored – that bargain may not seem such a good buy in the long run.

constantly changing direction, a voltage is built up in the stator. When the points open, the electrical energy is released to the primary side of the transformer (coil) which then converts it into an extremely high voltage.

There are basically three magnetos available for the VW engine, two of which are manufactured by Vertex/Scintilla, the third by Mallory. The Vertex magnetos are certainly the most common, particularly the OAC model which has the power coil - or transformer - incorporated in the main body. The Vertex OXC is a more recent design and has a separate external transformer. Both are suitable for use on either hot street or race-only cars. The OXC has the advantage of having a large diameter cap which discourages cross-firing between cylinders. The OXC model also produces approximately 20% more energy than the older Vertex OAC and is perfect for use with high-compression, high-rpm race engines which need to burn a lot of fuel as quickly as possible. The standard OAC produces around 540 volts at 10,000rpm, while the OXC produces some 600 volts at the same engine speed.

The Mallory Super Mag is similar in some ways to the Vertex OXC in that it features an external transformer. The primary voltage is between 350 and 400 volts and, as with the Vertex, it is necessary to re-gap the plugs to rather less than the stock figure of 0.025in - a gap in

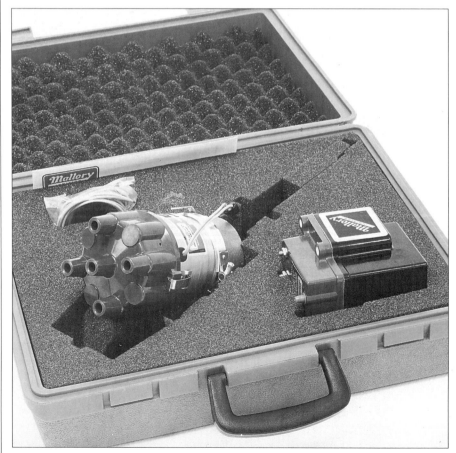

The Mallory Super Mag is an external coil design, as is the Vertex OXC. Mallory unit is supplied with spare bob-weights to allow the engine builder to adjust the spark advance to suit the chosen application.

Magnetos can be used to good effect on street engines without any problem. However, it is worth noting that you need to use a matching tachometer as a regular battery-ignition tacho will not work – companies like Autometer can supply a suitable unit.

the region of 0.018in is commonplace.

Magnetos have been the mainstay of VW drag race ignition systems for over thirty years and are generally extremely reliable. However, it is possible to experience problems with magnetos which have been stored in poor conditions. Many Vertex units were purchased by NATO for use with stationary engines and these units frequently appear on the European market new and at an appealing price.

However, there are two things to consider: the first is that the advance curve will not be suitable for use with an engine which runs at varying rpm, and second, there are problems regarding the condition of the internal coils due to poor storage. These problems manifest themselves by the magneto suddenly ceasing to function once the unit becomes hot. When it cools down, more often than not the engine will restart OK, but hot starting remains a problem unless the coils are replaced. This is not to say that these 'bargain' magnetos are not suitable for use on modified VW engines, as there are several companies which can repair or modify them, but be prepared to spend some extra money to get one sorted out.

RECOMMENDATIONS

Street	Bosch 009; Bosch 010; Bosch 050; Mallory (all with Bosch Blue Coil); Ignitor; Stinger GB629; Magnaspark; Jacobs 'Bug-Pack'; Crane Cams XR7000; Compu-Fire
Hot Street	Bosch 009; Bosch 010; Mallory (all with Bosch Blue coil); Stinger GB629; Vertex OAC; MSD6AL; Crane Cams XR3000; Crane Cams HI-6; Compu-Fire; MSD6A and 6AL
Competition	Stinger GB629A and GB629B; Crane Cams HI-6R; MSD7AL-2; Vertex OAC and OXC; Mallory Super Mag

LUBRICATION AND COOLING

It takes more than air to cool a Volkswagen engine

Although we always refer to the Beetle engine as being aircooled, it is not strictly true. Many Volkswagen owners are not aware that their engine is kept cool almost as much by the lubrication system as it is by the passage of air over the cylinders and heads. We are all taught to keep a watch on the condition of the fan belt, which turns the cooling fan, in case it breaks and the engine is 'cooked', but how many people realize that correct maintenance of the oiling system is just as important?

In a conventional, watercooled, engine, the cylinders and cylinder head are surrounded by a series of passageways through which a steady supply of coolant is pumped. This coolant absorbs much of the heat generated by the engine which is then dissipated to the atmosphere via the radiator. It is a very efficient way to keep an engine cool. The aircooled engine, on the other hand, has to rely on a large volume of air being passed over the motor. On the Volkswagen engine there is also an oil cooler, which acts in much the same way as the radiator on a water-cooled vehicle: the oil passes round the crankcase, absorbing heat from the engine, and is then directed through the cooler where cool air from the fan helps to dissipate the heat.

Air cooling

In the early Volkswagen engines, the oil cooler was located within the confines of the fan-housing, directly in the path of air which was intended to cool number 3 cylinder. As a result, this cylinder always ran a little hotter than the rest, resulting in problems, such as a dropped valve or cracked cylinder head, after a high

mileage. The factory was well aware of this problem but, rather than address it head on and redesign the cooling system, resorted to using a distributor which retarded the spark to number 3 cylinder. This was not the best solution to a problem which could have been solved by relocating the oil cooler outside the fan-housing - this step was finally taken in 1971 when an all-new cooling system was introduced which placed the cooler outside the fan-housing, with air being

supplied to it by some extra ducting. This is the so-called 'dog-house' design, so named because of its 'add-on' appearance.

When any engine is first started, it does not run at its most efficient until it has reached its optimum operating temperature. Watercooled cars have thermostats fitted which restrict the flow of coolant through the radiator until the correct operating temperature has been reached. In Volkswagens built prior to 1966, the flow of cooling air over the

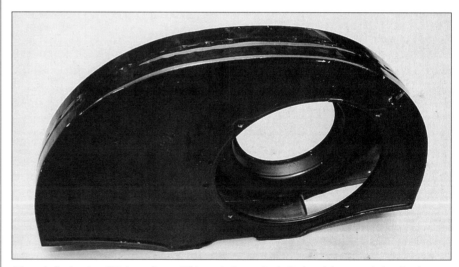

The early fan-housings (this is one from a 25bhp engine) were simple D-shaped designs with the oil cooler mounted internally. This style of shroud was used, virtually unchanged, up until the end of 1962 when a redesigned heating system was introduced.

Inside the fan-housing, a series of ducts ensured the cooling air was evenly distributed over the cylinders and heads. Many aftermarket housings do not have this all-important ducting.

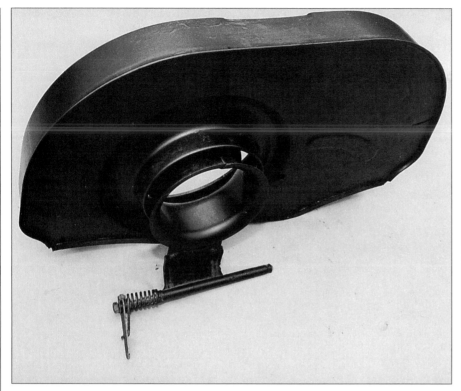

Late non-fresh-air fan-housing used this control-ring over the fan to restrict cooling air when the engine was still cold. This design lasted until the advent of new cooling flaps in 1965.

Difference in width of early and late fan-housings is clearly seen here. With some dual-carburetor installations, there may be a clearance problem when using the later shrouds.

cylinders was limited, until the engine was completely warm, by an annular ring which opened and closed about the cooling fan, this being operated by a pushrod from a bellows-type thermostat located below numbers 1 and 2 cylinders.

This design was changed in 1965 for a more sophisticated system of cooling flaps located within the lower part of the fan-housing, above the cylinders. When the engine is cold, these flaps remain closed but, as it warms up, the thermostat opens them via a pushrod, directing air over the cylinders and heads. There is always a temptation when rebuilding an engine to leave these cooling flaps out in the belief that they restrict the flow of cooling air to the engine. However, it is very important they remain in place to allow the engine to warm up in a controlled manner - without them, the engine will not reach its optimum operating temperature quickly, which can lead to increased cylinder wear.

The shape of the fan-housing has changed quite a lot over the years, with the original 25, 30 (US 36hp) and early 34bhp (US 40hp) engines all making use of simple D-shaped shrouds without extra ducting of any kind (part number 111 119 025A). With the advent of the so-called 'fresh-air' cooling system, in December 1962, the fan-housing was redesigned to incorporate outlets, one on each side, to allow air to be passed through the heating system. This fan-shrouding carried the part number 113 119 025B through to H. In 1965, when the cooling flaps were added, the width of the fan-housing was increased (part number 113 119 025J through to L). Later still, in 1971, the fan-housing was further redesigned to accept the dog-house cooler (shroud part number 113 119 025N through to Q).

The design of the cooling fan also changed over the years, with the number of blades being increased to coincide with the introduction of the 34bhp (US 40hp) engine in 1960 (part number 113 119 031A). The fan was over-driven (ie, rotated faster than the crankshaft by a factor of 1.8 - when the engine was revved to 3000rpm, the fan would be turning at some 5400rpm. However, the most significant change took place in

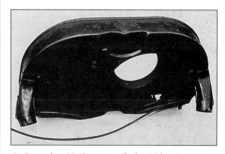

In December 1962, a new 'fresh-air' heating system was introduced – this may be easily identified by the appearance of two heater outlets on the front of the fan-housing.

1971 when the width was increased by 4.5mm and the over-drive factor reduced to 1.75 (ie, 5250rpm fan speed at 3000rpm engine speed). Despite the lower rotational speed, the new fan (part number 113 119 031B) was far more efficient (see note on power pulleys at end of chapter). However, it should be noted that it cannot be used in the earlier-style fan-housings due to its increased width.

It is often thought that the earlier D-shaped ('30bhp') fan-housings are more efficient due to their simple shape. However, this is not so and a look inside any of the later fan-housings will show

The late 'dog-house' fan-shrouding is so-called because of the add-on oil cooler ducting on the rear of the shroud. This is by far the most efficient factory cooling system of all.

offer superior cooling, even those which resemble the early 30bhp fan-housings yet are in fact designed to accept the later dog-house cooling system. The main drawbacks with the majority of these shrouds are that they lack either the correct internal vanes or any provision to fit the factory thermostatically-controlled cooling flaps. Of the aftermarket fan-housings, that manufactured by Scat Enterprises is probably the best and is well-finished, fits (many cheaper ones do not fit without extra work by the customer) and features nine directional vanes to correctly channel the cooling air.

Some resourceful people have cut open the later fan-housing and fitted the vanes and dog-house shrouding into an earlier 30bhp housing. To carry out this surgery correctly requires a great deal of patience, as you must drill out the numerous spot welds which hold the

that a great deal of time and effort (let alone money) was spent in developing the complex system of directional vanes which correctly route the cooling air over the cylinders and heads. The early fan-housing, with its internal oil cooler, had relatively few directional vanes to control the air flow, nor did the first of the 'fresh-air' units.

It is worth also dispelling another common misconception. Although it is fairly evident that the original location of the oil cooler within the fan-housing was less than ideal, simply removing and remotely mounting it via an adaptor fitting (an 'oil cooler block-off') will not improve the cooling of the engine. If anything, this will tend to make things worse as the location of the factory cooler is an important factor in the air flow management within the early-style shrouding. The major drawback was that the cooling air destined for number 3 cylinder passed through the cooler and became pre-heated by the hot oil - attempting to cool an engine with warm air is not a recipe for success.

Currently on sale are several aftermarket versions of the fan-housing, some offered as cosmetic dress-ups, others claiming to offer greater efficiency than the original. Without putting too fine a point on it, few of these accessory shrouds

Many companies market custom fan-housings and engine tinware, but few are as good as those sold by Scat Enterprises. Scat's fit well and feature all the factory-style internal ductwork. Chrome finish is attractive but not recommended for efficient heat dissipation.

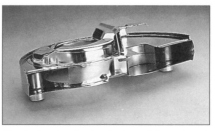

Scat fan-housing showing the internal ductwork and the external 'dog-house' cooler shrouding.

components together, and a high level of proficiency in welding, as the metal used to manufacture the shrouds is very thin.

There are other aftermarket fan-shroudings on sale which allow the generator or alternator to be center-mounted, as opposed to offset to the right side of the engine. Others are in the form of a wedge shape, the intention being to channel air more directly to the cylinders.

Neither of these types of shroud have any provision for use of the stock oil cooler (see note below on remote oil coolers) and, therefore, cannot be recommended for any street application. They may be OK on a show car which rarely sees any use, or a sand rail which burns alcohol (and therefore runs extremely cool), but forget the good looks and stay with your factory-style tinware.

Also commonly available is what is known as 'cool tin'. This is a piece of cylinder shrouding (part number 311 119 451), originally developed for the Type 3 engine, which wraps around the lower half of the cylinders. The idea behind this was to duct the cooling air more evenly round the cylinders, but only on the Type 3 models. In fact, when this tinware first became available, Volkswagen sent its dealers a bulletin stating that it should not be used on Type 1 engines as it disrupted

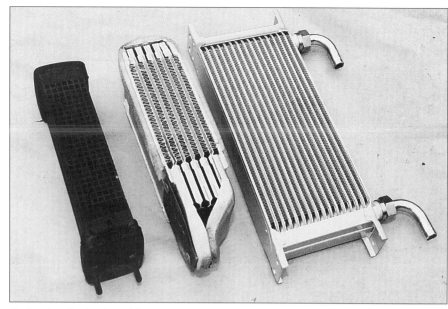

Stock early-style oil cooler on left was mounted inside fan-housing, while later dog-house cooler (center) was mounted externally. Aftermarket Serck oil cooler on right may be used in conjunction with an external oil system to provide extra cooling – a useful addition on a hard-working Type 2.

the cooling airflow. Indeed, it was strongly emphasized that only the original Type 1 shrouding should be used. Although cool tin is frequently recommended for use on modified VWs, it is worth bearing in mind that the factory spent much time and money developing the cooling system of this amazing engine.

Oil coolers

The original internal oil cooler (part number 111 117 021) was perfectly adequate in its job of maintaining oil temperatures at an acceptable level, but proved to be prone to fracturing due to vibration. The design was changed,

Pauter Machine have developed this Porsche-style fan set-up for its Super Pro VW engine. Similar conversions are available to fit the Type 1 engine from other manufacturers but few are as efficient as the factory tinware.

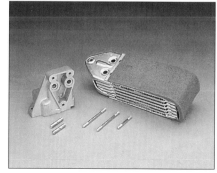

The dog-house cooler was in fact a Type 3 oil cooler mounted on a special adaptor which allowed it to be used vertically on the Type 1 engine. Foam helps to seal the cooler against the tinware.

In the late 1960s, EMPI developed this dual-external oil cooler system which used a pair of Type 3 coolers mounted under the rear window on a cast adaptor. Not very pretty and not all that effective, either!

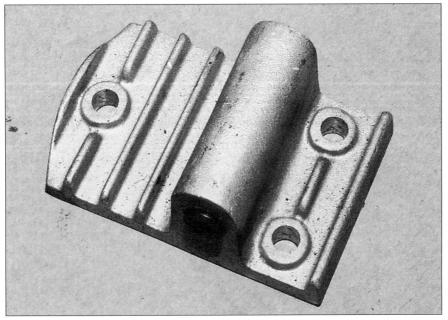

In race applications, where no oil cooler is necessary, it is possible to seal off the oilways using a block-off plate. This simply bolts in place using the oil cooler mountings.

therefore, to make provision for a tab which was bolted to the fan-housing to hold the cooler steady (part number 111 117 021A). With the advent of the 34bhp engine, the cooler was further redesigned (111 117 021D), this being a much more substantial item, slightly shorter and heavier in appearance - this was then supplied as a retro-fitment for all engines, on exchange, as part number 111 117 021DY. When the factory redesigned the cooling system in 1971, it decided to use the cooler previously fitted to the Type 3 range of 'pancake' engines. This cooler, part number 311 117 021A, is manufactured from aluminum and is far more efficient than its predecessor. However, it is fitted horizontally on the Type 3 engine and to use this on the Type 1 requires a special adaptor (part number 113 117 301) which turns the cooler through 90°, enabling it to be fitted

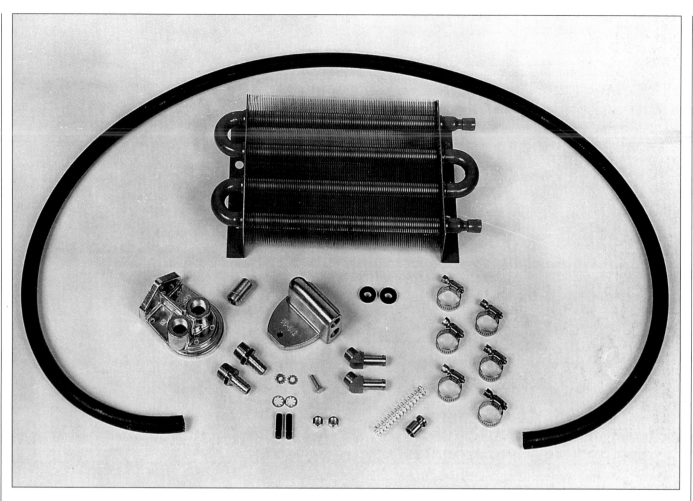

The worst type of external cooler you can fit is one that replaces the stock cooler with one which is bolted over the fan inlet. Not only does this restrict the flow of air to the fan but it also means that the cooling air will have been pre-heated by the oil cooler.

vertically at the rear of the fan-housing. This cooler/adaptor/dog-house shroud combination is the best that has been offered by the factory and has proved to be more than adequate for virtually any road-going VW Beetle.

The question of whether an external auxiliary oil cooler should be used in conjunction with the factory installation is open to debate. There are those who feel, not without reason, that there is the risk of the oil being kept too cool for too long by an auxiliary cooler, unless it can be isolated by a thermostat of some kind. On a Beetle, there is also the problem of where to mount an extra cooler - in the late 1960s, EMPI offered a kit which allowed the fitment of two Type 3 coolers, with a special adaptor, on the louvers under the rear window. This was a popular location among those people who raced or rallied Beetles in the '60s and

'70s, as the cooler was kept out of harm's way. However, on a road car, this is hardly an aesthetically-pleasing solution, so other popular sites are under the rear fender (preferably protected by a stone guard) or alongside the transmission. It is also possible to front-mount a cooler in or below the front bumper but, once again, the merits of this are open to debate. Many people feel that using an auxiliary oil cooler makes the oil lines too long and this can result in a drop in oil pressure. There is also an increased risk of damage to the lines, especially if they run underneath the car.

One popular modification has always been to fit an extra oil cooler across the rear of the fan-shrouding, covering the fan inlet. Worse still, there have been - and still are - kits on the market that allow you to do away completely with the stock factory cooler in favor of this aftermarket

system. The thinking behind this was that a larger-than-stock cooler could be fitted, through which the fan would draw air. This is not a good idea as it means that all the fresh air intended to cool the engine will already have been pre-heated by the external cooler. There will also be a restriction in the flow of air into the fan. Do not use this system - we can only repeat that the stock factory dog-house cooler is more than adequate for most situations.

Oil system

Before proceeding any further, it is worth taking a look in detail at the way the stock oil system works. The starting point, so to speak, is a sump which is an integral part of the crankcase and which holds 4.4 pints (that's 5.3 US pints or 2.5 liters) of oil. Lubricant is drawn from the sump by a pick-up tube which leads to an

Sectioned single-relief valve crankcase showing the oilways, all of which are located in the left half of the case. Lower gallery, just above the sump, is the principal one, feeding the main bearings, lifters and, indirectly, the rod bearings.

oil gallery in the crankcase and then to the pump. The pick-up tube measures approximately $9/16$in in diameter in German single relief-valve engine cases from 1961 to 1969 and $5/8$in or $3/4$in in 1970 and later crankcases - the former in Brazilian cases, the latter in German, Mexican and some late-Brazilian cases. The pick-up tube draws its oil through a crude strainer gauze located in the base of the sump and, although this may seem like a pretty ineffective form of filtration, it does at least keep any larger pieces of debris out of the oil pick-up - this is especially pertinent when a freshly-rebuilt engine is fired up, for it is common to find surprisingly large pieces of gasket sealant in the sump filter.

The stock oil pump is an aluminum casting which contains two steel gears: the upper is driven off the end of the camshaft, while the lower is an idler gear. As the engine turns, the two gears intermesh and draw the oil from the sump before forcing it through a gallery located in the left side of the crankcase (as viewed from the rear of the vehicle). After leaving the pump, oil is allowed to flow into a series of galleries drilled within the

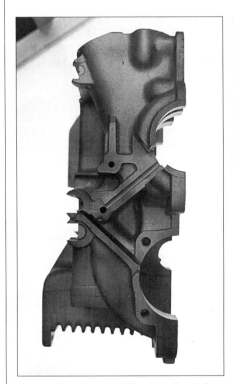

From the front, you can see the oilway (lower left) leading up from the pump at 45° and a second one leading to the number four main bearing.

Inside the case, it is just possible to see the oil feed to the lifters. Note also the oil feed to the main bearings – the lower hole on the center (number two) main bearing saddle is the feed, the upper one is the hole for the dowel which locates the bearing shell.

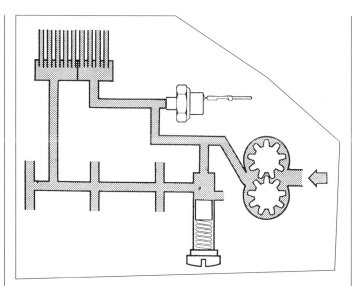

Diagram of the oil pressure relief system: when the oil is cold, the pressure relief valve is forced open by the high pressure, allowing oil to enter the main oil gallery without first passing through the oil cooler (at top).

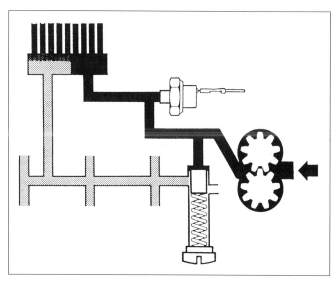

Once oil warms up and the pressure begins to fall, the relief valve closes, blocking off the main oil gallery and diverting all the oil up through the filter. Oil pressure switch can be seen above relief valve.

crankcase where it is passed either up to the oil cooler, or along the main oil gallery, from which feeds are taken to the main bearings, camshaft and lifter bores (see illustration). The valve gear is kept lubricated by oil which is forced from the lifters and up hollow pushrods (and which drains back into the sump via the pushrod tubes), while the cylinders, pistons and camshaft rely on splash lubrication.

To prevent cold, thick oil from passing through the oil cooler and thereby

allow it to warm up quickly, a spring-loaded bypass valve is located at the front of the crankcase (ie, the end adjacent to the crankshaft pulley) which opens when the engine is cold to allow excess oil to drain back into the sump. As the oil temperature rises and the pressure begins to fall, the valve gradually closes to direct oil up to the cooler, from where it flows back down a vertical gallery located between the bores for numbers three and four cylinders. You will note that all

principal oil galleries are located within the left half of the case.

The spring-loaded bypass valve also serves to help regulate the maximum oil pressure within the system, so as to prevent damage to the cooler which was not designed to withstand excessive pressures. In August 1969, a second spring-loaded valve was incorporated into the system at the rear of the main oil gallery adjacent to the flywheel, the purpose of which is to act as a relief valve

Pump draws oil from sump via this pick-up tube which can be found behind the sump plate. A crude 'tea-strainer' mesh filter fits over this tube and provides all the filtering the factory deemed necessary.

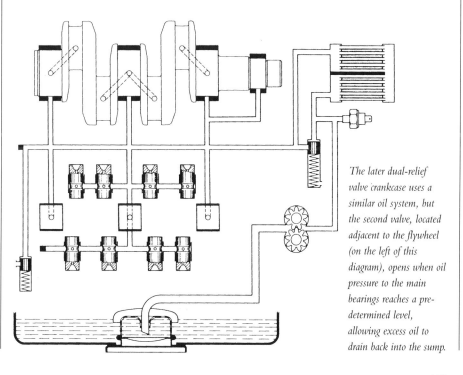

The later dual-relief valve crankcase uses a similar oil system, but the second valve, located adjacent to the flywheel (on the left of this diagram), opens when oil pressure to the main bearings reaches a pre-determined level, allowing excess oil to drain back into the sump.

Gene Berg Enterprises maintain that you should not use an aftermarket cast-iron oil pump due to the differing rates of expansion between the pump body and the crankcase. GBE markets this blue-printed factory pump which is said to be more than adequate for all high-performance applications.

adjustable pressure relief valve kit which allows you to increase or decrease the maximum pressure at the turn of an Allen key. These kits are normally used in conjunction with the stock relief valves, although they can be used with aftermarket ones where an oil cooler is not fitted, such as with an engine used for drag racing.

The factory oil pump is fine for use with an engine which has only been modestly modified, but any application which sees the engine turning at higher rpm, or where the compression ratio is significantly increased, will require the use of a high-volume oil pump of some form. In the early days of Volkswagen tuning, the popular trick among the racers was to use a modified oil pump from a semi-automatic Beetle. This pump is, in effect, two pumps in one: one set of gears flows

to regulate maximum oil pressure. The valve at the front of the engine remained as a bypass for the oil cooler as before.

Aside from the fitment of the extra relief valve, later crankcases also featured oil galleries which are some 0.050in larger in diameter than those of the early, pre-'70 cases. While it is possible to modify an earlier case by drilling out the galleries to approximately $^3/_8$in in diameter, it is questionable whether such measures are worth the effort when the improved later cases are so readily available.

In order to increase the oil pressure of the Volkswagen engine, it is possible to buy heavy-duty relief valve kits which feature stronger springs and longer valves. These are designed to open at higher pressures than normal, thereby increasing the pressure in the oil system. Some kits include a grooved valve (similar to that used by the factory in later engines) which must be fitted to the bypass system, the aim being to allow some oil to bleed past and find its way to the cooler before the valve fully opens. Many of these oil pressure relief valve kits have springs which are too heavy and can lead to problems with burst coolers or leaking oil fittings. Many specialists recommend using the aftermarket valves with the stock springs, or simply shimming these with a suitably-sized washer. However, perhaps the best solution is to fit an

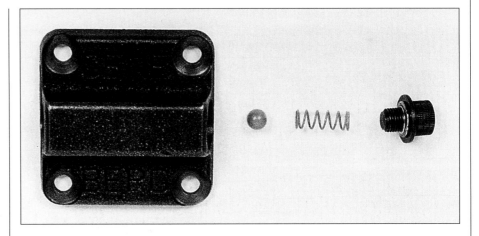

GBE also offers this oil pressure relief valve pump cover, which returns oil to the sump when the pressure exceeds 125psi (a figure often exceeded when the oil is cold, even on a stock engine).

lubricant round the engine, while another pressurizes the transmission fluid. The secret was to modify the pump so that both sets of gears pumped oil round the engine. However, people soon began to realize that it was possible to obtain superior flow by using a 'blue-printed' stock oil pump. By blueprinted, we mean a pump which has been carefully modified to bring it up to optimum efficiency.

Gene Berg Enterprises (GBE) only sells blueprinted factory pumps, these being available with either 26mm- or

Berg cast-iron pump cover allows oil to be fed to an external oil filter and cooler. These covers are the best available and far superior to the less expensive aluminum covers sold by some companies, which tend to wear quickly, resulting in a fall in oil pressure.

The Melling cast-iron pump is the most widely-used of all aftermarket pumps. Equipped with 30mm gears, the Melling is a well-made part but can suffer from leakage where it slips into the crankcase.

30mm-long gears (early factory pumps came with a range of gears from 19mm up to 25mm and are not really suitable for performance applications). The 30mm pumps are only available to fit the 1970 and later crankcases, with their larger oil galleries, whereas the 26mm pumps are available to fit both early and late cases. GBE feels that the 30mm pumps are more than adequate for use in high-performance applications, even all-out race engines turning to 10,000rpm. All the pumps are available with the outlet blocked off for use with a take-off plate and an external oil system (see below).

There are a number of aftermarket pumps available, some of which are manufactured from aluminum, others from cast iron. Of the latter, the most popular is that made by Melling which is a good quality pump with 30mm gears. The main problem with any cast iron pump is that there is a difference in expansion rates between the pump and the crankcase as the engine warms up, which can lead to oil leaks from around the pump. For this reason, GBE does not sell or recommend using a cast iron pump,

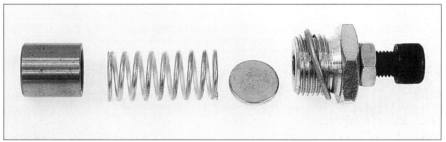

An adjustable oil pressure relief valve enables you to increase (or decrease) the oil pressure at the turn of an Allen key. Heavy-duty springs can also be used to increase the pressure on a performance engine.

feeling that any leakage will result in a drop in oil pressure.

Dry-sump oil systems are not a common sight on VW engines, largely because there is not a great deal of need for them. The exception is a situation where the oil is thrown about inside the sump, with the risk of the oil pump sucking in air, rather than oil - midget oval-track racing, for example. Dry-sump pumps work by having two sets of gears: one set sucks, or 'scavenges' oil from the sump before pumping it back to the main oil tanks, while the second set pumps oil from the tank into the engine's oil galleries. Dry-sumping an engine does have some other advantages, one being that there is always a plentiful supply of fresh, cool oil, another being that, on an engine using an aftermarket crankcase, it is possible to gain some extra ground clearance by doing away with a separate wet sump.

The main disadavantages of fitting a dry-sump system are the increased cost and complexity (a remote oil tank, extra

Auto-Craft Machine manufacturers a superb range of dry-sump oil pumps for the VW engine, including models to accept a Hilborn fuel-injection pump. All pumps are machined from billet aluminum.

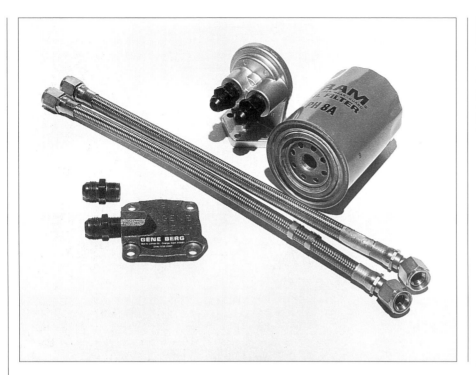

Another possibility is to fit the filter on the side of the sump using the stud which originally located the thermostat. Braided lines and anodized aluminum fittings are expensive but worth it in the long run.

An external oil filter is an absolute must on even the mildest modified VW engine. The factory wire-mesh filter in the sump simply is not good enough and needs to be augmented by a system such as this from Gene Berg Enterprises.

oil lines, special oil pump) and the increase in weight. the latter may not be a major problem on a road car, but it is anathema as far as drag racers are concerned. However, dry-sump oil systems are starting to find favor with some drag race engine builders who recognize the benefits of a large oil supply where high-horsepower, high-rpm engines are concerned.

Other aftermarket pumps incorporate an oil filter, commonly referred to as 'filter pumps'. Here, the oil is routed out of the pump, though the filter and back into the discharge side of the pump before passing into the main oil galleries. This type of pump, although popular, cannot really be recommended for two reasons: the first is that they are very restrictive and the second is that they place the oil filter in close proximity to the exhaust system, thereby warming the oil even before it enters the engine. If a proper oil filter is required then it is far better to modify the engine for a full-flow oil system.

This is achieved by drilling out the

There are various solutions to the problem of where to fit an external filter on a Beetle, one of which is to place it under the rear fender, using the bumper mount as a fixing point. GBE system is neat and tidy.

soft aluminum plug at the front end of the main oil gallery, to the left of the oil pump as viewed from the rear of the car. This gallery is then tapped, usually with a $3/8$ NPT thread, to accept a screw-in fitting. The outlet of the pump is blocked off with a plug and the stock oil pump cover replaced by a take-off plate which

allows oil to flow out of the pump. An oil line, fitted to the take-off plate, routes the oil to an external oil filter (and cooler if needs be) while another returns the oil to the crankcase at the main oil gallery. These oil lines can be the more costly steel braided hose (Earl's, Aeroquip etc) or the less expensive reinforced rubber type –

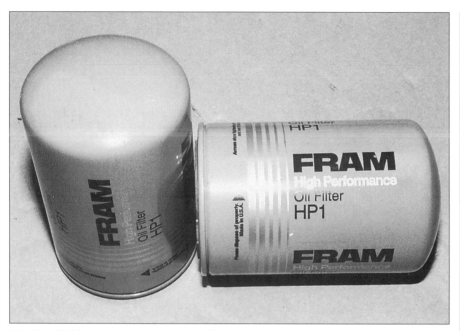

The Fram HP1 has become the industry standard filter on high-performance VW engines as it is capable of withstanding extremely high pressures without splitting.

It is possible to buy three different types of filter mounting – one which exits to the right, another which exits to the left and a third with the fittings in the top. One of these will be right for you.

An alternative to the regular cartridge-type filter is the System One, which is fully rebuildable and allows the owner to take a peek at what is happening inside his engine as he can now examine all the debris in the oil system.

either way, make certain that they are suited for use with oil and the high temperatures and pressures involved. As far as sizes are concerned, it is usual to use either $1/2$in rubber hose or -6 or -8 braided lines. If rubber hosing is used, it is perfectly acceptable to use the relatively low cost brass NPT/barbed fittings which are readily available, while braided hoses are normally used with the special screw-together aluminum fittings supplied by the hosing manufacturer.

Incidentally, while it could be argued that any oil filter is going to be better than no filter at all, do not be tempted to use one of the oil pump covers on the market which allow you to add a full-flow external filter to your engine without drilling and tapping the case. These covers work by directing the oil out of the pump through a small orifice to the filter and then back into the pump via a second orifice. Such covers offer too great a restriction to oil flow and should not be used, especially in any high-performance application.

Be aware that even the stock oil system is capable of showing over 150psi on a pressure gauge when the oil is cold. If a high-volume pump is used, especially in conjunction with aftermarket relief valves, pressures of as much as 300psi are not uncommon when the engine is first fired up, even when the stock by-pass (relief) valve is used! For this reason, it is important to use a filter which is capable of withstanding high pressures, the most popular of these being the Fram HP1. This is a bypass type filter which incorporates a spring-loaded ball-valve which opens when the pressure is very high to allow oil to bypass the filter element. To address the problem of excessively high pressure on initial fire-up, GBE manufactures an oil pump cover, with oil take-off, which incorporates an extra pressure relief valve. This is designed to route excess oil back into the inlet (scavenge) side of the pump until the oil has warmed up and the pressure begins to fall.

There are other filters on the market which can be dismantled and the filter screen examined for contamination, the most popular of these being either the O-Berg or the System One. Both of these filters are excellent for the person who wishes to closely monitor the wear on engine components - all material removed from bearings, piston rings, cam gear etc, finds its way into the filter screen where it can be easily examined. Anyone who has taken a close look at the contents of such a filter, even after just a few minutes running of a brand new engine, will need little convincing of the worth of a good quality filtration system: without this extra safeguard, all the debris which can be seen would be passed round the engine and through the bearings, causing further damage.

The stock oil sump has limited capacity, so Gene Berg Enterprises, along with a number of others, manufactures a sump extension which adds 1.5 US qts (0.69 liters) to the capacity. This simply bolts on in place of the sump plate. Note the extended pick-up tube.

Sump extensions

One of the drawbacks of the stock oil system is that the sump only holds a relatively small amount of oil compared to other engines of a similar capacity. As soon as any modifications are made to the VW engine, from modest performance tuning to even simply fitting a high-volume oil pump, the sump capacity becomes inadequate. The problem is that the lubricant cannot drain back to the sump fast enough to keep up with demand, running the risk of starving the oil pump of oil. By adding a sump extension, the capacity is increased to more acceptable levels. Several companies offer sump extensions with capacities varying from 1.5 US qts (1.2 Imp pts or 0.69 liters) up to 4 US qts (3.2 Imp pts/1.82 liters), the latter from GBE being intended for race use where the engine will be turning over at high rpm. The one to watch with this particular extension is that the ground clearance is reduced quite considerably. If this is a problem, then the alternative 3.5 US qts (2.8 Imp pts or 1.6 liters) extension is probably the best choice.

All sump extensions require the fitting of an extension to the oil pick-up tube. Usually this comes in the form of a short piece of pipe which is held in place with a hose clip. Ideally, this pipe should

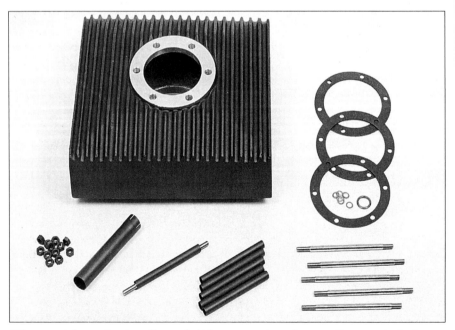

Where ground clearance is not a problem, or for high-rpm race engines, a larger capacity sump extension is available. This carries an extra 4 US qts (1.82 liters) but does significantly reduce the clearance under the vehicle.

Where ground clearance is limited, GBE offers this wide sump extension – part number GB210A) which still contains an extra 3.5 US qts (or 1.6 liters) of oil.

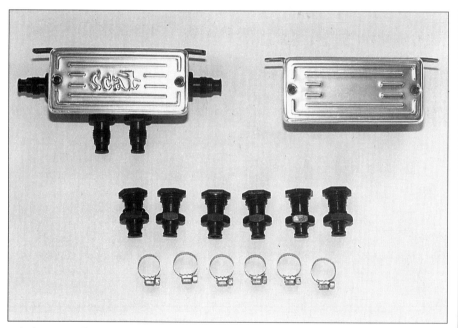

A high-revving Volkswagen engine needs to be able to breath and adding a set of breather lines to the valve covers and fuel pump take-off (when an electric pump is used) will help prevent the engine from leaking oil at high rpm. Small breather boxes like this are OK for street use, but not large enough to cope with race situations.

during violent manoeuvres and causing oil starvation. However, a sump extension does a far better job. If the problem is one of oil being forced up the pushrod tubes during hard cornering, then it is probably better to fit what are referred to as windage tubes - these are pushrod tubes which have been extended where they fit into the crankcase. These do a perfectly adequate job of controlling the oil movement under hard cornering.

Crankcase breathers

When a Volkswagen engine is run at high rpm, there is a problem with crankcase breathing - as the crankshaft rotates and the pistons move up down in the cylinders, they displace a large volume of air. At low rpm, this does not present any problem, but increase the engine speed, or fit a stroker crank and/or larger pistons and cylinders, and the amount of air being displaced becomes more than the stock breather system can cope with. Add to this the fact that there is always a certain amount of blow-by past the piston rings which will tend to pressurize the crankcase, and it is easy to see why many high-performance engines 'weep' oil from valve covers, behind the crankshaft pulley or around any poorly sealed joint.

The solution is to fit an improved breathing system - many racers will fit breather lines to each valve cover and another to the crankcase, either at the location of the stock fuel pump, the

be spot welded to the original pick-up to prevent it from working loose. Obviously this can only be done while the engine is apart. It is worth noting that, as certain manufacturers are at pains to point out, not all sump extensions are the same: some are very poor quality castings which can prove to be porous. Others do not have any internal reinforcement and can be easily damaged by careless use of a trolley (floor) jack. When installing a sump extension, always use a gasket

between the extension and the crankcase, and always fit the factory oil strainer gauze.

Another benefit of a sump extension is that it ensures there is always a supply of oil close to the pick-up tube under hard cornering or acceleration. This can also be achieved, to a degree, by fitting a windage tray - this is a pressed steel tray which locates in the crankcase below the crankshaft and is intended to prevent the oil from being thrown about too much

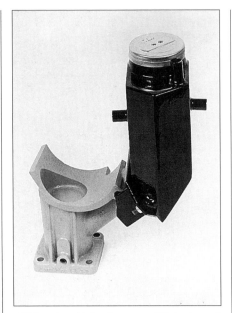

GBE markets this breather tower which has internal baffles to separate the oil from the air, allowing it to drain back into the engine. Extra fittings allow breather lines from the valve covers to be hooked up.

Gene Berg Enterprises manufactures the Equalizer – a heavyweight crankshaft pulley which acts as a damper to remove harmonics from the crankshaft at high engine speeds. The narrower stock-sized pulley weighs 6.25lbs, while the thicker power-pulley type weighs in at 7.5lbs.

Pauter Machine makes a high-quality steel pulley which is virtually bullet-proof. Machined degree marks on the edge of the pulley make setting the ignition timing a simple matter.

generator mounting or the oil filler. These lines will often terminate in what is known as a breather tank, or 'puke tank' to give it its popular name among racers. All this does is collect any oil which is blown out of the crankcase in the form of oil mist, thus preventing it from finding its way onto the track. However, it is important to regularly check the contents of the breather tank to see if it has filled up. Also, take care when positioning the tank not to place it where rainwater can seep in.

There are, however, a number of breather boxes on the market which allow the engine to breath more easily without actually collecting the oil. Some of these breathers are little more than small cast aluminum boxes containing a pad of foam rubber, with a lid bolted on. A small gap around the edge of the lid allows air to escape, while the foam absorbs any oil mist. The main problem with these simple breathers is that they do not have a large enough volume to be really effective. They also tend to leak oil as the foam becomes saturated. A better system is that offered by GBE which markets a breather box which fits onto the stock oil filler assembly. Inside the breather is a series of baffles which prevent excess oil from being forced out. Two basic designs are

listed (two inlets only or two inlets and an outlet for connection to an air-cleaner), each in turn being available for use with either the factory generator or an alternator.

For most applications, the breather lines need only be 3/8in (or -6 steel braided) in diameter, while racers may prefer to use 1/2in (or -8) hoses. It is not really necessary to use anything more

exotic than rubber oil hose for the breather lines, although there is little doubt that expensive braided steel hosing, with anodized aluminum fittings, does wonders for the appearance of an engine bay. Beware, however, of using the thin-wall hose supplied with some inexpensive breather boxes, for this can become very soft and collapse when warm, thus effectively sealing the breather system.

Choosing your oil pump

When selecting you oil pump, ensure that it is compatible with your camshaft. All aftermarket cams come with three fixing bolts holding the timing gear in place, while stock cams from 1971 on had four bolts. These late-model cams have a dished face and require an oil pump with a longer driveshaft. Also check that the oil pump has the correct size of inlet and outlet to match the oil galleries in your engine case. When the oil galleries in the factory crankcase were enlarged, so were the inlet and outlet holes in the oil pump body.

Power pulleys and Berg Achievers

One of the simplest ways to obtain more usable horsepower from your engine is to

Where a fan belt is not needed, this 'drag button' from Pauter Machine will do the trick. Again, degree marks are machined on the edge for accurate timing.

For off-road use, a sand-seal pulley should be used. This features an oil seal which prevents dirt and dust being drawn into the engine past the end of the crankshaft. Some drag racers use these to prevent oil leaks from the front of the crankcase caused by crankshaft flexing at high rpm.

fit what is referred to as a 'power pulley'. This is a smaller crankshaft pulley which is 5.70in in diameter, as opposed to the stock 6.70in, and has the effect of reducing the speed of the power-sapping cooling fan. Now, immediately we can see a potential problem: the slower the fan turns, the less cooling the engine receives. However, the stock fan is only intended to work efficiently at engine speeds up to 6,000rpm - above that the fan 'stalls' and cannot pass any more air. A power pulley slows the fan, allowing it to work at anything up to 8,000rpm. On a high-rpm street or race engine, fitting a power pulley is fine - indeed, it could be considered a must - but on an engine

There are many aftermarket pulleys available, some good, some bad. The poor ones tend to crack along the key-way. Smaller diameter power-pulleys reduce the fan speed and help prevent the fan from stalling at high rpm,

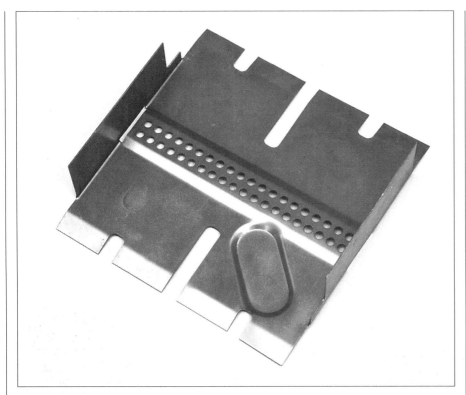

One product that is not really necessary on anything except, possibly, a VW used for slalom or road racing, is a sump baffle (windage tray). If you have any concerns about oil surge, far better solution is to fit a sump extension and windage pushrod tubes.

Once installed, the serpentine belt conversion looks quite impressive. Doing away with the stock split-pulley and shim set-up makes it far easier to adjust the belt tension. Crank pulley is only available in stock diameter at time of writing.

CB Performance's serpentine fan-belt system is a well-engineered conversion which should put an end to thrown belts at high rpm. Flat belt requires the use of specially-designed crank and generator pulleys. Jockey wheel is used to tension belt.

which sees regular street use at low rpm, it is better to stay with the stock-size pulley.

Gene Berg Enterprises offers a range of crankshaft pulleys under the Achiever and Equalizer brand name. The Achiever is a high-quality steel pulley which helps to dampen vibrations which are set up in the crankshaft at higher rpm. The lighter Achiever pulley weighs 3.5lb and is intended for use on engines that see occasional use above 6,000rpm. The substantial (6.25lb!) Equalizer pulley is for those engines which regularly see use over 5,500rpm and acts almost as a secondary flywheel, thus helping drag race cars leave the startline harder. Both Achiever and Equalizer pulleys are available in stock and power pulley diameters.

RECOMMENDATIONS

Mild Street	Blueprinted stock oil pump with 26mm gears; Melling-style 30mm pump; full-flow filter system; factory oil cooler (dog-house type preferred)
Hot Street	Blueprinted stock oil pump with 26mm or 30mm gears; Melling-style 30mm pump; full-flow filter system (remote cooler optional); dog-house oil cooler/fanhousing; uprated relief valves
Competition	Blueprinted stock oil pump with 30mm gears; Melling-style 30mm pump; full-flow filter system; uprated relief valves (adjustable if preferred); dry-sump oil system (optional)

LIST OF MANUFACTURERS AND SUPPLIERS
(in alphabetical order)

Autocavan Components Ltd
103 Lower Weybourne lane,
Badshot Lea, Farnham
Surrey GU9 9LG, England
Tel: (01252) 333891
Fax: (01252) 343363

Auto-Craft Machine
1050 S. Cypress #K, La Habra,
California 90631, USA
Tel: (714) 870-7223
Fax: (714) 525-8511

Benchmark Systems
2960 La Vista, Corona
California 91719, USA
Tel: (714) 734-2022

Gene Berg Enterprises
1725 North Lime street,
Orange, California 92665, USA
Tel: (714) 998-7500
Fax: (714) 998-7528

Bernie Bergmann
340 North Hale Avenue,
Escondido
California 92029, USA
Tel: (619) 747-4649
Fax: (619) 740-8522

Bugpack
Dee Engineering Inc
3560 Cadillac Avenue
Costa Mesa
California 92626, USA
Tel: (714) 979-4990
Fax: (714) 979-3468

Carrillo Industries Inc
990 Calle Amanecer
San Clemente
California 92672, USA
Tel: (714) 498-1800
Fax: (714) 498-2355

CB Performance
28813 Farmersville Blvd,
Farmersville
California 93223, USA
Tel: (209) 733-8222
Fax: (209) 733-7967

Chassis Shop
1931 North 24th Avenue
Mears, Michigan
Missouri 49436, USA
Tel: (616) 873-3640
Fax: (616) 873-0218

Compufire Ignition
Engine Electronics Inc
20290 Carrey Road, Walnut
California 91789, USA
Tel: (909) 598-5485
Fax: (909) 598-5695

Crane Cams
530 Fentress Blvd, Daytona
Beach, Florida 32014, USA
Tel: (904) 252-1151
Fax: (904) 258-6167

Crower Cams Inc
3333 Main Street, Chula Vista
California 91911-5898, USA
Tel: (619) 422-1191
Fax: (619) 422-9067

Del West Engineering
24711 Rockefeller Av, Valencia
California 91355, USA
Tel: (805) 295-5700

Engle Racing Cams
1621 12th Street, Santa Monica
California 90404, USA
Tel: (213) 450-0806
Fax: (213) 452-3753

Erson Cams
550 Mallory way, Carson City
Nevada 89701, USA
Tel: (702) 882-1622
Fax: (702) 887-4326

Fat Performance
1558 North Case, Orange
California 92667, USA
Tel: (714) 637-2889
Fax: (714) 637-7352

Hilborn Fuel Injection
Engineering Co Inc
25891 Crown Valley parkway
South laguna
California 92677, USA
Tel: (714) 582-1170

Holley Fuel Systems
PO Box 10360, Bowling Green
Kentucky 42102-7360, USA
Tel: (502) 781-9741

Jacobs Electronics Inc
500 North Baird Street
Midland, Texas 79701, USA
Tel: (800) 627-8800

JayCee Enterprises
7442 Talbert Avenue
Huntington Beach
California 92647, USA
Tel: (714) 848-9898
Fax: (714) 848-5558

J & E Pistons
15681 Computer lane,
Huntington Beach
California 92649, USA
Tel: (714) 898-9763
Fax: (714) 893-8297

Jet Engineering
5212 Aurelius Road, Lansing
Michigan 48911, USA
Tel: (517) 882-4311
Fax: (517) 882-2330

Johnny's Speed & Chrome
6411 Beach Boulevard
Buena Park
California 90621-2896, USA
Tel: (714) 994-4022
Fax: (714) 228-0136

Kawell Racing Engines
Route 2, Box 144, Friendship
Tennessee 38034, USA
Tel: (901) 677-2160
Fax: (901) 677-2143

Dick Landy Industries
19743 Bahama Street,
Northridge
California 91324, USA
Tel: (818) 341-4143

Ron Lummus Racing
15632 Product Lane, Unit B
Huntington Beach
California 92649, USA
Tel: (714) 895-5574
Fax: (714) 895-3006

Mallory Ignition
550 Mallory way, Carson City
Nevada 89701, USA
Tel: (702) 882-6600
Fax: (702) 887-4326

Manley Valves
1960 Swarthmore Avenue,
Lakewood
New jersey 08701, USA
Tel: (908) 905-3366

Mofoco
102 West Capitol Drive,
Milwaukee
Wisconsin 53212, USA
Tel: (414) 963-1020
Fax: (414) 963-2045

MSD Ignition Systems
Automotive Controls
Corporation
1490 Henry Brennan Drive
El Paso, Texas 79936, USA
Tel: (915) 857-5200
Fax: (915) 857-3344

Nitrous Oxide Systems Inc
5930 Lakeshore Drive, Cypress
California 90630, USA
Tel: (714) 821-0592

Oberg Enterprises
12414 Highway 99 South
Bay 80, Everett
Washington 98204, USA
Tel: (206) 353-2595

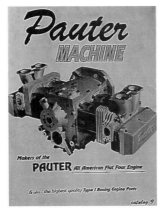

Pauter Machine Co Inc
367 Zenith Street, Chula Vista
California 92011, USA
Tel: (619) 422-5384
Fax: (619) 422-1924

Performance Technology
1631 Placentia, Unit N
Anaheim, California 92805,
USA
Tel: (714) 526-0533

Rimco Riddle Machine Co
520 East Dyer Road, Santa Ana
California 92707, USA
Tel: (714) 549-0357
Fax: (714) 549-0627

S&S Headers
1401 East Ball Road
Suite C, Anaheim
California 92805, USA
Tel: (714) 758-0355
Fax: (714) 758-0350

Scat Enterprises Inc
1400 Kingsdale Avenue,
Redondo Beach
California 90278-3983, USA
Tel: (310) 370-5501
Fax: (310) 214-2285

System One Filtration
1822 East main Street #A
Visalia, California 93291, USA
Tel: (209) 732-1955
Fax: (209) 732-1982

Top Gun Nitrous Systems
5111 Troup Highway, Tyler
Texas 75707, USA
Tel: (903) 581-4878
Fax: (903) 581-2993

Total Seal Piston Rings
2225 West Mountain View #6
Phoenix, Arizona 85021, USA
Tel: (602) 678-4977
Fax: (602) 678-4991

Venolia Pistons
Tor-Cam Industries Inc
2160 Cherry Industrial Circle
Long Beach
California 90805, USA
Tel: (310) 531-8463
Fax: (310) 633-9439

Vertex Magnetos
212 Roesch Avenue, Oreland
Pennsylvania 19075, USA
Tel: (215) 884-0440
Fax: (215) 828-9529

Web-Cam
1815 Massachusetts Avenue,
Riverside
California 92507, USA
Tel: (909) 369-5144
Fax: (909) 369-7266

Weber Cams
1663 Superior Avenue
Costa Mesa
California 92627, USA
Tel: (714) 631-4884
Fax: (714) 631-4968

Wiseco Pistons Inc
7201 Industrial Park Blvd,
Mentor, Ohio 44060, USA
Tel: (216) 951-6600
Fax: (216) 951-6606